BARCLAYS de ZOETE WEDD

THE RATE REFERENCE GUIDE

TO THE

U.S. TREASURY MARKET

STEVEN R. RICCHIUTO

PROBUS PUBLISHING COMPANY
Chicago, Illinois

Library of Congress Cataloging-in-Publication Data Available

ISBN 1-55738-166-6

Printed in the United States of America

Cover Illustration by Rick Brown

1   2   3   4   5   6   7   8   9   0

TABLE OF CONTENTS

ABOUT THE AUTHOR

Steven R. Ricchiuto, Director and Chief Economist, joined Barclays de Zoete Wedd Securities Inc. in June 1988. His major responsibilities include providing fixed income sales and trading with current, detailed analyses of the major factors which influence the direction of interest rates. Additionally, Mr. Ricchiuto is an integral member of the Barclays de Zoete Wedd worldwide research network, which covers all of the major global financial markets.

Before joining BZW Securities Inc., Mr. Ricchiuto was Senior Vice President and Money Market Economist at Kidder, Peabody & Co. from 1984-1988 following five years at Donaldson, Lufkin and Jenrette where he was Associate Money Market Economist.

Mr. Ricchiuto holds a B.S. degree in Mathematics and Economics from St. Peter's College, New Jersey, and a M.A. in Economics from Columbia University. He has completed the course requirements at Fordham University for his Ph.D. in Economics, and has embarked on his dissertation.

ACKNOWLEDGMENTS

I would like to thank those who helped in the preparation, research, and writing of this reference guide. First, I would like to thank Elder Maxwell, Financial Markets Analyst for Barclays Bank PLC (North America), and Lucy Mullins, Oil Analyst at BZW Research, London, for their valuable contributions to the analyses presented in this guide. I would also like to thank Bernard C. Grigsby and Samuel R. Marrone, co-Chief Executives of Barclays de Zoete Wedd Securities Inc., for their encouragement of this project through its various stages from manuscript to completed book. I would also like to thank Carol Bere for her editorial comments and continued patience. Among the many others who should be remembered are Michael Au and Seton Seremba for their organizational skills and dedication to this undertaking. Finally, Rick Brown should be noted for his excellent cover illustration.

PREFACE

Barclays Bank PLC, which traces its roots to the seventeenth century, is among the world's largest, best regarded financial institutions with a "AAA" rating and assets of $205 billion as of 1989. The Group provides a comprehensive range of services to a diverse universe of clients, with a presence in 75 countries. Barclays de Zoete Wedd (BZW), the international investment banking arm of Barclays PLC, was created in 1986 through the union of stockbrokers de Zoete & Beven and stock-jobbers Wedd Durlacher Mordaunt with Barclays Merchant Bank and Barclays Investment Management. BZW was formed in response to the growing volume of international securities businesses—the "globalization" and "securitization" of the marketplace—and the far-reaching changes in the British financial markets, which became effective on 27 October 1986 and are known as "Big Bang," whereby the fixed scale of London Stock Exchange commissions was terminated, enforced single capacity in dealing was eliminated, and outside investors were permitted to own Stock Exchange firms.

BZW, with offices in Europe, the Far East, and North America and a staff of 3,000, provides a broad range of investment and merchant banking services, including comprehensive dealing services in U.K. securities, global economic analysis and investment research, asset and portfolio management, and origination, distribution, and trading in international stock and bond markets. BZW is a premier participant in the British fixed income securities markets, and an active dealer in the securities of the U.S., Germany, Holland, France, Australia, and Japan, as well as in Eurobonds denominated in a menu of currencies. Additionally, the Group is a leader in foreign exchange, the global swaps market, and is an important participant in structured finance and derivative products.

Within the investment bank, Barclays de Zoete Wedd Securities Inc. (BZW Securities), a wholly-owned Group subsidiary established in 1987, has worldwide responsibility for sales, trading, and research in the full range of U.S. government and federal agency securities, their derivatives and related financial instruments. BZW Securities was named "Primary Dealer" in U.S. government securities in December 1989.

Barclays de Zoete Wedd Securities Inc. is headquartered in New York, with financial futures operations in Chicago and full dealing capabilities in London and Tokyo to provide 24-hour transactional services for institutional investors. BZW Securities' global client base includes money managers, insurance companies, pension funds, depository institutions, corporate treasuries, trust banks, investment trusts, domestic and international governmental agencies, official institutions, and central banks.

The Board of Directors of Barclays de Zoete Wedd Securities Inc. is chaired by Sir Martin Jacomb, Deputy Chairman of Barclays PLC and Chairman of BZW, and includes Barclays PLC Board of Directors members David Band, CEO of BZW, Lord Camoys, Deputy Chairman of BZW, and Kenneth B. Sinclair, Chairman of BZW Fixed Income Division. Bernard C. Grigsby and Samuel R. Marrone serve as co-Chief Executives of BZW Securities Inc.

INTRODUCTION

During the latter half of the 1980s, as the American economy embarked on one of the longest postwar expansions on record, the determination of benchmark interest rates in the United States was increasingly influenced by international considerations. Indeed, of the major financial events which occurred between 1984 and 1989, most were international in origin: the 1985 Plaza Accord wherby the "G-5" effected the lowering of the dollar's foreign exchange value; the volatility of the oil market, including the 1986 price collapse and the 1989 price recovery; increased cooperation among the major industrial nations on statutory and market concerns; and the recent political upheaval in Eastern Europe. All of these events have important long-term ramifications for the global capital markets. Domestically, the 1985 passage of the Gramm-Rudman amendment and the October 1987 stock market crash had the most lasting effects on the direction of yields over the 1984-1989 period. All of these events took place in a general market environment of financial innovation, deregulation and consolidation.

Of major consequence is that these important events have significantly influenced the patterns of global investing and, more important, investment activity in the U.S. Treasury market during the years of 1984 through 1989. In the United States, swelling Treasury budget deficits and the prolonged economic expansion of the 1980s have resulted in an ongoing need for overseas capital. This need for foreign capital is best exemplified by the deterioration of the merchandise trade position, which began the decade in a surplus and is now in an annual deficit position of approximately $110 billion.

As the financial markets have become increasingly globalized, the significance of the U.S. Treasury market to international investors cannot be underestimated. Therefore, to provide those involved either directly or indirectly in today's market—investors, salespersons, traders, analysts, professors, and students of international finance—Barclays de Zoete Wedd Securities Inc. has compiled this comprehensive guide to the events which influenced the U.S. Treasury market during 1984-1989. This important reference work—the first historical guide to recent events in the U.S. Treasury market—provides a detailed catalogue of the events that have determined the structure of benchmark interest rates in the U.S. Treasury market. Readers will be afforded not only a historical perspective on this important, rapidly changing financial period, but will also gain a better understanding of how a great variety of occurrences—often seemingly unrelated—can either singularly or in combination move the financial markets.

This book is meant to be used as a reference guide. As such, four summary sections, which address the events that have shaped the structure of interest rates during 1984-1989, form the basis of this study. These sections are followed by more descriptive, in-depth analyses which detail significant events—on both a monthly and a yearly basis—which occured from 1984 through 1989. Although the organization of this guide is such that market-moving events in specific months or years can be referred to directly, for greater understanding of the U.S. Treasury market, readers may find it beneficial to do so within the context of the overview provided on pages 3–16.

These overview sections cover significant events that influenced the structure of rates over this six-year period; movements in the currency and commodity markets; and oil price developments. Illustrative charts accompany each of these sections which indicate how important events affected yields in the U.S. Treasury market; for

1

example, changes in prime rates; the dollar's performance against the Deutsche mark and the yen in response to both domestic and international events; and the complex history of oil production quotas. Additionally, separate groupings of charts profile movements in the U.S. Treasury market and present a chronology of shifts in monetary policy during this period.

The separate monthly sections form a composite of all significant events which influenced the pattern of interest rates during a specific month. For ease of reference, these monthly breakdowns are presented in two-page units: the right-hand page details important events that occurred during the month, while the left-hand page graphically describes how these events influenced yields on the 3-month Treasury bill, the 30-year Treasury bond, and the resulting spreads between the two maturities. Additionally, a table is included which breaks down yields on T-bills, notes, and bonds on a daily basis for each month. Overall, with the historical perspective and the detailed analyses provided, those involved in the global capital markets will be able to evaluate more accurately market direction, spread relationships, and, consequently, the risk potential at any given time for benchmark investments.

OVERVIEW

SELECTED MARKET EVENTS

3-MONTH TREASURY BILL
(Weekly At Friday Close)

30-YEAR TREASURY BOND
(Weekly At Friday Close)

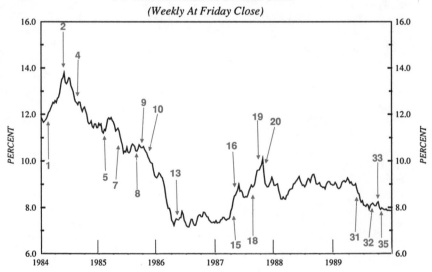

SELECTED MARKET EVENTS

1 Major U.S. banks raised their prime lending rate from 11% to 11 1/2%, the first increase since August 1983.

2 Long-term bond yields began to fall as growth in the nation's money supply fell within the Federal Reserve's target ranges.

3 Short-term interest rates continued to rise as a result of a record $13.2 billion Treasury auction of 13-week and 26-week Treasury bills.

4 The prime lending rate declined by 1/4 percentage point from 13% to 12 3/4%. This was the first industry-wide decline in more than a year and a half.

5 Interest rates on both ends of the curve moved up sharply after testimony by Federal Reserve Chairman Paul Volcker that the Fed had stopped easing. Coupled with the recent strong growth in the nation's money supply, this prompted many analysts to forecast higher interest rates.

6 In a prepared speech for the Export-Import Bank Conference, Chairman Volcker suggested that the Fed would ease rates soon to stimulate the sluggish manufacturing sector.

7 A weak 0.9% increase in April retail sales, following a 0.7% decline in March, caused renewed speculation about a Fed easing in the near future. The long end of the curve was helped by strong foreign demand for the Treasury's 30-year bond offering.

8 The flash report pegging second-quarter GNP growth at 3.1% caused a rise in interest rates.

9 The Gramm-Rudman amendment, which was passed in conjunction with an increase in the statutory debt limit, enhanced prospects for a balanced budget.

10 Spot market oil prices plunged for a fourth consecutive trading session, reflecting the disarray of OPEC following Saudi Arabia's netback pricing structure.

11 Both the Federal Reserve and the central bank of Japan cut their respective discount rates by 50 basis points. These moves were in response to an easing of inflation expectations in the U.S., and the desire to keep the dollar on a steady downward trend. The Bundesbank had made a similar move a day earlier, cutting its rate by 50 basis points.

12 Reduced inflationary pressures prompted a second 50 basis point reduction in the U.S. discount rate to 6.50%. Again, this move was quickly followed by the Bundesbank and the central bank of Japan (from 3.5% to 3.0%, and from 4.0% to 3.5%, respectively).

13 The Treasury announced a record $27 billion refunding package, about $4 billion above the previous quarterly financing.

14 Citing a pattern of relatively sluggish domestic growth and excess capacity in the industrialized world, the Fed executed a unilateral discount rate reduction to 6%.

15 Weak growth in the economy and stress in the financial system were highlighted as the Fed undertook an additional 50 basis point discount rate reduction. The move to 5.5% occurred on the day following the FOMC meeting in August 1986.

16 In testimony before a panel of the House Banking Committee, Chairman Volcker indicated that the Fed had "snugged reserve market conditions in response to the latest collapse in the dollar."

17 Commodity price gains, which ranged across most raw material markets, resulted in one of the largest single-day advances in the Commodity Research Bureau futures index (+2.7% or 6.17 points).

18 The dollar plunged by nearly 2.0% against the yen and 1.4% against the mark in response to a $1.7 billion widening in the June 1987 trade deficit. This currency move forced the Fed to return to a back-filling operating style.

19 As the dollar moved sharply lower against both the yen and the mark, the Fed raised the discount rate by 50 basis points, citing evidence of accelerating growth and building inflation pressures.

20   The Dow Jones Industrial Average plummeted an astonishing 508.32 points, or 22.6% to 1738.42. The one-day drop far exceeded the 12.8% decline of the notorious stock market crash of October 29, 1929.

21   Speaking at a conference sponsored by the Cato Institute, the Federal Reserve Board's Governor Manual Johnson commented that the central bank should use the interest rate yield curve, the value of the dollar, and commodity prices as substitutes for money in gauging the effects of policy.

22   In response to survey evidence of strong economic growth in all regions of the economy, the Fed began to tighten reserve market conditions slowly.

23   In his mid-year review of monetary policy, Federal Reserve Chairman Greenspan affirmed that monetary policy makers would assume a restrictive stance because the economy was close to the threshold on capacity and unemployment.

24   The Federal Reserve raised the discount rate from 6.0% to 6.5%, citing growing inflation pressures and a wide discount rate-fed funds spread.

25   A sharp downturn in the dollar prompted tighter reserve market conditions, despite evidence of a summer slowdown in real growth.

26   The Bundesbank increased the Lombard rate by 50 basis points to 5.5%, while the Federal Reserve tightened the funds rate from 8 5/8% to 8 7/8%.

27   Following a disastrous 1.0% pop in January wholesale prices, commercial banks raised the prime lending rate, which had been in place since late November 1988, from 10.5% to 11.0%.

28   In his monetary policy report to Congress, Federal Reserve Chairman Greenspan served notice that he would push rates higher to head off inflation. The CPI rose by 0.6% in January after a 0.3% rise the previous month. The discount rate was raised by 50 basis points to 7.0% in response to growing inflation pressures.

29   Wholesale prices rose by 1.0% in February for the second consecutive month as accelerating food and energy prices added to a sizable 0.6% rise in the core rate of inflation.

30   A sharp deceleration in the underlying rate of wholesale prices in March (+0.3% vs. +0.6% in February), combined with an unexpectedly aggressive Fed operating style, prompted renewed speculation about a monetary policy easing.

31   Student protests in China produced an international "flight to quality," which was reflected in a dollar rally and large overseas purchases of Treasury bonds. Many Street analysts incorrectly projected a recession as a sluggish hiring report for April indicated that manuacturing payroll employment had inched 9,000 lower.

32   A second consecutive +5.0% rise in non-defense capital goods orders in July, combined with evidence of a bottoming out in the manufacturing sector, ended speculation on an imminent recession environment.

33   Aggressive foreign interest failed to materialize for the 10-year August issue, producing the lowest received-to-accepted application cover in the past twelve offerings.

34   For a third consecutive month, wholesale prices fell by 0.4%, reflecting a drop in finished energy and food prices. This temperate inflation environment and shakeout in the junk bond market following Campeau Corp.'s cash crunch, reignited speculation about a Fed easing, which was validated in early October with a 25 basis point decline in the acceptable funds rate.

35   The Dow Jones Industrial Average fell 190.58 points following the announcement that a takeover group for UAL could not arrange financing for the leveraged buyout.

36   The Fed eased the fed funds rate to 8 1/2% as evidence of a broad-based slowing in the economy continued to emerge.

37   A third consecutive 25 basis point easing in monetary policy was executed in late December, bringing the funds rate down to an 8 1/4% level.

CURRENCY RATES: YEN/DOLLAR VS. MARK/DOLLAR
(Weekly At Friday Close)

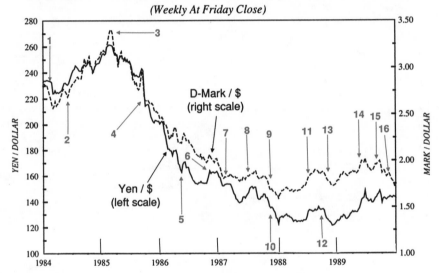

SELECTED MARKET EVENTS

1   A correction in the dollar's advance was precipitated by the combination of investor concerns about the United States' ability to finance projected currency account deficits at prevailing exchange rates and narrowing interest rate differentials.

2   A large U.S. bank experienced funding difficulties amidst heightened concern about potential LDC debt complications.

3   Shortly after the dollar peaked, President Reagan officially offered support for intervention as a means of containing the dollar.

4   The G-5 agreed to work together to encourage "an orderly appreciation of the non-dollar currencies."

5   The G-7 was formed by adding Italy and Canada to the original G-5, while also establishing an economic indicator system to monitor relative economic performance.

6   Baker and Miyazawa unilaterally decided to make the first moves at stabilizing the Dollar-Baker-Miyazawa Pact. One month later, the central bank of Japan cut its discount rate to stimulate domestic demand.

7   At a meeting in Paris, the G-7 endorsed exchange rate stability. The Louvre Accord established the reference range principle for central bank currency intervention.

8   At the Venice Economic Summit, the leaders of the G-7 countries reaffirmed their finance ministers' commitment to maintain currency stability and vowed complementary fiscal restraint.

9   Following the stock market crash, the G-7 countries temporarily abandoned the Louvre Accord.

10   With the crash causing only a limited downturn in real growth, the G-7 called an emergency meeting to reinstate the Louvre Accord. In fact, the directive stated that any "further decline or rise of the dollar, to an extent that it becomes destabilizing, is counterproductive."

11   After the Toronto Summit, a communique was issued which allowed for dollar retracement to higher levels.

12   The G-7 Berlin communique endorsed currency market stability followed by coordinated central bank dollar sales.

13   U.S. Presidential election: the market became increasingly pessimistic regarding official resolve to reduce the budget deficit, and was uncertain about G-7 determination to establish direction during the policy void.

14   Market reports of a secret G-3 agreement for the purpose of maneuvering the dollar lower contrasted with earlier comments by G-7 officials regarding the absence of dollar targets and the long-term ineffectiveness of intervention. Coordinated intervention followed, accompanied by official rate increases in Europe and an easing by the Federal Reserve two weeks later.

15   Coordinated intervention and official rate increases in Europe and Japan followed G-7 warnings issued at the Washington Summit about potential problems associated with a higher dollar.

16   As the political reform process began in Eastern Europe, East Germany relaxed border controls and began dismantling parts of the Berlin wall.

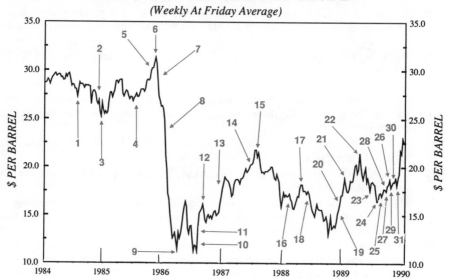

WEST TEXAS INTERMEDIATE CRUDE
(Weekly At Friday Average)

SELECTED MARKET EVENTS

1   OPEC decided to establish contact with non-OPEC producers.

2   Extraordinary meeting was called in response to decision by U.K. and Norwegian governments to cut official crude prices. Ministers agreed to an overall production cut of 1.5m b/d, bringing the ceiling down to 16m b/d.

3   Non-OPEC members Brunei, Egypt, Malaysia, and Mexico attended the meeting as observers.

4   Price differentials between crude blends eased downward. Algeria, Iran, and Libya disassociated themselves from the decision.

5   Saudi Arabia began selling its crude at prices linked to spot product prices, (netback system of pricing), guaranteeing a margin to refiners and encouraging refiners to seek progressively lower prices.

6   Extraordinary meeting: ministers agreed to maintain 16m b/d ceiling but deferred redistribution of individual quotas.

7   OPEC decided to pursue market share at the expense of prices.

8   Extraordinary meeting: 10 members of OPEC agreed that OPEC's production should be realistically set at 16.7m b/d and 16.3 b/d and 17.3 b/d for the third and fourth quarters, respectively. Talks held with non-OPEC countries on possible cooperation.

9   Brioni: OPEC meeting adjourned with no clear output or price decisions. Oil ministers returned home to consult their governments.

10 Saudi output reached 6.2m b/d.

11 The deterioration in the oil price led to the adoption by OPEC of a temporary production ceiling for September/October of 16m b/d, distributed among members with the same quotas as established in 1984; Iraq excluded.

12 Extraordinary meeting: OPEC agreed to extend its interim production agreement into November and December.

13 OPEC decided to return to fixed prices set at a level of $18/bbl. New OPEC production ceiling set at 15.8m b/d for Q1 and Q2 1987.

14 Escalation of Gulf tensions led to a U.S. agreement to escort reflagged Kuwaiti tankers through the Gulf.

15 Mecca Riots: hundreds of Iranian pilgrims were killed by Saudi forces during the Haj at Mecca, inflaming Gulf hostilities.

16 OPEC set production ceiling at 15.06m b/d; Iraq excluded.

17 Representatives from seven non-OPEC oil producers—Angola, China, Columbia, Egypt, Malaysia, Mexico, and Oman met with the OPEC Committee which comprised ministers from Algeria, Indonesia, Kuwait, Nigeria, Saudi Arabia, and Venezuela. Non-OPEC producers offered to cut back production in May and June by 5% contingent upon a proportional response from OPEC.

18 OPEC consultative meeting did not ratify proportional cuts. OPEC President Lukman, while welcoming the moves from non-OPEC producers, did not agree to implement proportional cuts and the offer lapsed.

19 Production reached record levels. OPEC's total production estimated at 22-23m b/d.

20 A Saudi cabinet meeting affirmed that the Saudi's were not prepared to lose market share to other members and would not check overproduction begun in September. Saudi output was 5.7m b/d.

21 New production accord brought Iraq back within quota. Total production restricted to 18.5m b/d. Saudi Arabia withdrew a last minute suggestion for for a $15/bbl support price when the agreement appeared to be faltering at the suggestion. Commitment to $18/bbl reaffirmed within communique.

22   North Sea production dropped as a series of accidents in the North Sea shut in 20% of the region's production.

23   Alaskan volumes were reduced in response to the Exxon Valdez oil spill.

24   May OPEC output estimated at 21m b/d as UAE and Kuwait boosted volumes.

25   Production ceiling raised 1m b/d to 19.5m b/d, to be distributed on a pro rata basis. Although all 13 ministers signed the agreement, UAE did not commit itself to honoring its new quota of 1.041m b/d.

26   All 13 members attended this committee meeting. Agreement was finally reached to increase the production ceiling to 20.5m b/d on a pro rata basis, after rejection of a plan which called for a sharp increase in UAE and Kuwaiti quotas at the expense of poorer OPEC states.

27   Spot prices fell as tropical storms caused Gulf of Mexico production to be shut down for several days.

28   Non-OPEC producers meeting in Juala Lumpar decided to remove voluntary output curb of 0.3m b/d on belief that supply and demand were in balance.

29   Prices declined on fears of an increasing OPEC production in November. Output estimated at 23.0m b/d.

30   At the biennial OPEC conference, members of the cartel agreed that production in November should be at 23.5m b/d. Kuwait agreed to new quota for first time in several years, and record low temperatures in parts of the U.S. raised spot prices.

31   Concern about the closing of the Panama Canal and Pipeline increased upward pressure on crude prices. These two facilities account for about 500,000-600,000 b/d of U.S. crude.

NON-FARM EMPLOYMENT
(Percent Change Year Ago)

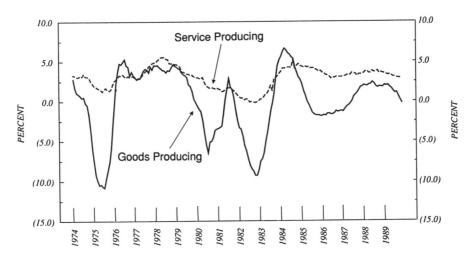

INDUSTRIAL PRODUCTION
(Percent Change Year Ago)

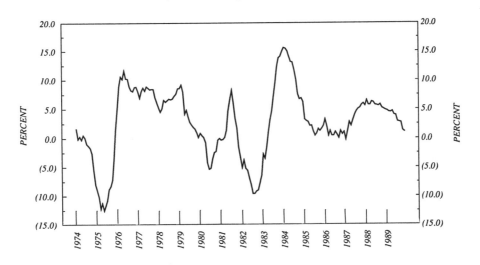

PERSONAL CONSUMPTION EXPENDITURES
(Percent Change Year Ago)

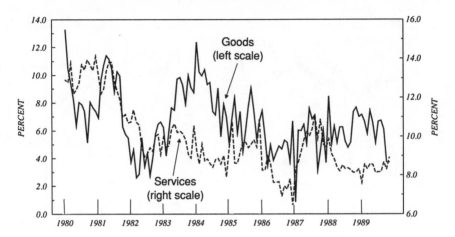

CONSTRUCTION EXPENDITURES
(Percent Change Year Ago)

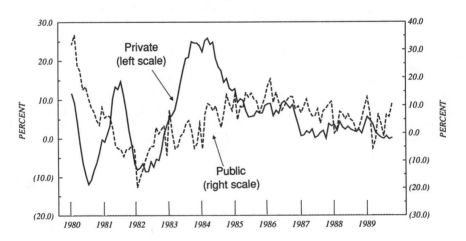

PRODUCER PRICE INDEX VS. AVG HOURLY EARNINGS
(Percent Change Year Ago)

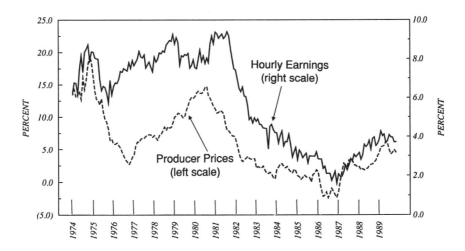

RESERVES
(Percent Change Year Ago)

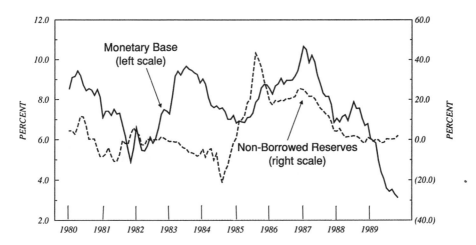

FED FUNDS VS. DISCOUNT RATE
(Monthly Average)

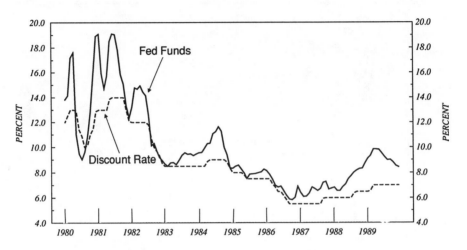

M2 MONEY SUPPLY
(Percent Change Year Ago)

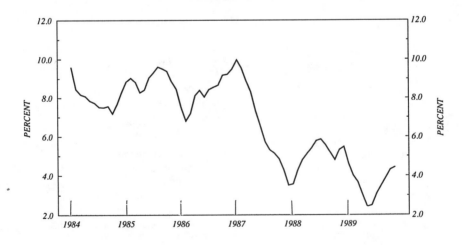

1984

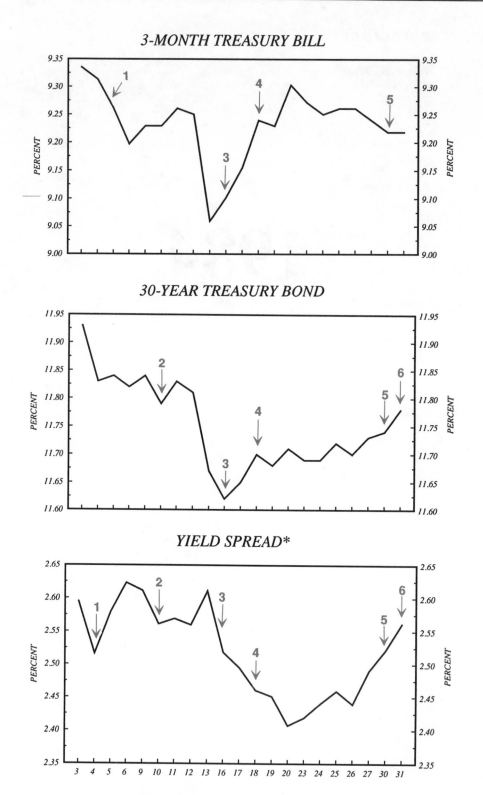

3-MONTH TREASURY BILL

30-YEAR TREASURY BOND

YIELD SPREAD*

*NOTE: SPREAD=30-YEAR BOND MINUS 3-MONTH BILL

SELECTED MARKET FACTORS

1   Short-term rates fell as anticipation of slower economic growth increased, but long-term yields held steady as a high fed funds rate, which reached an intra-day high of 11 1/2%, caused uneasiness among traders.

2   Bond prices rose due, in part, to a relatively large injection of funds into the banking network by the Federal Reserve.

3   Interest rates plummeted in response to news of a meager 0.1% rise in retail sales and a small 0.5% rise in industrial production.

4   The recent decline in rates was stalled as market participants awaited further indications that the economy was slowing.

5   The markets continued to be listless prior to the Open Market Committee meeting.

6   Bond prices declined as dealers and investors braced for a $16 billion to $17 billion supply of U.S. government securities to be offered during the following week.

U.S. TREASURY YIELDS
(Bond Equivalent Yields)

	Fed Funds	3-Month Bill	6-Month Bill	1-Year Bill	2-Year Note	3-Year Note	5-Year Note	7-Year Note	10-Year Note	30-Year Bond	Spread*
January											
3	10.15	9.34	9.74	10.11	10.87	11.10	11.59	11.79	11.86	11.93	2.59
4	9.96	9.31	9.71	10.03	10.77	11.05	11.50	11.70	11.78	11.83	2.52
5	9.62	9.26	9.68	9.99	10.75	11.00	11.47	11.69	11.77	11.84	2.58
6	9.43	9.20	9.63	9.93	10.68	10.99	11.43	11.64	11.73	11.82	2.62
9	9.55	9.23	9.67	9.98	10.73	11.02	11.47	11.69	11.75	11.84	2.61
10	9.42	9.23	9.62	9.92	10.66	10.98	11.44	11.63	11.71	11.79	2.56
11	9.83	9.26	9.64	9.99	10.72	11.03	11.46	11.68	11.76	11.83	2.57
12	9.61	9.25	9.64	9.98	10.71	11.03	11.48	11.69	11.76	11.81	2.56
13	9.40	9.06	9.36	9.66	10.50	10.82	11.26	11.48	11.59	11.67	2.61
16	9.51	9.10	9.44	9.76	10.52	10.79	11.25	11.44	11.55	11.62	2.52
17	9.45	9.16	9.47	9.85	10.55	10.85	11.28	11.49	11.57	11.65	2.50
18	10.04	9.24	9.51	9.97	10.58	10.86	11.30	11.52	11.61	11.70	2.46
19	9.63	9.23	9.51	9.88	10.57	10.87	11.29	11.50	11.60	11.68	2.45
20	9.48	9.30	9.58	9.86	10.60	10.91	11.32	11.53	11.64	11.71	2.41
23	9.66	9.27	9.57	9.87	10.61	10.88	11.31	11.52	11.63	11.69	2.42
24	9.57	9.25	9.57	9.88	10.63	10.90	11.31	11.53	11.63	11.69	2.44
25	9.44	9.26	9.57	9.87	10.65	10.91	11.31	11.53	11.64	11.72	2.46
26	9.48	9.26	9.53	9.87	10.62	10.90	11.31	11.52	11.63	11.70	2.44
27	9.31	9.24	9.52	9.85	10.62	10.88	11.31	11.52	11.63	11.73	2.49
30	9.34	9.22	9.52	9.83	10.57	10.88	11.31	11.53	11.66	11.74	2.52
31	9.35	9.22	9.52	9.85	10.58	10.89	11.34	11.56	11.67	11.78	2.56

3-MONTH TREASURY BILL

30-YEAR TREASURY BOND

YIELD SPREAD*

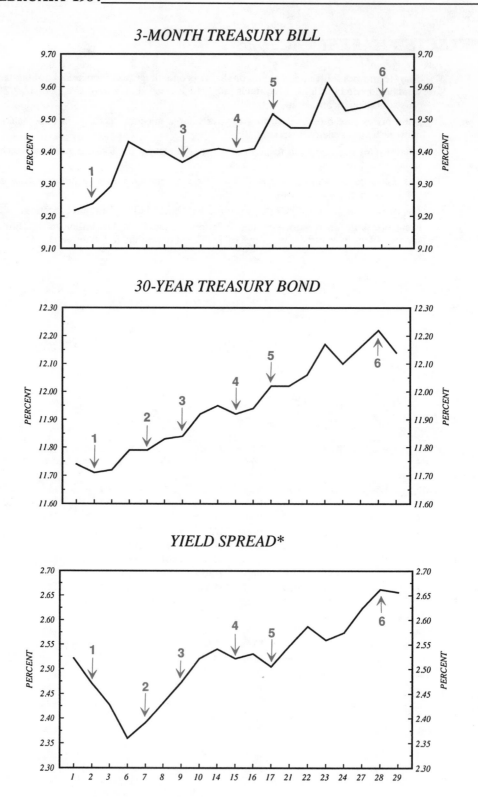

*NOTE: SPREAD=30-YEAR BOND MINUS 3-MONTH BILL

SELECTED MARKET FACTORS

1   The Reagan administration projected a $180.4 billion federal budget deficit for the fiscal year beginning October 1.

2   Analysts began to turn bearish on bonds, citing the Federal Reserve's unwillingness to ease credit because of the huge budget deficit.

3   Rates continued to drift higher as the long-awaited Fed easing failed to materialize.

4   Rates edged only slightly higher, despite a stronger than expected 2.2% jump in retail sales.

5   Bonds fell as the economy showed further signs of robust growth. Personal income rose 1.1% and housing starts surged 15.0%.

6   January's economic strength, coupled with rapid money supply growth in recent months, prompted many analysts to predict that the Fed would assume a tighter credit stance.

U.S. TREASURY YIELDS
(Bond Equivalent Yields)

	Fed Funds	3-Month Bill	6-Month Bill	1-Year Bill	2-Year Note	3-Year Note	5-Year Note	7-Year Note	10-Year Note	30-Year Bond	Spread*
February											
1	9.74	9.22	9.51	9.80	10.56	10.87	11.31	11.53	11.64	11.74	2.52
2	9.60	9.24	9.51	9.78	10.54	10.84	11.28	11.49	11.60	11.71	2.47
3	9.51	9.29	9.54	9.80	10.53	10.85	11.31	11.52	11.60	11.72	2.43
6	9.69	9.43	9.68	9.97	10.67	10.96	11.40	11.60	11.70	11.79	2.36
7	9.69	9.40	9.68	9.95	10.66	10.93	11.40	11.61	11.71	11.79	2.39
8	9.57	9.40	9.64	9.94	10.65	10.95	11.41	11.63	11.72	11.83	2.43
9	9.49	9.37	9.66	9.90	10.66	10.96	11.43	11.64	11.73	11.84	2.47
10	9.44	9.40	9.69	9.95	10.73	10.99	11.52	11.75	11.83	11.92	2.52
14	9.67	9.41	9.76	10.02	10.78	11.03	11.54	11.77	11.85	11.95	2.54
15	9.83	9.40	9.73	9.96	10.73	10.98	11.50	11.72	11.81	11.92	2.52
16	9.64	9.41	9.76	10.01	10.75	11.02	11.51	11.71	11.83	11.94	2.53
17	9.56	9.52	9.91	10.20	10.87	11.11	11.63	11.81	11.92	12.02	2.50
21	9.64	9.47	9.88	10.18	10.85	11.12	11.62	11.81	11.91	12.02	2.55
22	9.67	9.47	9.87	10.17	10.92	11.13	11.61	11.81	11.93	12.06	2.59
23	9.72	9.61	10.00	10.29	11.03	11.26	11.76	11.94	12.05	12.17	2.56
24	9.63	9.53	9.88	10.18	10.94	11.17	11.69	11.90	11.99	12.10	2.57
27	9.72	9.54	9.90	10.26	11.02	11.27	11.77	11.97	12.05	12.16	2.62
28	9.53	9.56	9.96	10.25	11.04	11.28	11.80	12.00	12.09	12.22	2.66
29	9.45	9.48	9.90	10.21	10.99	11.22	11.74	11.97	12.04	12.14	2.66

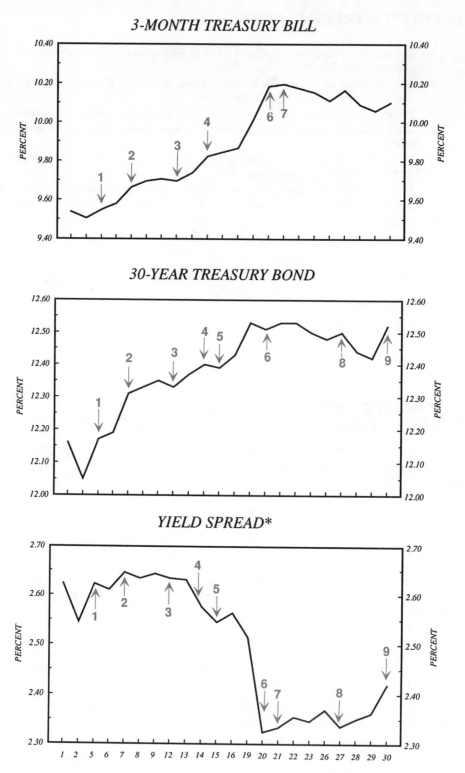

3-MONTH TREASURY BILL

30-YEAR TREASURY BOND

YIELD SPREAD*

*NOTE: SPREAD=30-YEAR BOND MINUS 3-MONTH BILL

SELECTED MARKET FACTORS

1. Interest rates rose sharply in response to increased concern about an overheating economy and a high fed funds rate of 9 13/16%.

2. The continued slide of the U.S. dollar in foreign exchange markets intensified concern about higher inflation. Bond prices also continued their recent slide.

3. Pressures mounted for an increase in the banking industry's prime lending rate, which is currently at 11%. The increase in banks' cost of funds is beginning to squeeze profit margins.

4. Rates rose in response to a White House release that President Reagan had lost some faith in bipartisan budget talks.

5. Bond prices surged after the Reagan administration announced an agreement with Republican Congressional leaders on a plan to cut the federal budget deficit.

6. Interest rates surged as the nation's major banks raised their prime lending rate from 11% to 11 1/2%. This is the first increase since August 1983.

7. Short-term rates rose in response to the Commerce Department's report that the economic growth was at a 7.2% annual rate in the current quarter.

8. The Federal Reserve System drained funds from the banking network in a move considered by some analysts as confirmation of a Federal Reserve tightening move.

9. Bond prices tumbled as dealers were disappointed with lackluster demand for the U.S. Treasury's latest offering of long-term bonds.

U.S. TREASURY YIELDS
(Bond Equivalent Yields)

March	Fed Funds	3-Month Bill	6-Month Bill	1-Year Bill	2-Year Note	3-Year Note	5-Year Note	7-Year Note	10-Year Note	30-Year Bond	Spread*
1	9.73	9.54	9.95	10.28	11.05	11.27	11.77	11.99	12.07	12.16	2.62
2	9.75	9.51	9.89	10.18	10.92	11.18	11.68	11.91	11.99	12.05	2.55
5	9.81	9.55	9.97	10.24	11.01	11.27	11.76	11.98	12.07	12.17	2.62
6	9.72	9.58	9.97	10.26	11.01	11.29	11.77	12.02	12.09	12.19	2.61
7	9.66	9.66	10.03	10.32	11.08	11.39	11.87	12.12	12.22	12.31	2.65
8	9.74	9.70	10.07	10.38	11.15	11.45	11.90	12.15	12.24	12.33	2.63
9	9.73	9.71	10.14	10.46	11.19	11.52	11.95	12.20	12.28	12.35	2.64
12	9.84	9.70	10.14	10.43	11.18	11.47	11.94	12.15	12.24	12.33	2.63
13	9.79	9.74	10.18	10.47	11.22	11.49	11.97	12.21	12.27	12.37	2.63
14	9.96	9.82	10.25	10.56	11.26	11.57	12.00	12.26	12.31	12.40	2.58
15	10.09	9.85	10.25	10.53	11.28	11.55	11.99	12.23	12.31	12.39	2.55
16	9.84	9.87	10.28	10.65	11.27	11.58	12.01	12.25	12.34	12.43	2.56
19	10.07	10.02	10.41	10.73	11.39	11.69	12.11	12.37	12.45	12.53	2.51
20	10.25	10.19	10.54	10.81	11.45	11.73	12.13	12.38	12.44	12.51	2.32
21	10.36	10.20	10.56	10.85	11.57	11.77	12.17	12.38	12.45	12.53	2.33
22	10.45	10.18	10.59	10.93	11.59	11.83	12.22	12.43	12.49	12.53	2.35
23	10.28	10.15	10.59	10.91	11.59	11.83	12.23	12.43	12.48	12.50	2.35
26	10.06	10.11	10.55	10.87	11.56	11.84	12.20	12.38	12.46	12.48	2.37
27	9.62	10.16	10.55	10.83	11.58	11.83	12.21	12.40	12.46	12.50	2.34
28	8.81	10.09	10.45	10.75	11.48	11.75	12.15	12.38	12.42	12.44	2.35
29	10.07	10.06	10.45	10.72	11.49	11.74	12.16	12.36	12.41	12.42	2.36
30	10.24	10.10	10.52	10.80	11.60	11.86	12.28	12.45	12.53	12.52	2.42

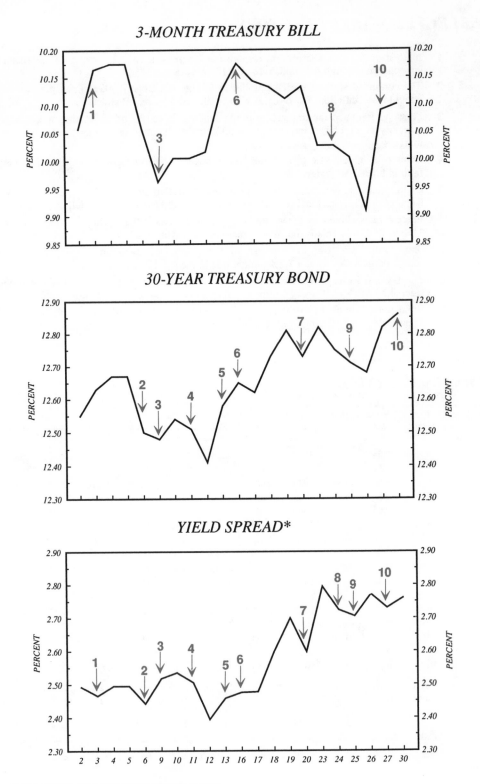

*NOTE: SPREAD=30-YEAR BOND MINUS 3-MONTH BILL

SELECTED MARKET FACTORS

1. Rates continued to rise amidst concern by dealers and investors that the Federal Reserve might be tightening credit further. Concern about Fed policy intensified because of an increase in the fed funds rate and rumors of an imminent discount rate hike.
2. Major U.S. banks raised their prime lending rate from 11 1/2% to 12% as a result of an increase in the bank's own cost for funds and stronger loan demand.
3. The Federal Reserve raised the discount rate from 8 1/2% to 9%, the first increase in nearly three years. Most economists and bond traders viewed the move as a catch-up move since most other interest rates had risen in recent months.
4. Bond prices fell in reaction to the report of large trading losses by Marsh & McLennan. Officials of Marsh & McLennan announced that the insurance and financial services company had been victimized by an employee's unauthorized trading. There was widespread speculation that the firm has already begun to liquidate its large holdings of U.S. government securities.
5. The M1 money supply plunged $5 billion in the week ending April 2, and March retail sales dropped 2.2%.
6. Long and short rates rose amidst renewed concern about inflation. Although the economy has shown signs of slowing, many analysts doubt that it will slow enough to contain inflation. The market was affected further by rumors that Federal Reserve Chairman Volcker had resigned.
7. Bond prices continued lower on a GNP report which was stronger than expected. Real GNP for the first quarter expanded at an 8.3% annual rate compared with the consensus 7.0% forecasted by many analysts.
8. Interest rates on short-term Treasury bills declined at the weekly auction. The declines reflected, in part, a reduction in the size of the offering from $12 billion to $10 billion at the previous sale.
9. The consumer price index rose 0.2% in March compared with 0.4% in February.
10. Interest rates rose on the report of an $844 million increase in commercial and industrial loans at 10 major New York City banks.

U.S. TREASURY YIELDS
(Bond Equivalent Yields)

April	Fed Funds	3-Month Bill	6-Month Bill	1-Year Bill	2-Year Note	3-Year Note	5-Year Note	7-Year Note	10-Year Note	30-Year Bond	Spread*
2	10.42	10.06	10.49	10.84	11.61	11.87	12.29	12.50	12.56	12.55	2.49
3	10.75	10.16	10.65	10.98	11.73	12.02	12.40	12.58	12.65	12.63	2.47
4	10.90	10.18	10.63	10.99	11.76	12.05	12.44	12.60	12.67	12.67	2.49
5	10.74	10.18	10.63	10.97	11.70	12.02	12.42	12.58	12.65	12.67	2.49
6	10.37	10.06	10.46	10.79	11.55	11.85	12.24	12.42	12.51	12.50	2.44
9	10.32	9.96	10.43	10.71	11.55	11.87	12.22	12.39	12.47	12.48	2.52
10	9.49	10.01	10.44	10.71	11.54	11.85	12.26	12.42	12.52	12.54	2.53
11	9.25	10.01	10.44	10.71	11.53	11.82	12.24	12.41	12.50	12.51	2.50
12	10.34	10.02	10.37	10.74	11.49	11.77	12.16	12.32	12.40	12.41	2.39
13	10.24	10.12	10.52	10.91	11.66	11.91	12.30	12.50	12.57	12.58	2.46
16	10.50	10.18	10.57	10.95	11.70	11.99	12.35	12.53	12.61	12.65	2.47
17	10.45	10.14	10.52	10.87	11.59	11.90	12.30	12.49	12.57	12.62	2.48
18	10.61	10.13	10.49	10.95	11.69	11.99	12.40	12.62	12.70	12.73	2.60
19	10.73	10.11	10.49	10.98	11.77	12.08	12.47	12.68	12.77	12.81	2.70
20	9.77	10.13	10.49	10.95	11.69	11.99	12.40	12.62	12.70	12.73	2.60
23	9.63	10.03	10.41	10.97	11.78	12.10	12.49	12.69	12.80	12.82	2.79
24	9.55	10.03	10.43	10.95	11.73	12.06	12.46	12.66	12.75	12.75	2.72
25	10.67	10.01	10.40	10.97	11.79	12.04	12.45	12.64	12.69	12.71	2.71
26	10.63	9.91	10.39	10.93	11.77	12.02	12.42	12.60	12.67	12.68	2.77
27	10.49	10.09	10.56	11.06	11.89	12.17	12.55	12.72	12.79	12.82	2.73
30	10.90	10.10	10.57	11.11	11.89	12.20	12.57	12.75	12.82	12.86	2.76

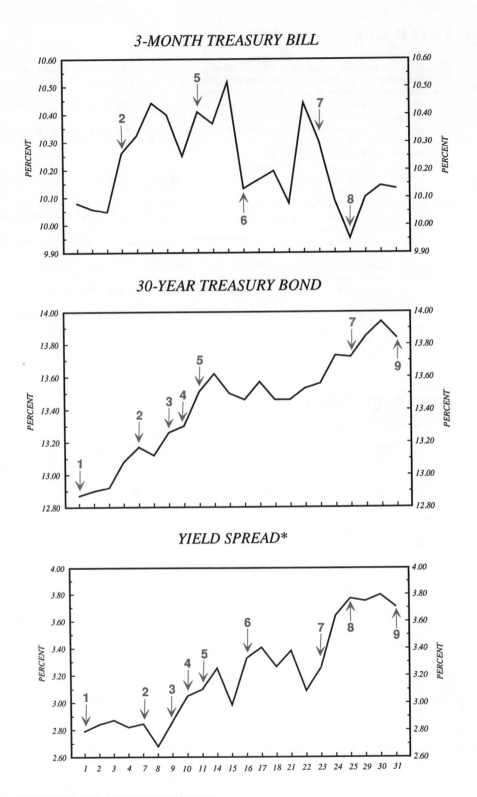

3-MONTH TREASURY BILL

30-YEAR TREASURY BOND

YIELD SPREAD*

*NOTE: SPREAD=30-YEAR BOND MINUS 3-MONTH BILL

SELECTED MARKET FACTORS

1   The Commerce Department's Composite Index of Leading Indicators fell 1.1% in March. This was the first decline since August 1982 in the index.

2   Long- and short-term interest rates surged in reaction to April's employment report. Payroll employment increased by 269,000 jobs, while the average workweek spurted to 35.6 hours from 35.2 hours the previous month.

3   Most of the nation's major banks boosted their prime lending rate from 12% to 12 1/2%, bringing the rate to its highest level since October 1982. The hike was attributed to continued increases in the banking industry's cost of raising funds.

4   Bond prices tumbled under the weight of the U.S. government's massive borrowing needs. The Treasury auctioned off $5.26 billion of 10-year notes. The average yield on the notes soared from 11.70% to 13.16% at the previous sale of similar securities in February.

5   Bonds suffered another setback as prices fell and investors shunned the Treasury's $4.75 billion auction of 30-year bonds. Short-term rates fell as the "flight to quality" continued with funds moving into debt instruments with shorter time commitments.

6   Short-term interest rates fell as most investors moved their funds from long bonds to CDs and Treasury bills.

7   Long and short rates surged as the fed funds rate rose to 10 5/8%, well above last week's average of 9 7/10%. This precipitated fears of another round of Fed tightening.

8   Investors bid up prices on Treasury bills as worries over the U.S. banking system increased. There were rumors that Manufacturers Hanover might be facing the same difficulties as the Continental Illinois National Bank & Trust Co. of Chicago. Less than two weeks ago, government officials set up a massive rescue operation for the failing bank.

9   Bonds continued to be battered on unconfirmed reports that Bolivia had decided to suspend payments on its international debt.

U.S. TREASURY YIELDS
(Bond Equivalent Yields)

May	Fed Funds	3-Month Bill	6-Month Bill	1-Year Bill	2-Year Note	3-Year Note	5-Year Note	7-Year Note	10-Year Note	30-Year Bond	Spread*
1	11.04	10.08	10.56	11.08	11.88	12.19	12.57	12.76	12.82	12.87	2.79
2	10.88	10.06	10.64	11.16	11.92	12.23	12.62	12.80	12.86	12.90	2.84
3	10.45	10.05	10.65	11.17	11.96	12.25	12.64	12.81	12.89	12.92	2.87
4	10.04	10.26	10.90	11.41	12.15	12.44	12.83	12.97	13.07	13.08	2.82
7	10.48	10.32	11.02	11.49	12.24	12.51	12.90	13.08	13.13	13.17	2.85
8	11.06	10.44	11.02	11.47	12.23	12.50	12.88	13.05	13.09	13.12	2.68
9	11.12	10.40	11.02	11.50	12.32	12.57	12.97	13.14	13.21	13.26	2.86
10	11.00	10.25	10.86	11.50	12.32	12.56	12.98	13.17	13.25	13.30	3.05
11	10.58	10.41	11.01	11.65	12.55	12.79	13.20	13.40	13.46	13.51	3.10
14	10.33	10.37	10.99	11.69	12.57	12.83	13.30	13.49	13.58	13.62	3.25
15	10.55	10.52	11.15	11.69	12.51	12.77	13.23	13.41	13.48	13.50	2.98
16	9.99	10.13	10.86	11.62	12.42	12.71	13.17	13.34	13.41	13.46	3.33
17	9.92	10.16	11.01	11.72	12.51	12.83	13.27	13.45	13.54	13.57	3.41
18	9.01	10.20	10.95	11.68	12.47	12.77	13.21	13.35	13.45	13.46	3.26
21	9.71	10.08	10.94	11.66	12.48	12.77	13.18	13.35	13.43	13.46	3.38
22	10.73	10.44	11.24	11.80	12.58	12.86	13.27	13.43	13.52	13.53	3.09
23	10.84	10.30	11.20	11.85	12.67	12.91	13.30	13.43	13.54	13.56	3.26
24	10.72	10.09	11.21	12.00	12.77	13.04	13.46	13.62	13.72	13.73	3.64
25	10.04	9.95	11.12	11.90	12.77	13.07	13.52	13.67	13.75	13.72	3.77
29	10.51	10.10	11.32	12.07	12.98	13.24	13.70	13.83	13.89	13.85	3.75
30	10.71	10.14	11.38	12.20	13.04	13.40	13.84	13.95	13.99	13.94	3.80
31	10.81	10.13	11.33	12.15	13.00	13.33	13.76	13.87	13.91	13.84	3.71

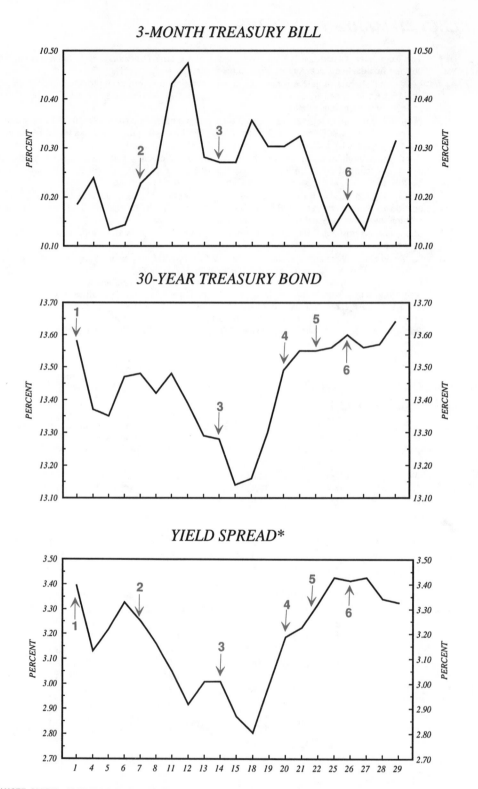

3-MONTH TREASURY BILL

30-YEAR TREASURY BOND

YIELD SPREAD*

*NOTE: SPREAD=30-YEAR BOND MINUS 3-MONTH BILL

SELECTED MARKET FACTORS

1   The Commerce Department's Index of Leading Indicators rose a moderate 0.5% in April, and new factory orders tumbled 3.6% during the month.

2   Short-term interest rates rose as the fed funds rate reached an intra-day high of 11.25% from yesterday's average of 10.65%.

3   Interest rates declined amidst growing dealer optimism as a result of the economy's recent slowdown, the Federal Reserve would ease up its reserve grip. The optimism was spurred by a Commerce Department report showing a much smaller than expected 0.2% rise last month in retail sales. Compared with last month's 3.1% surge, this was well below the 1%–2% increase many analysts had been expecting.

4   Bond prices dropped in response to news from the Commerce Department that personal consumption expenditures rose 1.1% in May, following a 1.6% jump in April.

5   The nation's money supply surged $3 billion, bringing it above the Federal Reserve's target range for the first time since late February.

6   Most big banks raised their prime lending rate by 1/2% to 13%. The increase was attributed to strong loan demand and higher cost of funds for banks.

U.S. TREASURY YIELDS
(Bond Equivalent Yields

June	Fed Funds	3-Month Bill	6-Month Bill	1-Year Bill	2-Year Note	3-Year Note	5-Year Note	7-Year Note	10-Year Note	30-Year Bond	Spread*
1	10.53	10.19	11.20	11.96	12.72	13.01	13.46	13.61	13.63	13.58	3.39
4	10.99	10.24	11.18	11.85	12.63	12.90	13.29	13.39	13.42	13.37	3.13
5	10.65	10.13	11.17	11.82	12.60	12.90	13.24	13.34	13.37	13.35	3.22
6	11.03	10.14	11.21	11.89	12.75	13.04	13.38	13.51	13.54	13.47	3.33
7	11.01	10.23	11.29	12.00	12.81	13.07	13.43	13.56	13.54	13.48	3.25
8	10.76	10.26	11.26	12.03	12.74	13.03	13.35	13.46	13.46	13.42	3.16
11	11.16	10.43	11.41	12.20	13.00	13.23	13.57	13.61	13.58	13.48	3.05
12	10.83	10.47	11.39	12.13	12.92	13.15	13.45	13.59	13.54	13.39	2.92
13	10.66	10.28	11.18	11.97	12.83	13.07	13.37	13.48	13.44	13.29	3.01
14	11.04	10.27	11.10	11.93	12.75	13.04	13.31	13.40	13.39	13.28	3.01
15	11.33	10.27	11.10	11.85	12.63	12.90	13.12	13.20	13.21	13.14	2.87
18	11.56	10.36	11.18	11.91	12.75	12.96	13.19	13.26	13.27	13.16	2.80
19	11.55	10.30	11.18	11.91	12.79	13.02	13.30	13.37	13.38	13.30	3.00
20	12.31	10.30	11.35	12.26	13.08	13.36	13.57	13.66	13.65	13.49	3.19
21	11.90	10.32	11.42	12.34	13.14	13.43	13.67	13.72	13.72	13.55	3.23
22	11.51	10.23	11.37	12.31	13.15	13.42	13.72	13.73	13.74	13.55	3.32
25	11.08	10.13	11.26	12.24	13.12	13.39	13.70	13.72	13.75	13.56	3.43
26	10.84	10.19	11.26	12.29	13.17	13.49	13.77	13.79	13.79	13.60	3.41
27	10.51	10.13	11.17	12.25	13.12	13.45	13.70	13.75	13.76	13.56	3.43
28	10.64	10.23	11.21	12.32	13.17	13.48	13.70	13.78	13.80	13.57	3.34
29	10.85	10.31	11.19	12.30	13.17	13.48	13.72	13.82	13.84	13.64	3.33

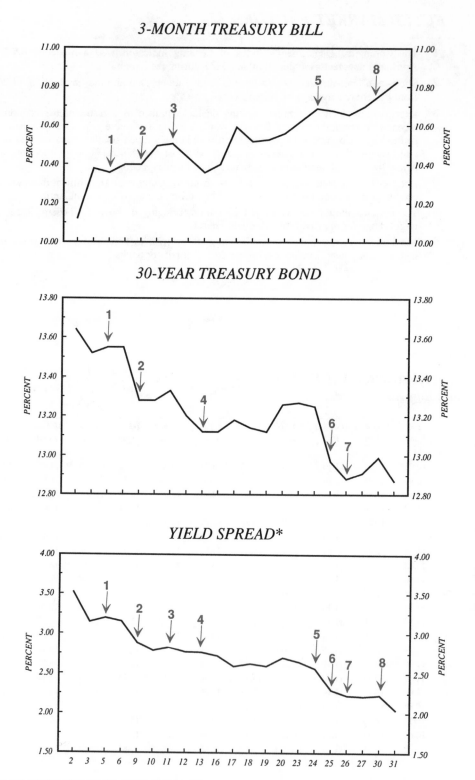

3-MONTH TREASURY BILL

30-YEAR TREASURY BOND

YIELD SPREAD*

*NOTE: SPREAD=30-YEAR BOND MINUS 3-MONTH BILL

SELECTED MARKET FACTORS

1 Bond prices rallied in response to demand, which was stronger than expected, at the Treasury's auction of $5.51 billion of new 7-year notes.

2 The civilian unemployment rate tumbled from 7.5% in May to 7.1% in June. Non-farm payroll employment increased by 301,000 jobs.

3 Short-term interest rates continued to rise as the Treasury announced plans to sell a record $13.2 billion of 13-week and 26-week Treasury bills.

4 Bond prices surged on the report that two of the three Fed money supply figures were within the central bank's target range for the year. Analysts hoped that this bill would reduce pressure on the Federal Reserve to tighten credit further.

5 Interest rates on short-term debt instruments continued to move higher before the Treasury's impending $13.2 billion bill auction during the week.

6 The Consumer Price Index rose 0.2% in June, while orders for durable goods fell 3.2% after rising by 4% in May.

7 Bond prices posted big gains as testimony by Federal Reserve Chairman Paul Volcker stated that the Fed expected slower economic growth in the second half of this year than in the first half.

8 The bond rally stalled as short-term interest rates continued their assent under the weight of heavy government borrowing needs. Later this week, the Treasury is expected to disclose plans to sell about $16.75 billion to $17.0 billion of new notes and bonds.

U.S. TREASURY YIELDS
(Bonds Equivalent Yields)

July	Fed Funds	3-Month Bill	6-Month Bill	1-Year Bill	2-Year Note	3-Year Note	5-Year Note	7-Year Note	10-Year Note	30-Year Bond	Spread*
2	11.43	10.12	11.12	12.23	13.17	13.43	13.73	13.83	13.87	13.64	3.52
3	10.88	10.38	11.19	12.19	13.12	13.37	13.67	13.79	13.80	13.52	3.14
5	11.25	10.36	11.13	12.10	13.07	13.33	13.64	13.73	13.77	13.55	3.19
6	11.13	10.40	11.18	12.15	13.13	13.38	13.65	13.74	13.75	13.55	3.15
9	11.52	10.40	11.16	12.05	12.96	13.23	13.40	13.48	13.48	13.28	2.88
10	11.37	10.50	11.28	12.10	13.00	13.24	13.46	13.52	13.53	13.28	2.79
11	11.22	10.51	11.32	12.23	13.06	13.26	13.45	13.55	13.55	13.33	2.82
12	11.03	10.43	11.24	12.13	12.96	13.19	13.39	13.43	13.42	13.20	2.77
13	11.00	10.36	11.17	11.99	12.85	13.04	13.24	13.21	13.30	13.12	2.76
16	11.45	10.40	11.27	12.07	12.89	13.07	13.24	13.32	13.32	13.12	2.72
17	11.40	10.59	11.37	12.11	12.93	13.12	13.29	13.37	13.37	13.18	2.59
18	11.60	10.52	11.26	12.01	12.89	13.06	13.22	13.31	13.32	13.14	2.62
19	11.36	10.53	11.24	11.95	12.82	12.99	13.17	13.23	13.25	13.12	2.59
20	11.09	10.56	11.30	12.00	12.85	13.06	13.24	13.32	13.36	13.26	2.70
23	11.49	10.62	11.35	12.06	12.87	13.06	13.25	13.34	13.35	13.27	2.65
24	11.21	10.69	11.36	12.00	12.85	13.02	13.24	13.30	13.31	13.25	2.56
25	11.02	10.68	11.28	11.86	12.64	12.81	12.95	13.04	13.06	12.97	2.29
26	11.29	10.66	11.22	11.76	12.55	12.67	12.80	12.89	12.89	12.88	2.23
27	11.33	10.70	11.32	11.80	12.59	12.76	12.89	12.95	12.95	12.91	2.21
30	11.53	10.76	11.39	11.90	12.66	12.84	13.00	13.05	13.05	12.99	2.23
31	11.83	10.83	11.39	11.86	12.57	12.70	12.85	12.91	12.91	12.87	2.04

3-MONTH TREASURY BILL

30-YEAR TREASURY BOND

YIELD SPREAD*

*NOTE: SPREAD=30-YEAR BOND MINUS 3-MONTH BILL

SELECTED MARKET FACTORS

1   A decrease in factory orders and construction spending caused the bond market to rally. The rally lost much of its steam, however, after the government announced plans to sell $16.75 billion in new notes and bonds in its quarterly financing operation.

2   The market continued to rally on optimism about the slowing economy and the decreased problem of tightening by the Federal Reserve.

3   Nervousness brought on by concern about the government's massive borrowing needs and the trade deficit (which widened to a record $26.29 billion), brought an end to a two-week rally.

4   A mood of euphoria swept through bond markets as an unexpectedly large drop in the nation's money supply and aggressive bidding at the Treasury's long-term bond auction sent bond prices soaring.

5   The bond market slumped as fed funds traded as high as 12% at one time during the day.

6   Bond prices advanced, despite increases in short-term interest rates. Fed funds traded between 11 13/16%-11 7/8%.

7   Interest rates rose as hopes of an easing in credit by the Federal Reserve dwindled.

U.S. TREASURY YIELDS
(Bond Equivalent Yields)

	Fed Funds	3-Month Bill	6-Month Bill	1-Year Bill	2-Year Note	3-Year Note	5-Year Note	7-Year Note	10-Year Note	30-Year Bond	Spread*
August											
1	12.04	10.86	11.39	11.82	12.48	12.63	12.74	12.82	12.81	12.78	1.92
2	11.65	10.89	11.39	11.85	12.48	12.61	12.71	12.75	12.74	12.70	1.81
3	11.50	10.89	11.35	11.75	12.30	12.39	12.55	12.61	12.61	12.59	1.70
6	11.76	10.98	11.45	11.88	12.42	12.53	12.66	12.74	12.73	12.69	1.71
7	11.74	10.97	11.39	11.85	12.41	12.45	12.64	12.71	12.69	12.64	1.68
8	11.50	10.90	11.34	11.80	12.37	12.43	12.62	12.69	12.66	12.62	1.72
9	11.62	10.84	11.25	11.74	12.33	12.40	12.59	12.65	12.61	12.47	1.63
10	11.57	10.86	11.28	11.73	12.35	12.41	12.63	12.68	12.68	12.47	1.61
13	11.73	10.88	11.36	11.81	12.45	12.52	12.71	12.79	12.74	12.54	1.66
14	11.52	10.72	11.24	11.71	12.34	12.40	12.62	12.68	12.67	12.48	1.76
15	11.82	10.61	11.22	11.70	12.39	12.45	12.68	12.76	12.74	12.57	1.96
16	11.74	10.68	11.24	11.70	12.40	12.46	12.66	12.73	12.70	12.51	1.83
17	11.77	10.75	11.25	11.73	12.40	12.44	12.67	12.73	12.70	12.46	1.71
20	11.87	10.87	11.32	11.80	12.42	12.45	12.66	12.74	12.69	12.41	1.54
21	11.83	10.85	11.34	11.80	12.41	12.44	12.64	12.67	12.62	12.35	1.50
22	11.61	10.84	11.28	11.78	12.45	12.48	12.66	12.69	12.65	12.43	1.59
23	11.57	10.88	11.30	11.81	12.44	12.49	12.68	12.72	12.69	12.45	1.57
24	11.53	10.91	11.34	11.81	12.41	12.45	12.67	12.69	12.66	12.44	1.53
27	11.68	11.12	11.52	11.95	12.54	12.57	12.80	12.84	12.81	12.60	1.48
28	11.47	11.09	11.53	11.97	12.54	12.59	12.82	12.84	12.81	12.57	1.48
29	11.20	11.10	11.52	11.97	12.56	12.61	12.78	12.88	12.83	12.57	1.47
30	11.65	11.09	11.52	11.99	12.56	12.62	12.79	12.89	12.84	12.56	1.47
31	11.64	11.07	11.50	11.96	12.54	12.61	12.77	12.85	12.79	12.51	1.44

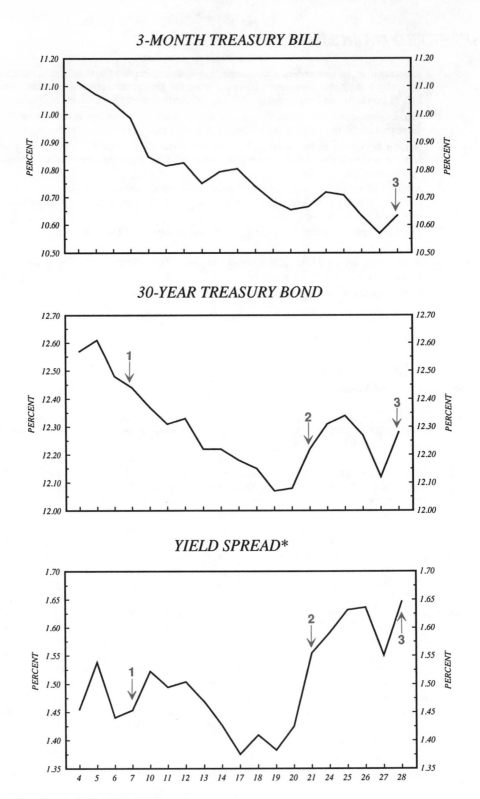

3-MONTH TREASURY BILL

30-YEAR TREASURY BOND

YIELD SPREAD*

*NOTE: SPREAD=30-YEAR BOND MINUS 3-MONTH BILL

SELECTED MARKET FACTORS

1   Bonds surged amidst speculation that the Fed might ease credit. The rally was attributed, in part, to the Federal Reserve's aggressive injection of reserves into the system, which led to short covering.

2   Bond prices slumped following the government's estimate that the economy was expanding at a 3.6% rate for the quarter. A large $7.8 billion surge in money supply also added to market jitters.

3   The prime lending rate declined by 1/4 point from 13% to 12 3/4%—the first industry-wide decline in more than a year and a half. Bond yields rose, however, as dealers and investors braced for a massive supply of Treasury notes and bonds.

U.S. TREASURY YIELDS
(Bond Equivalent Yields)

September	Fed Funds	3-Month Bill	6-Month Bill	1-Year Bill	2-Year Note	3-Year Note	5-Year Note	7-Year Note	10-Year Note	30-Year Bond	Spread*
4	11.81	11.12	11.54	12.01	12.59	12.65	12.85	12.94	12.88	12.57	1.46
5	11.72	11.07	11.54	12.02	12.63	12.71	12.92	13.01	12.92	12.61	1.54
6	11.71	11.04	11.47	11.95	12.54	12.63	12.82	12.88	12.81	12.48	1.44
7	11.56	10.99	11.43	11.83	12.45	12.52	12.75	12.80	12.70	12.44	1.45
10	11.36	10.85	11.28	11.65	12.27	12.39	12.65	12.72	12.62	12.37	1.52
11	11.23	10.82	11.26	11.68	12.26	12.39	12.59	12.64	12.54	12.31	1.50
12	11.66	10.83	11.30	11.69	12.30	12.39	12.62	12.65	12.55	12.33	1.50
13	11.55	10.75	11.19	11.56	12.21	12.28	12.47	12.52	12.44	12.22	1.47
14	11.38	10.79	11.18	11.48	12.15	12.23	12.42	12.49	12.42	12.22	1.43
17	11.64	10.81	11.18	11.53	12.16	12.23	12.42	12.49	12.40	12.18	1.38
18	11.53	10.74	11.09	11.45	12.10	12.19	12.33	12.43	12.35	12.15	1.41
19	11.35	10.69	11.01	11.34	11.94	12.12	12.26	12.33	12.25	12.07	1.38
20	11.12	10.66	10.99	11.30	11.94	12.12	12.27	12.35	12.28	12.08	1.43
21	10.89	10.67	11.06	11.43	12.06	12.27	12.44	12.51	12.45	12.22	1.55
24	10.94	10.72	11.10	11.49	12.10	12.31	12.51	12.58	12.52	12.31	1.59
25	10.52	10.71	11.09	11.43	12.12	12.34	12.53	12.61	12.56	12.34	1.63
26	9.84	10.63	11.04	11.42	12.05	12.28	12.47	12.54	12.46	12.27	1.64
27	11.00	10.57	10.97	11.32	11.95	12.13	12.31	12.38	12.31	12.12	1.55
28	11.23	10.63	11.06	11.43	12.07	12.28	12.48	12.54	12.47	12.28	1.65

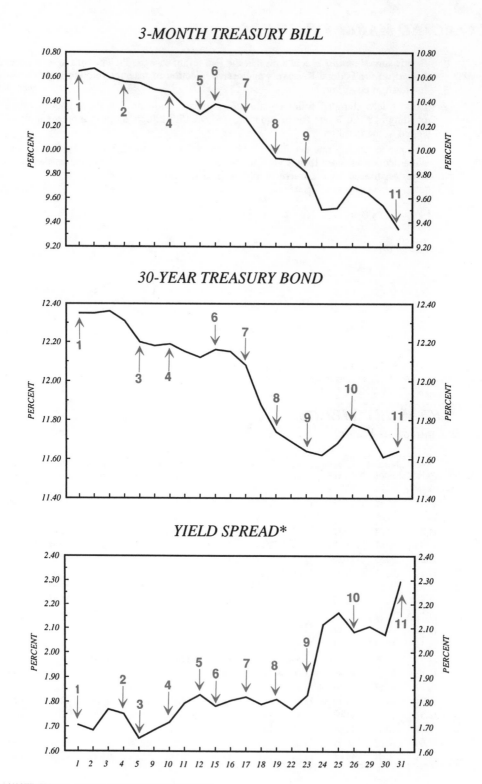

3-MONTH TREASURY BILL

30-YEAR TREASURY BOND

YIELD SPREAD*

*NOTE: SPREAD=30-YEAR BOND MINUS 3-MONTH BILL

SELECTED MARKET FACTORS

1   The Commerce Department reported a 0.5% increase in its Composite Index of Leading Economic Indicators for August. The increase followed successive declines of 1.8% in July and 1.1% in June.

2   Treasury bill rates declined in a "flight to quality" move by many dealers in response to renewed worries about the stability of the banking system. First Chicago Corp. announced that it expected a sizable loss in the third-quarter because of sharply increased loan-loss reserves.

3   Bonds rallied in response to an unexpectedly large $2.4 billion decline in the nation's money supply.

4   Interest rates declined as the closely watched fed funds rate traded at 10.21%, down sharply from 11.25% a week ago.

5   Treasury bill rates continued to decline, reflecting renewed concern about the stability of the banking system.

6   Producer prices fell 0.2% in September.

7   Most major banks lowered their prime lending rate from 12 3/4% to 12 1/2%.

8   Interest rates dropped sharply on the report of a $2 a barrel cut in oil prices and an unexpected drop in the nation's money supply.

9   Rates continued their decline as the fed funds rate traded below 10%.

10   An unexpectedly large $1.8 billion increase in the nation's money supply ended the bond rally.

11   President Reagan's statement that interest rates "should drop further in the days ahead," spurred a rally in the bill and bond markets.

U.S. TREASURY YIELDS
(Bond Equivalent Yields)

	Fed Funds	3-Month Bill	6-Month Bill	1-Year Bill	2-Year Note	3-Year Note	5-Year Note	7-Year Note	10-Year Note	30-Year Bond	Spread*
October											
1	11.38	10.64	11.08	11.44	12.09	12.31	12.51	12.60	12.54	12.35	1.71
2	11.42	10.67	11.07	11.44	12.07	12.29	12.52	12.61	12.54	12.35	1.68
3	10.91	10.59	11.01	11.40	12.06	12.29	12.49	12.59	12.54	12.36	1.77
4	10.58	10.56	10.98	11.37	12.02	12.25	12.45	12.57	12.52	12.31	1.75
5	10.21	10.55	10.94	11.31	11.93	12.15	12.35	12.44	12.39	12.20	1.65
9	9.91	10.50	10.90	11.25	11.87	12.12	12.32	12.43	12.36	12.18	1.69
10	8.72	10.47	10.86	11.23	11.89	12.13	12.32	12.44	12.36	12.19	1.72
11	10.25	10.36	10.77	11.12	11.78	12.02	12.23	12.37	12.31	12.15	1.79
12	10.02	10.29	10.68	11.03	11.72	11.98	12.17	12.32	12.28	12.12	1.83
15	10.54	10.38	10.76	11.11	11.78	12.04	12.24	12.38	12.34	12.16	1.78
16	10.45	10.35	10.75	11.10	11.77	12.01	12.25	12.33	12.32	12.15	1.80
17	10.27	10.26	10.66	10.99	11.70	11.95	12.21	12.27	12.28	12.08	1.82
18	9.92	10.09	10.47	10.82	11.53	11.75	11.98	12.07	12.09	11.88	1.79
19	9.83	9.93	10.20	10.61	11.39	11.63	11.82	11.91	11.93	11.74	1.81
22	9.95	9.92	10.21	10.62	11.35	11.63	11.82	11.87	11.90	11.69	1.77
23	9.24	9.81	10.10	10.45	11.17	11.44	11.62	11.72	11.78	11.64	1.83
24	7.53	9.51	9.90	10.29	11.10	11.34	11.55	11.68	11.74	11.62	2.11
25	9.24	9.52	9.95	10.35	11.13	11.41	11.65	11.77	11.83	11.68	2.16
26	9.59	9.70	10.20	10.59	11.33	11.59	11.82	11.95	11.99	11.78	2.08
29	9.99	9.64	10.17	10.55	11.30	11.56	11.79	11.89	11.95	11.75	2.11
30	10.10	9.54	9.98	10.37	11.13	11.37	11.63	11.69	11.75	11.61	2.07
31	9.99	9.35	9.86	10.26	11.09	11.36	11.59	11.70	11.79	11.64	2.29

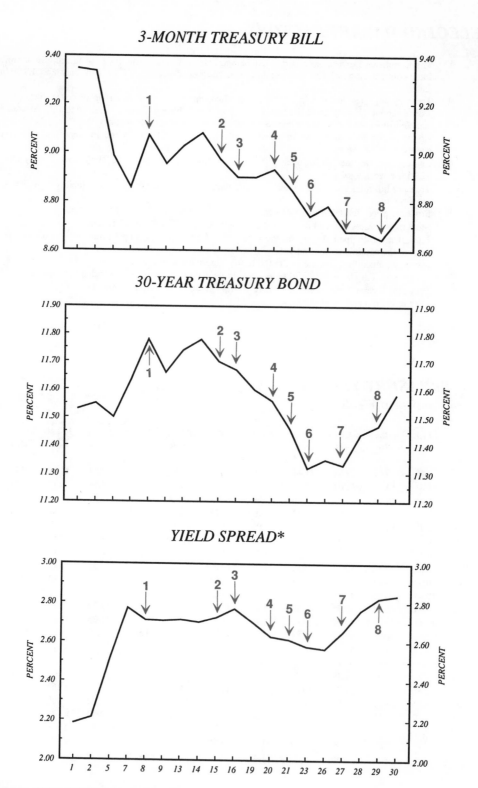

*NOTE: SPREAD=30-YEAR BOND MINUS 3-MONTH BILL

SELECTED MARKET FACTORS

1 Several major banks cut their prime lending rates from 12.0% to 11 3/4%. Bond prices fell, partially in response to the disappointment of market participants when the Republicans failed to make substantial gains in Congressional races, despite President Reagan's landslide victory.

2 Interest rates rose in response to a bleak budget outlook. Reagan administration officials expected the deficit for the current year to exceed $205 billion, which easily eclipsed the record $195 billion set in fiscal 1983.

3 Bond and bill prices rallied after the Federal Reserve unexpectedly injected reserves into the banking system. This prompted many analysts to call for a future cut in the discount rate.

4 Interest rates fell in response to an aggressive injection of reserves into the banking system.

5 The Commerce Department lowered its estimate of third-quarter economic growth to an annual rate of 1.9%, down from their earlier projection of 2.7%.

6 The Federal Reserve cut its discount rate from 9.0% to 8 1/2%. October durable goods orders fell 4.1%, following a 3.3% decline in September.

7 Citibank and several other major banks trimmed their prime lending rates from 11 3/4% to 11 1/2%, a much smaller cut than had generally been expected.

8 Some banks cut their prime lending rates to 11 1/4%, while others held the line at 11 1/2%.

U.S. TREASURY YIELDS
(Bonds Equivalent Yields)

	Fed Funds	3-Month Bill	6-Month Bill	1-Year Bill	2-Year Note	3-Year Note	5-Year Note	7-Year Note	10-Year Note	30-Year Bond	Spread*
November											
1	10.26	9.35	9.78	10.18	10.93	11.18	11.45	11.57	11.66	11.53	2.18
2	10.15	9.34	9.81	10.17	10.96	11.20	11.46	11.58	11.66	11.55	2.22
5	9.57	8.99	9.58	10.01	10.79	10.99	11.40	11.52	11.60	11.50	2.52
7	9.35	8.86	9.40	9.93	10.80	11.05	11.45	11.63	11.72	11.63	2.77
8	9.76	9.07	9.57	10.06	10.95	11.15	11.55	11.74	11.81	11.78	2.71
9	9.50	8.95	9.46	9.91	10.81	11.05	11.47	11.63	11.71	11.66	2.71
13	9.51	9.03	9.58	10.06	10.89	11.10	11.55	11.69	11.78	11.74	2.71
14	9.56	9.08	9.59	10.08	10.91	11.11	11.59	11.72	11.81	11.78	2.70
15	9.62	8.98	9.44	9.95	10.78	11.01	11.52	11.65	11.73	11.70	2.72
16	9.54	8.90	9.39	9.85	10.71	10.97	11.46	11.59	11.69	11.67	2.77
19	9.45	8.90	9.36	9.85	10.67	10.92	11.41	11.54	11.61	11.60	2.70
20	9.28	8.93	9.30	9.76	10.59	10.83	11.29	11.46	11.53	11.56	2.63
21	9.32	8.85	9.07	9.53	10.39	10.69	11.14	11.29	11.39	11.46	2.61
23	8.97	8.74	8.95	9.43	10.29	10.56	10.99	11.15	11.24	11.32	2.58
26	9.03	8.78	9.00	9.48	10.33	10.57	11.05	11.19	11.28	11.35	2.57
27	8.96	8.68	9.02	9.51	10.31	10.61	11.05	11.19	11.28	11.33	2.65
28	8.78	8.68	9.05	9.51	10.35	10.65	11.03	11.31	11.38	11.44	2.76
29	8.63	8.65	9.05	9.52	10.37	10.67	11.07	11.34	11.42	11.47	2.82
30	8.92	8.74	9.19	9.71	10.50	10.86	11.25	11.56	11.58	11.58	2.84

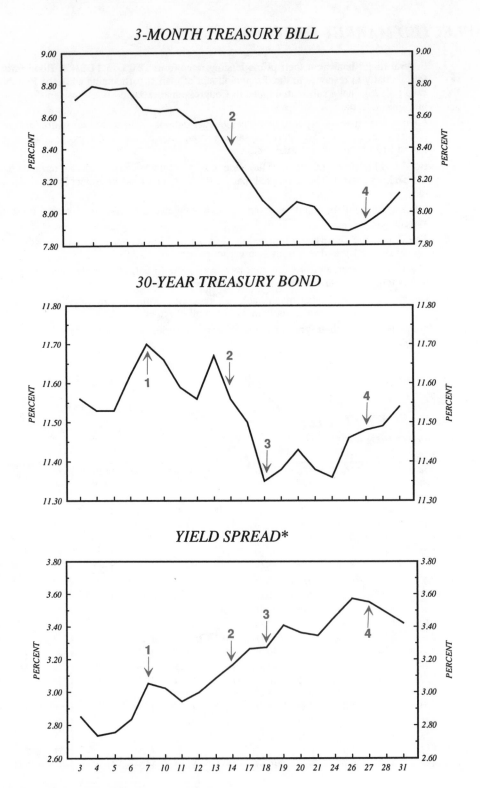

3-MONTH TREASURY BILL

30-YEAR TREASURY BOND

YIELD SPREAD*

*NOTE: SPREAD=30-YEAR BOND MINUS 3-MONTH BILL

SELECTED MARKET FACTORS

1   Bond prices edged lower amidst growing fears that the recent surge in money supply would prevent the Federal Reserve from easing further.

2   The bond market fell after a surprisingly strong increase in retail sales.

3   Manufacturers Hanover reduced its prime lending rate by 50 basis points from 11 1/4% to 10 3/4%. Interest rates fell amidst mounting evidence that the Fed had eased.

4   Bonds declined as the market tried to absorb the government's huge borrowing needs.

U.S. TREASURY YIELDS
(Bond Equivalent Yields)

December	Fed Funds	3-Month Bill	6-Month Bill	1-Year Bill	2-Year Note	3-Year Note	5-Year Note	7-Year Note	10-Year Note	30-Year Bond	Spread*
3	9.27	8.71	9.12	9.66	10.50	10.84	11.23	11.51	11.56	11.56	2.85
4	8.80	8.80	9.10	9.59	10.44	10.74	11.16	11.45	11.52	11.53	2.73
5	8.35	8.77	9.09	9.58	10.40	10.74	11.14	11.46	11.52	11.53	2.76
6	8.93	8.78	9.18	9.68	10.49	10.81	11.23	11.55	11.61	11.62	2.84
7	8.62	8.65	9.12	9.65	10.51	10.85	11.31	11.64	11.70	11.70	3.05
10	8.75	8.64	9.08	9.63	10.47	10.84	11.26	11.61	11.66	11.66	3.02
11	8.75	8.65	9.02	9.57	10.40	10.75	11.18	11.53	11.57	11.59	2.94
12	8.58	8.56	8.87	9.44	10.35	10.67	11.14	11.51	11.54	11.56	3.00
13	8.42	8.58	8.95	9.54	10.40	10.72	11.27	11.67	11.70	11.67	3.09
14	8.26	8.39	8.72	9.26	10.20	10.57	11.08	11.50	11.56	11.56	3.17
17	7.83	8.23	8.60	9.18	10.07	10.42	11.01	11.43	11.49	11.50	3.27
18	6.93	8.08	8.43	9.01	9.85	10.24	10.83	11.25	11.29	11.35	3.27
19	7.98	7.97	8.45	9.04	9.89	10.29	10.86	11.28	11.34	11.38	3.41
20	8.29	8.07	8.49	9.14	9.94	10.34	10.89	11.28	11.37	11.43	3.36
21	8.06	8.03	8.44	9.10	9.94	10.31	10.89	11.29	11.34	11.38	3.35
24	7.53	7.90	8.41	9.02	9.83	10.27	10.85	11.26	11.31	11.36	3.46
26	8.12	7.89	8.48	9.08	9.95	10.37	10.97	11.42	11.45	11.46	3.57
27	8.51	7.93	8.49	9.11	9.96	10.43	10.98	11.43	11.45	11.48	3.55
28	8.62	8.00	8.55	9.17	10.02	10.48	11.03	11.44	11.46	11.49	3.49
31	8.74	8.12	8.66	9.22	10.02	10.52	11.08	11.52	11.55	11.54	3.42

1985

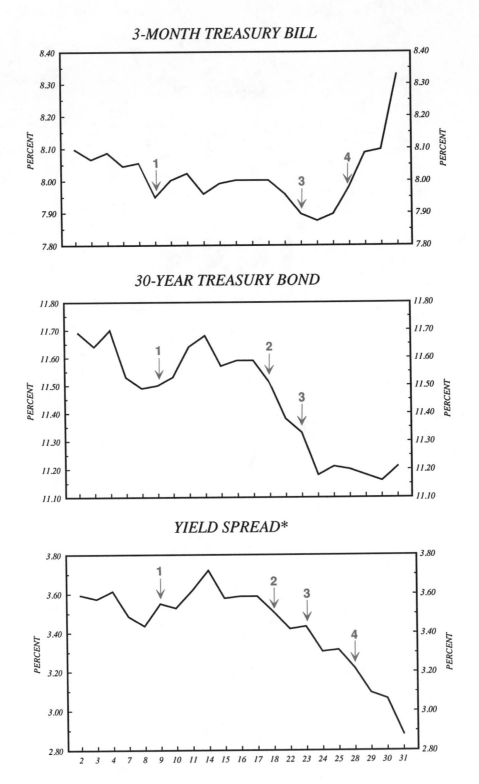

3-MONTH TREASURY BILL

30-YEAR TREASURY BOND

YIELD SPREAD*

*NOTE: SPREAD=30-YEAR BOND MINUS 3-MONTH BILL

SELECTED MARKET FACTORS

1. A 25 basis point decline in the prime lending rate by Southwest Bank in St. Louis prompted speculation on similar moves by other commercial banks. At the same time, a rise in payroll employment for December, which was stronger than expected, caused analysts to increase inflation warnings.

2. M1 rose $2.1 billion in the week ending January 7. This increase, which was lower than expected, caused bond prices to rally and yields to fall from 11.61% to 11.51%.

3. Personal income rose a solid 0.5% for December 1984, with consumer spending up a strong 1.2%. Fourth-quarter GNP rose at a 3.9% annual rate; however, the implicit price deflator rose by only 2.4%, causing bond prices to rally on an improved inflation outlook.

4. An upward rebound in the fed funds rate following five weeks of consecutive declines was quickly reflected in the Treasury bill market.

U.S. TREASURY YIELDS
(Bond Equivalent Yields)

	Fed Funds	3-Month Bill	6-Month Bill	1-Year Bill	2-Year Note	3-Year Note	5-Year Note	7-Year Note	10-Year Note	30-Year Bond	Spread*
January											
2	9.37	8.10	8.63	9.19	10.03	10.61	11.22	11.68	11.70	11.69	3.59
3	8.77	8.07	8.63	9.17	10.06	10.55	11.13	11.54	11.62	11.64	3.57
4	8.18	8.09	8.63	9.17	10.08	10.62	11.19	11.61	11.67	11.70	3.61
7	8.23	8.05	8.49	9.03	10.01	10.50	11.09	11.41	11.50	11.53	3.48
8	7.79	8.06	8.48	9.04	9.99	10.48	11.04	11.36	11.45	11.49	3.44
9	8.02	7.95	8.30	8.95	9.95	10.45	11.03	11.36	11.47	11.50	3.55
10	8.23	8.00	8.37	9.05	10.00	10.52	11.05	11.37	11.48	11.53	3.53
11	8.24	8.02	8.48	9.13	10.08	10.59	11.14	11.47	11.59	11.64	3.62
14	8.15	7.96	8.47	9.12	10.07	10.59	11.13	11.47	11.60	11.68	3.72
15	8.03	7.99	8.42	9.04	10.00	10.49	11.01	11.33	11.49	11.57	3.58
16	8.51	8.00	8.43	9.04	9.99	10.51	11.02	11.37	11.51	11.59	3.59
17	8.27	8.00	8.42	9.04	9.98	10.47	10.99	11.34	11.48	11.59	3.59
18	8.10	8.00	8.38	8.99	9.91	10.38	10.89	11.25	11.39	11.51	3.51
22	8.29	7.96	8.37	8.91	9.83	10.30	10.79	11.13	11.27	11.38	3.42
23	8.36	7.90	8.35	8.90	9.83	10.26	10.74	11.06	11.21	11.33	3.43
24	8.33	7.88	8.32	8.88	9.74	10.18	10.61	10.91	11.06	11.18	3.30
25	8.37	7.90	8.35	8.90	9.76	10.24	10.66	10.98	11.11	11.21	3.31
28	8.62	7.98	8.44	8.95	9.79	10.30	10.70	10.98	11.11	11.20	3.22
29	8.61	8.09	8.47	8.97	9.79	10.28	10.70	10.98	11.11	11.18	3.09
30	8.49	8.10	8.46	8.95	9.76	10.27	10.68	10.96	11.08	11.16	3.06
31	8.73	8.33	8.63	9.09	9.90	10.36	10.77	11.07	11.17	11.21	2.88

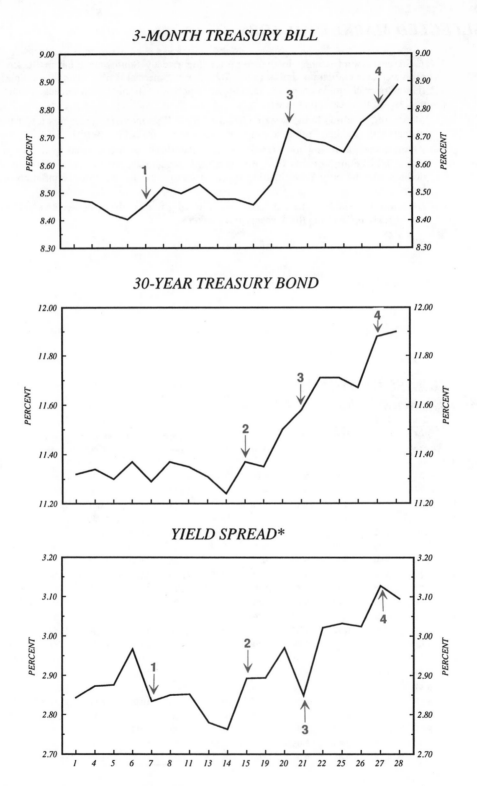

3-MONTH TREASURY BILL

30-YEAR TREASURY BOND

YIELD SPREAD*

*NOTE: SPREAD=30-YEAR BOND MINUS 3-MONTH BILL

SELECTED MARKET FACTORS

1   Despite a $1.9 billion drop in M1 for the most recent reporting week, market analysts have begun to speculate on a new round of credit tightening following two weeks of a higher fed funds rate.

2   The Treasury's $19 billion first-quarter refinancing settled amidst growing concern that money supply growth had started to force the Federal Reserve into a tightening posture.

3   At the semi-annual Humphrey-Hawkins testimony, Paul Volcker stated that the Federal Reserve had clearly stopped easing rates but had also not begun tightening. The Fed faces a dilemma caused by soaring money supply growth and the recent rally in the exchange value of the dollar.

4   Rates rose sharply at both ends of the yield curve as Chairman Volcker told the House Banking Committee that recent dollar intervention had not been aggressive enough to halt the dollar's rise.

U.S. TREASURY YIELDS
(Bond Equivalent Yields)

February	Fed Funds	3-Month Bill	6-Month Bill	1-Year Bill	2-Year Note	3-Year Note	5-Year Note	7-Year Note	10-Year Note	30-Year Bond	Spread*
1	8.74	8.48	8.77	9.21	10.04	10.48	10.93	11.20	11.29	11.32	2.84
4	8.61	8.47	8.78	9.20	10.03	10.51	10.99	11.25	11.35	11.34	2.87
5	8.36	8.42	8.72	9.14	9.99	10.37	10.93	11.21	11.30	11.30	2.88
6	8.22	8.40	8.71	9.15	10.03	10.40	11.00	11.31	11.40	11.37	2.97
7	8.41	8.46	8.77	9.21	10.06	10.44	11.04	11.34	11.41	11.29	2.83
8	8.49	8.52	8.78	9.18	10.03	10.40	11.00	11.30	11.37	11.37	2.85
11	8.30	8.50	8.80	9.22	10.06	10.45	11.05	11.35	11.42	11.35	2.85
13	8.61	8.53	8.78	9.22	10.03	10.44	11.02	11.32	11.39	11.31	2.78
14	8.59	8.48	8.75	9.18	9.98	10.33	10.93	11.22	11.29	11.24	2.76
15	8.53	8.48	8.75	9.15	10.02	10.38	10.98	11.32	11.38	11.37	2.89
19	8.63	8.46	8.74	9.13	10.01	10.37	10.95	11.27	11.37	11.35	2.89
20	8.67	8.53	8.84	9.24	10.13	10.47	11.09	11.43	11.52	11.50	2.97
21	8.67	8.73	9.03	9.40	10.29	10.64	11.29	11.58	11.64	11.58	2.85
22	8.50	8.69	9.05	9.44	10.34	10.74	11.35	11.71	11.76	11.71	3.02
25	8.52	8.68	9.03	9.41	10.36	10.75	11.40	11.70	11.75	11.71	3.03
26	8.04	8.65	9.03	9.41	10.36	10.75	11.35	11.67	11.72	11.67	3.02
27	8.06	8.75	9.23	9.64	10.56	10.93	11.51	11.87	11.89	11.88	3.13
28	8.74	8.81	9.33	9.72	10.66	11.03	11.55	11.87	11.91	11.90	3.10

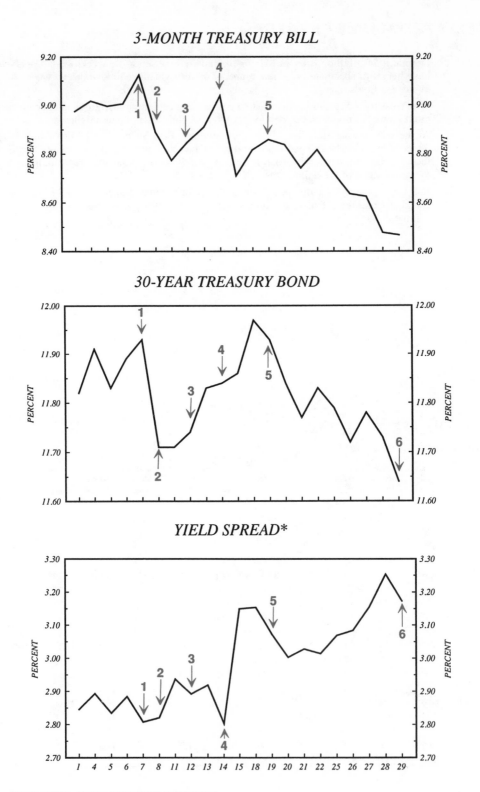

3-MONTH TREASURY BILL

30-YEAR TREASURY BOND

YIELD SPREAD*

*NOTE: SPREAD=30-YEAR BOND MINUS 3-MONTH BILL

SELECTED MARKET FACTORS

1 A drop in the fed funds rate to about 8.5% reduced speculation on an imminent tightening that had been touched off by Federal Reserve Chairman Volcker's February testimony.

2 Interest rates fell at both ends of the yield curve as Chairman Volcker indicated that a drop in the U.S. dollar would not prompt any increase in monetary restraint.

3 The dollar plunged sharply as prospects of lower short-term rates increased in the absence of a Federal Reserve tightening move.

4 Retail sales for February were up 1.4%, suggesting strong consumer spending, despite a weak manufacturing sector.

5 A run on Ohio's S&Ls sent many investors scrambling to buy Treasury bills as a safe haven. The Governor of Ohio closed 71 state-chartered S&Ls following the run.

6 A sharp uptrend in the dollar ended following Chairman Volcker's statement that the Federal Reserve had not tightened policy, and that he considered the dollar's value to be too high.

U.S. TREASURY YIELDS
(Bond Equivalent Yields)

	Fed Funds	3-Month Bill	6-Month Bill	1-Year Bill	2-Year Note	3-Year Note	5-Year Note	7-Year Note	10-Year Note	30-Year Bond	Spread*
March											
1	8.74	8.98	9.49	9.87	10.73	11.09	11.52	11.81	11.86	11.82	2.85
4	8.73	9.02	9.56	9.91	10.78	11.12	11.57	11.87	11.93	11.91	2.89
5	8.53	9.00	9.49	9.84	10.71	11.05	11.49	11.80	11.86	11.83	2.83
6	8.21	9.01	9.49	9.88	10.75	11.09	11.53	11.86	11.92	11.89	2.88
7	8.47	9.12	9.69	10.08	10.83	11.19	11.61	11.91	11.94	11.93	2.81
8	8.42	8.89	9.39	9.76	10.56	10.90	11.37	11.69	11.71	11.71	2.82
11	8.26	8.77	9.32	9.71	10.56	10.92	11.38	11.71	11.72	11.71	2.94
12	8.53	8.85	9.39	9.80	10.62	10.99	11.45	11.76	11.78	11.74	2.89
13	9.12	8.91	9.57	9.95	10.79	11.13	11.59	11.88	11.90	11.83	2.92
14	9.12	9.04	9.70	10.07	10.86	11.19	11.63	11.91	11.92	11.84	2.80
15	8.81	8.71	9.53	10.00	10.82	11.17	11.63	11.92	11.93	11.86	3.15
18	8.62	8.82	9.62	10.09	10.89	11.22	11.70	12.00	12.02	11.97	3.15
19	8.62	8.86	9.58	10.04	10.85	11.19	11.67	11.97	11.99	11.93	3.07
20	8.49	8.84	9.51	10.00	10.85	11.17	11.62	11.90	11.91	11.84	3.00
21	8.60	8.74	9.38	9.84	10.69	11.02	11.48	11.78	11.82	11.77	3.03
22	8.61	8.82	9.44	9.89	10.75	11.05	11.55	11.83	11.88	11.83	3.01
25	8.45	8.72	9.41	9.83	10.71	11.05	11.53	11.80	11.86	11.79	3.07
26	7.99	8.64	9.33	9.77	10.63	10.97	11.45	11.73	11.77	11.72	3.08
27	7.79	8.63	9.26	9.71	10.63	10.99	11.49	11.82	11.84	11.78	3.15
28	8.89	8.48	9.11	9.61	10.53	10.86	11.38	11.69	11.75	11.73	3.25
29	8.58	8.47	9.06	9.49	10.43	10.79	11.29	11.59	11.65	11.64	3.17

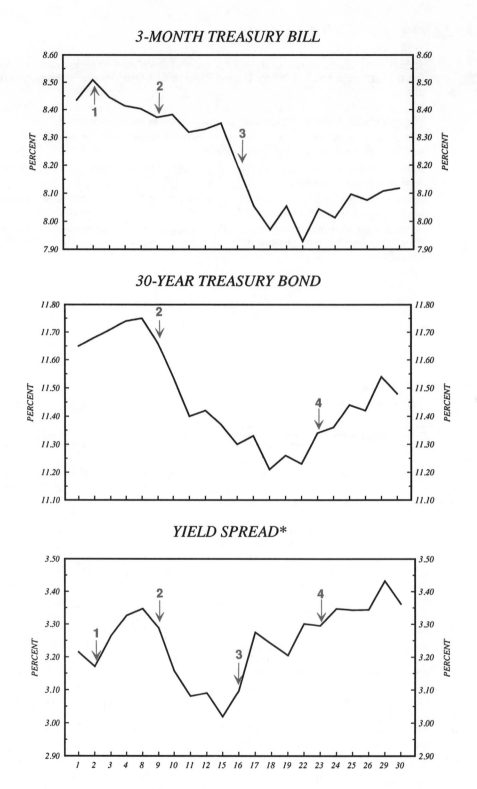

3-MONTH TREASURY BILL

30-YEAR TREASURY BOND

YIELD SPREAD*

*NOTE: SPREAD=30-YEAR BOND MINUS 3-MONTH BILL

SELECTED MARKET FACTORS

1   Although factory orders for February fell 0.2% in response to a large drop in orders for defense goods, non-defense capital goods orders were up a solid 2.1% for the month. At the same time, construction spending for February rose 1.4% as building outlays rose for single-family homes, office buildings, and industrial structures.

2   Bevill, Bresler-GSI was put into Chapter 11 proceedings and charged with fraud by the SEC.

3   In a speech prepared for the Export-Import Bank Conference, Federal Reserve Chairman Volcker suggested that the Fed would soon begin to ease rates in light of a six- to nine-month downturn in manufacturing, which was caused by a record flow of imports into the economy. An unexpected reserve add executed by the Federal Reserve pushed the funds rate down sharply. Fed funds traded most of the day in the 8 1/8% to 8 3/8% range, down from 8.57% average on Monday.

4   With the value of the dollar moving lower, and the Federal Reserve in an easing mode for several weeks, a 0.5% jump in the March CPI caught the markets by surprise. The 0.5% increase in CPI represents a 5.8% compounded annual increase, the largest increase recorded in over a year.

U.S. TREASURY YIELDS
(Bond Equivalent Yields)

April	Fed Funds	3-Month Bill	6-Month Bill	1-Year Bill	2-Year Note	3-Year Note	5-Year Note	7-Year Note	10-Year Note	30-Year Bond	Spread*
1	8.83	8.44	9.06	9.51	10.45	10.81	11.28	11.57	11.66	11.65	3.22
2	8.79	8.51	9.09	9.54	10.48	10.83	11.33	11.64	11.70	11.68	3.17
3	8.49	8.45	9.10	9.55	10.49	10.83	11.34	11.65	11.73	11.71	3.26
4	8.56	8.41	9.12	9.54	10.53	10.87	11.35	11.70	11.75	11.74	3.33
8	8.58	8.40	9.09	9.53	10.49	10.84	11.36	11.69	11.77	11.75	3.35
9	8.68	8.37	8.98	9.40	10.38	10.77	11.28	11.60	11.66	11.66	3.29
10	8.94	8.38	8.93	9.36	10.31	10.67	11.20	11.50	11.58	11.54	3.16
11	8.81	8.32	8.76	9.14	10.12	10.51	11.05	11.31	11.42	11.40	3.08
12	8.49	8.33	8.74	9.15	10.13	10.52	11.05	11.33	11.43	11.42	3.09
15	8.57	8.35	8.75	9.15	10.09	10.49	11.02	11.29	11.37	11.37	3.02
16	8.30	8.20	8.52	8.95	9.86	10.25	10.80	11.14	11.25	11.30	3.10
17	8.09	8.06	8.57	9.01	9.93	10.33	10.86	11.19	11.29	11.33	3.28
18	7.84	7.97	8.33	8.77	9.73	10.17	10.69	11.05	11.13	11.21	3.24
19	7.60	8.06	8.43	8.86	9.81	10.17	10.69	11.06	11.16	11.26	3.21
22	7.52	7.93	8.32	8.77	9.72	10.15	10.67	11.03	11.13	11.23	3.30
23	7.88	8.05	8.46	8.90	9.88	10.29	10.79	11.13	11.25	11.34	3.30
24	7.81	8.01	8.44	8.88	9.81	10.27	10.77	11.15	11.25	11.36	3.35
25	8.23	8.10	8.53	8.96	9.90	10.37	10.87	11.27	11.37	11.44	3.34
26	8.14	8.08	8.49	8.93	9.88	10.36	10.87	11.23	11.35	11.42	3.34
29	8.41	8.11	8.58	9.07	9.97	10.47	10.96	11.35	11.47	11.54	3.43
30	8.58	8.12	8.57	8.99	9.91	10.39	10.91	11.31	11.41	11.48	3.36

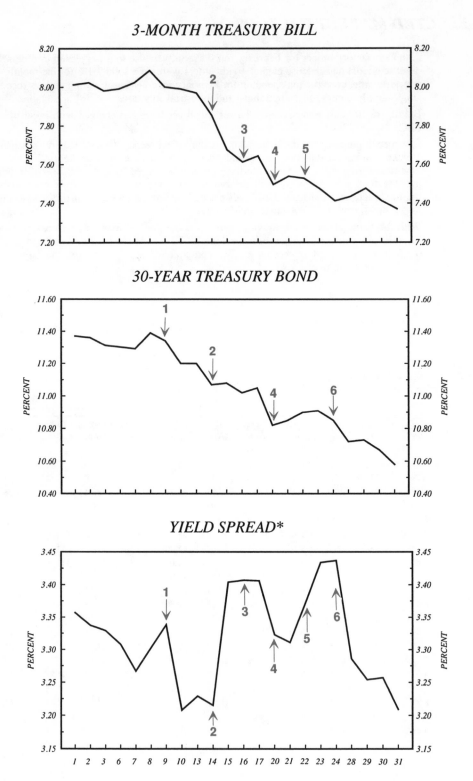

*NOTE: SPREAD=30-YEAR BOND MINUS 3-MONTH BILL

SELECTED MARKET FACTORS

1   Bond yields declined as strong foreign demand surfaced for the Treasury 30-year bond offering. The high degree of interest in the third part of the refunding was highlighted by the $15.9 billion in tenders received for the $6.0 billion offering.

2   A sharp rally at both ends of the yield curve was sparked by renewed speculation about a Federal Reserve easing following the April retail sales report. Retail sales rose by 0.9% in April, barely reversing a 0.7% decline reported for the previous month.

3   Industrial production dropped by 0.2% in April, confirming other signs that manufacturers had experienced practically no growth since last July. Bankers Trust cut the prime lending rate to 10%, the lowest rate in six and one-half years, following the April output report.

4   The Federal Reserve reduced the discount rate to 7 1/2%, bringing it to its lowest rate since August 1978.

5   First-quarter real GNP for 1985 grew at a sluggish 0.7%.

6   Bond prices edged upward yesterday amidst renewed investor optimism about a plan to reduce the government's massive budget deficit that would soon be enacted.

U.S. TREASURY YIELDS
(Bond Equivalent Yields)

	Fed Funds	3-Month Bill	6-Month Bill	1-Year Bill	2-Year Note	3-Year Note	5-Year Note	7-Year Note	10-Year Note	30-Year Bond	Spread*
May											
1	8.83	8.01	8.46	8.89	9.82	10.28	10.81	11.15	11.27	11.37	3.36
2	8.83	8.02	8.48	8.91	9.86	10.31	10.83	11.17	11.29	11.36	3.34
3	8.28	7.98	8.34	8.73	9.71	10.17	10.74	11.09	11.21	11.31	3.33
6	7.97	7.99	8.37	8.76	9.70	10.15	10.71	11.07	11.19	11.30	3.31
7	7.98	8.02	8.34	8.72	9.66	10.04	10.68	11.06	11.17	11.29	3.27
8	7.71	8.09	8.41	8.76	9.73	10.11	10.74	11.17	11.26	11.39	3.30
9	8.08	8.00	8.35	8.73	9.67	10.04	10.68	11.08	11.20	11.34	3.34
10	8.18	7.99	8.32	8.68	9.62	9.95	10.57	10.93	11.04	11.20	3.21
13	8.16	7.97	8.33	8.69	9.64	9.95	10.56	10.93	11.04	11.20	3.23
14	8.02	7.86	8.19	8.58	9.47	9.79	10.39	10.78	10.87	11.07	3.22
15	8.17	7.68	8.03	8.49	9.40	9.74	10.39	10.78	10.89	11.08	3.40
16	8.24	7.61	7.97	8.38	9.31	9.62	10.28	10.69	10.81	11.02	3.41
17	8.00	7.64	8.00	8.45	9.37	9.65	10.32	10.72	10.84	11.05	3.41
20	7.75	7.50	7.82	8.21	9.10	9.38	10.04	10.45	10.56	10.82	3.32
21	7.65	7.54	7.82	8.23	9.11	9.39	10.07	10.45	10.60	10.85	3.31
22	7.76	7.53	7.79	8.21	9.11	9.43	10.05	10.45	10.62	10.90	3.37
23	7.80	7.48	7.81	8.25	9.21	9.51	10.11	10.47	10.64	10.91	3.43
24	7.46	7.41	7.76	8.19	9.13	9.46	10.05	10.43	10.57	10.85	3.44
28	7.71	7.43	7.75	8.14	9.05	9.38	9.95	10.28	10.43	10.72	3.29
29	7.87	7.48	7.77	8.15	9.05	9.42	9.90	10.31	10.46	10.73	3.25
30	7.71	7.41	7.69	8.09	9.03	9.36	9.84	10.25	10.39	10.67	3.26
31	7.64	7.37	7.62	7.98	8.92	9.27	9.68	10.15	10.28	10.58	3.21

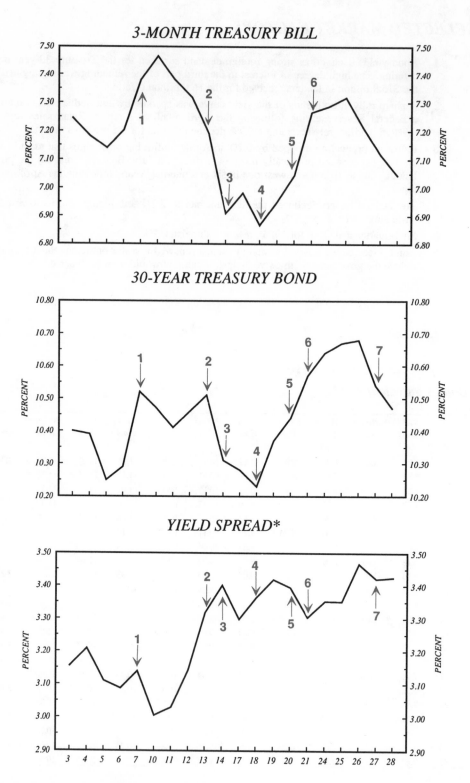

3-MONTH TREASURY BILL

30-YEAR TREASURY BOND

YIELD SPREAD*

*NOTE: SPREAD=30-YEAR BOND MINUS 3-MONTH BILL

SELECTED MARKET FACTORS

1 The unemployment rate held steady at 7.3% in May, indicating continued moderate growth in the economy. Total payroll employment rose by 345,000 workers in May as manufacturing jobs dropped 28,000 in the month.

2 Retail sales declined by 0.8% in May after a disappointing April rebound in sales activity.

3 Factory output moved lower again in May (-0.1%), while wholesale prices gained 0.2% during the same month.

4 Major money center banks cut the prime lending rate by 50 basis points to 9 1/2%. Recent reductions in CD rates suggested that additional reductions would be possible in the near future.

5 Consumer spending rebounded in May, up 0.7% as personal income fell by 0.5% for the same month.

6 The flash report which placed second-quarter GNP growth at 3.1% sent interest rates higher. The preliminary GNP report was complemented by an unexpected rise in M1 during the latest reporting period.

7 Enthusiastic investor response to a $17 billion end-of-quarter financing was sparked by declines in prices prior to the auction, which brought yields back to levels that attracted foreign demand.

U.S. TREASURY YIELDS
(Bond Equivalent Yields)

June	Fed Funds	3-Month Bill	6-Month Bill	1-Year Bill	2-Year Note	3-Year Note	5-Year Note	7-Year Note	10-Year Note	30-Year Bond	Spread*
3	7.84	7.25	7.50	7.83	8.72	9.07	9.50	9.93	10.05	10.40	3.16
4	7.91	7.18	7.50	7.81	8.68	9.01	9.47	9.93	10.05	10.39	3.21
5	7.87	7.14	7.30	7.63	8.42	8.77	9.26	9.75	9.83	10.25	3.11
6	7.77	7.20	7.37	7.72	8.51	8.83	9.33	9.84	9.89	10.29	3.09
7	7.60	7.38	7.65	7.99	8.82	9.15	9.67	10.18	10.19	10.52	3.14
10	7.76	7.47	7.73	8.04	8.87	9.21	9.68	10.13	10.16	10.47	3.01
11	7.62	7.38	7.61	7.92	8.78	9.15	9.63	10.04	10.08	10.41	3.03
12	7.40	7.32	7.55	7.88	8.76	9.10	9.65	10.09	10.16	10.46	3.14
13	7.38	7.19	7.51	7.87	8.76	9.07	9.67	10.14	10.21	10.51	3.32
14	7.27	6.91	7.19	7.54	8.45	8.78	9.39	9.90	9.98	10.31	3.40
17	7.25	6.98	7.27	7.59	8.48	8.86	9.45	9.92	9.97	10.28	3.30
18	6.77	6.87	7.15	7.48	8.37	8.73	9.33	9.85	9.90	10.23	3.36
19	6.73	6.95	7.25	7.60	8.50	8.84	9.46	9.97	10.04	10.37	3.42
20	7.34	7.05	7.33	7.70	8.59	8.93	9.51	10.06	10.14	10.44	3.39
21	7.41	7.27	7.59	7.94	8.80	9.15	9.75	10.26	10.34	10.57	3.30
24	7.59	7.29	7.65	7.98	8.87	9.26	9.83	10.37	10.45	10.64	3.35
25	7.60	7.32	7.66	8.02	8.96	9.37	9.95	10.45	10.50	10.67	3.35
26	7.46	7.21	7.57	7.98	8.94	9.37	9.97	10.43	10.54	10.68	3.47
27	7.74	7.12	7.45	7.86	8.81	9.25	9.83	10.25	10.39	10.54	3.42
28	7.95	7.05	7.32	7.71	8.67	9.08	9.65	10.08	10.25	10.47	3.43

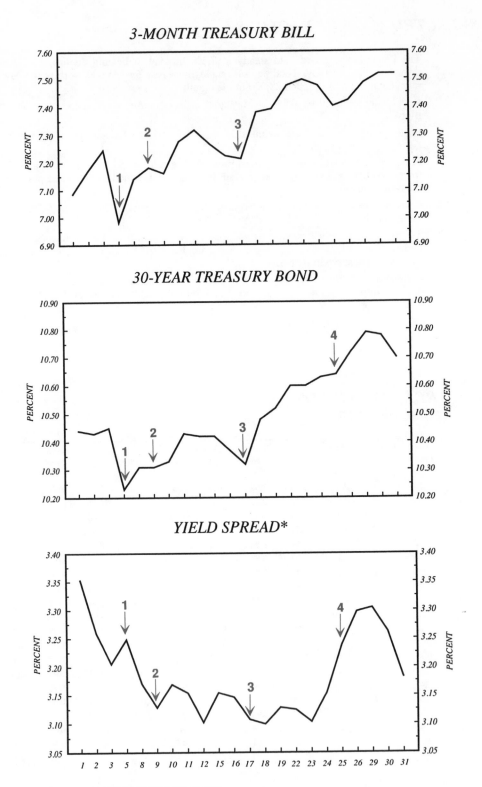

3-MONTH TREASURY BILL

30-YEAR TREASURY BOND

YIELD SPREAD*

*NOTE: SPREAD=30-YEAR BOND MINUS 3-MONTH BILL

SELECTED MARKET FACTORS

1 The unemployment rate remained unchanged in June at 7.3% for the fifth consecutive month, and factory payroll employment dropped 45,000 during the month.

2 Short yields rose amidst growing concern that a weak dollar would prohibit the Federal Reserve from easing credit, despite the weakening in the economy.

3 The Federal Reserve was rumored to be restrained from easing rates by a budgetary impasse.

4 The long end of the Treasury market began to weaken under the weight of coming supply in the August refunding.

U.S. TREASURY YIELDS
(Bond Equivalent Yields)

July	Fed Funds	3-Month Bill	6-Month Bill	1-Year Bill	2-Year Note	3-Year Note	5-Year Note	7-Year Note	10-Year Note	30-Year Bond	Spread*
1	8.12	7.09	7.38	7.72	8.66	9.06	9.58	10.04	10.19	10.44	3.35
2	8.13	7.17	7.41	7.73	8.66	9.08	9.61	10.05	10.20	10.43	3.26
3	8.58	7.25	7.43	7.75	8.66	9.06	9.62	10.07	10.23	10.45	3.20
5	8.05	6.98	7.13	7.43	8.36	8.72	9.30	9.76	9.93	10.23	3.25
8	8.13	7.14	7.33	7.60	8.52	8.84	9.41	9.87	10.05	10.31	3.17
9	7.96	7.18	7.40	7.65	8.52	8.86	9.41	9.87	10.05	10.31	3.13
10	7.70	7.16	7.40	7.66	8.55	8.89	9.45	9.91	10.07	10.33	3.17
11	7.80	7.28	7.55	7.84	8.73	9.11	9.61	10.08	10.22	10.43	3.15
12	7.67	7.32	7.57	7.88	8.78	9.11	9.63	10.12	10.23	10.42	3.10
15	7.71	7.27	7.52	7.84	8.76	9.10	9.63	10.10	10.22	10.42	3.15
16	7.58	7.22	7.49	7.76	8.67	9.07	9.59	10.01	10.15	10.37	3.15
17	8.26	7.21	7.45	7.71	8.63	9.03	9.54	9.97	10.12	10.32	3.11
18	8.01	7.38	7.63	7.88	8.76	9.21	9.71	10.15	10.30	10.48	3.10
19	7.91	7.39	7.65	7.92	8.82	9.25	9.72	10.18	10.34	10.52	3.13
22	8.07	7.48	7.73	8.02	8.95	9.39	9.87	10.31	10.46	10.60	3.12
23	7.83	7.50	7.75	8.05	8.97	9.41	9.91	10.32	10.47	10.60	3.10
24	7.55	7.48	7.76	8.04	8.99	9.42	9.92	10.36	10.51	10.63	3.15
25	7.49	7.40	7.73	8.01	8.96	9.40	9.91	10.38	10.52	10.64	3.24
26	7.41	7.42	7.74	8.02	8.98	9.44	9.96	10.45	10.59	10.72	3.30
29	7.60	7.49	7.80	8.07	9.03	9.50	10.02	10.50	10.67	10.79	3.30
30	7.57	7.52	7.85	8.14	9.04	9.51	10.02	10.50	10.66	10.78	3.26
31	8.61	7.52	7.81	8.12	9.01	9.47	9.98	10.41	10.57	10.70	3.18

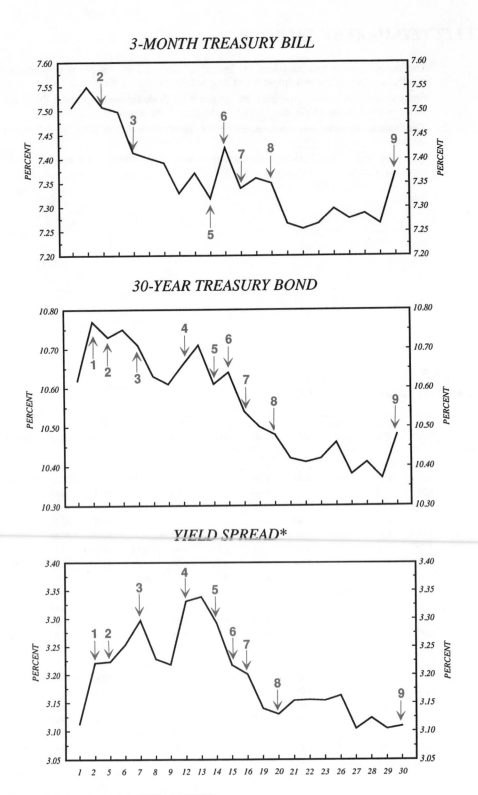

3-MONTH TREASURY BILL

30-YEAR TREASURY BOND

YIELD SPREAD*

*NOTE: SPREAD=30-YEAR BOND MINUS 3-MONTH BILL

SELECTED MARKET FACTORS

1   Bond prices tumbled on an increase of 243,000 in July payroll employment, which was larger than expected.

2   Automobile sales came in at a moderate seasonally-adjusted annual rate of 7.0 million units, which helped to ease fear of higher rates.

3   Yields on Treasury auction notes were slightly lower than expected.

4   Bond prices declined as fed funds traded between 7 3/4% and 7 7/8%. This occurred in the high end of its range and surprised many traders.

5   Long bond yields fell sharply on the report of a 0.4% rise in business inventories coupled with sharply declining sales. The relative increase in inventories was generally perceived as contributing to a weak manufacturing sector. Short-term rates continued to be mixed due to the weak economic news and a high fed funds of 8 1/4% - 9.0%.

6   An unexpected jump of $5.3 billion in money supply caused rates to increase on speculation of Federal Reserve policy tightening.

7   Housing starts slumped 2.4% during July despite lower mortgage rates in August.

8   Treasury bonds and bills rallied sharply as fed funds dropped below 8% and expectations of weak economic data increased.

9   Fixed income securities retreated from recent gains as a result of the cloudy interest rate outlook for strong growth in money supply.

U.S. TREASURY YIELDS
(Bond Equivalent Yields)

August	Fed Funds	3-Month Bill	6-Month Bill	1-Year Bill	2-Year Note	3-Year Note	5-Year Note	7-Year Note	10-Year Note	30-Year Bond	Spread*
1	8.26	7.51	7.84	8.12	9.04	9.47	9.95	10.36	10.51	10.62	3.11
2	7.94	7.55	7.89	8.23	9.15	9.60	10.09	10.49	10.66	10.77	3.22
5	7.85	7.51	7.88	8.22	9.13	9.59	10.06	10.48	10.64	10.73	3.22
6	7.76	7.50	7.88	8.18	9.13	9.53	10.08	10.48	10.65	10.75	3.25
7	7.73	7.41	7.82	8.16	9.08	9.49	10.01	10.41	10.55	10.71	3.30
8	7.68	7.40	7.80	8.11	8.99	9.37	9.91	10.30	10.43	10.63	3.23
9	7.61	7.39	7.77	8.08	8.95	9.30	9.86	10.24	10.37	10.61	3.22
12	7.85	7.33	7.75	8.07	8.95	9.29	9.86	10.25	10.38	10.66	3.33
13	8.02	7.37	7.74	8.10	8.96	9.33	9.92	10.32	10.46	10.71	3.34
14	8.75	7.32	7.70	8.05	8.96	9.28	9.84	10.25	10.38	10.61	3.29
15	8.53	7.42	7.75	8.10	8.96	9.28	9.83	10.23	10.36	10.64	3.22
16	8.22	7.34	7.68	8.01	8.90	9.21	9.74	10.13	10.26	10.54	3.20
19	7.99	7.36	7.69	8.00	8.89	9.20	9.74	10.09	10.23	10.50	3.14
20	7.67	7.35	7.67	8.00	8.86	9.20	9.70	10.08	10.20	10.48	3.13
21	7.57	7.27	7.55	7.92	8.82	9.16	9.63	10.02	10.12	10.42	3.15
22	7.79	7.26	7.51	7.91	8.81	9.14	9.62	9.99	10.10	10.41	3.16
23	7.69	7.27	7.55	7.94	8.87	9.20	9.67	10.02	10.14	10.42	3.15
26	7.86	7.30	7.61	7.98	8.88	9.22	9.70	10.06	10.18	10.46	3.16
27	7.93	7.28	7.55	7.94	8.81	9.18	9.65	10.00	10.12	10.38	3.10
28	7.82	7.29	7.55	7.95	8.85	9.20	9.63	10.03	10.16	10.41	3.12
29	7.81	7.27	7.57	7.94	8.81	9.17	9.58	10.00	10.12	10.37	3.10
30	7.80	7.37	7.69	8.03	8.96	9.33	9.74	10.17	10.28	10.48	3.11

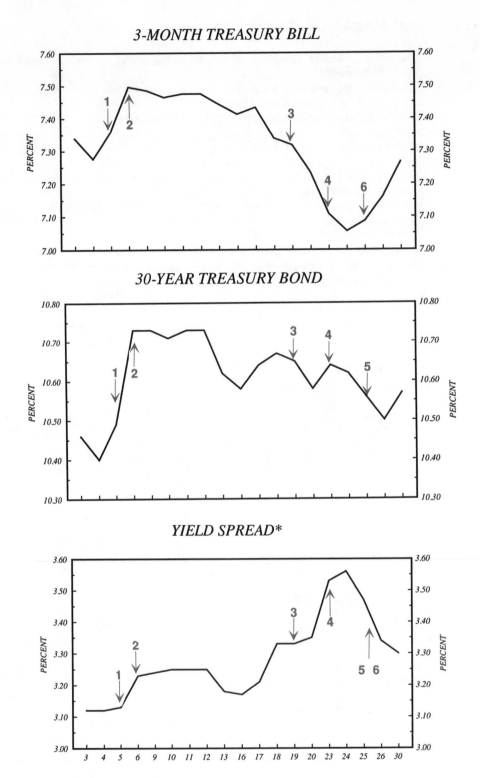

*NOTE: SPREAD=30-YEAR BOND MINUS 3-MONTH BILL

SELECTED MARKET FACTORS

1 Security prices at both ends of the yield curve fell on news of strong late-August auto sales of 11.87 million units. Coupled with the recent large expansion in the money supply, this prompted fears of a stronger economy and a possible Federal Reserve tightening.

2 The civilian unemployment rate dropped sharply from 7.3% in July to 7.0% in August on strong household employment growth.

3 Interest rates fell in response to rumors that the Commerce Department would report a mere 2.8% annual rate of growth in the current quarter as measured by real GNP.

4 Following a coordinated G-5 action to lower the dollar, short-term rates declined and bond yields rose.

5 Bond prices rose after the Federal Reserve injected funds into the banking system. This prompted speculation about a possible easing of credit in support of the international agreement to lower the dollar.

6 The Federal Reserve sold $500 million of Treasury bills on behalf of a customer account. This sale was presumed to be for a foreign central bank which had intervened in foreign exchange markets Tuesday by selling dollars.

U.S. TREASURY YIELDS
(Bond Equivalent Yields)

	Fed Funds	3-Month Bill	6-Month Bill	1-Year Bill	2-Year Note	3-Year Note	5-Year Note	7-Year Note	10-Year Note	30-Year Bond	Spread*
September											
3	8.24	7.34	7.66	8.02	8.95	9.32	9.71	10.14	10.24	10.46	3.12
4	7.91	7.28	7.59	7.92	8.85	9.24	9.64	10.06	10.16	10.40	3.12
5	7.72	7.36	7.68	8.02	8.92	9.31	9.71	10.15	10.27	10.49	3.13
6	7.68	7.50	7.84	8.22	9.15	9.56	9.97	10.37	10.49	10.73	3.23
9	7.95	7.49	7.84	8.22	9.13	9.53	9.97	10.37	10.49	10.73	3.24
10	7.83	7.47	7.80	8.19	9.10	9.52	9.96	10.35	10.48	10.71	3.25
11	8.03	7.48	7.82	8.23	9.13	9.53	9.98	10.39	10.51	10.73	3.25
12	7.95	7.48 .	7.82	8.21⊦	9.15	9.54	9.97	10.40	10.52	10.73	3.25
13	7.77	7.44	7.78	8.14	9.03	9.43	9.87	10.29	10.40	10.62	3.18
16	8.06	7.41	7.73	8.09	8.99	9.39	9.83	10.24	10.37	10.58	3.17
17	7.82	7.43	7.76	8.13	9.05	9.42	9.85	10.28	10.41	10.64	3.21
18	7.82	7.34	7.70	8.12	9.07	9.45	9.87	10.30	10.43	10.67	3.33
19	8.03	7.32	7.73	8.16	9.13	9.48	9.89	10.30	10.43	10.65	3.33
20	7.93	7.23	7.65	8.07	9.01	9.40	9.81	10.22	10.36	10.58	3.35
23	7.92	7.11	7.52	7.94	8.89	9.25	9.74	10.23	10.39	10.64	3.53
24	7.85	7.06	7.41	7.90	8.82	9.22	9.69	10.17	10.33	10.62	3.56
25	8.15	7.09	7.21	7.81	8.71	9.09	9.59	10.09	10.27	10.56	3.47
26	7.87	7.16	7.28	7.87	8.72	9.12	9.61	10.05	10.22	10.50	3.34
30	8.84	7.27	7.42	7.99	8.88	9.27	9.73	10.15	10.31	10.57	3.30

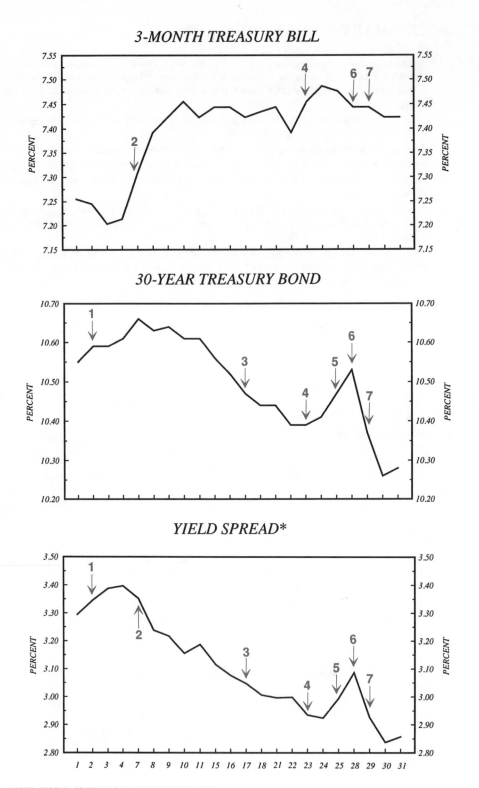

3-MONTH TREASURY BILL

30-YEAR TREASURY BOND

YIELD SPREAD*

*NOTE: SPREAD=30-YEAR BOND MINUS 3-MONTH BILL

SELECTED MARKET FACTORS

1   Bond prices fell on rumors that Paul Volcker would resign as Chairman of the Federal Reserve Board.

2   Short-term rates rose on expectations that the government would auction at least $5 billion of short-term "cash management" bills.

3   Bond prices surged following a report by the Commerce Department that the economy had grown at a 3.3% annual rate for the quarter, after adjusting for inflation. Housing starts also slumped 9.3% in September.

4   Consumer prices in September increased a slim 0.2% for the fifth consecutive month.

5   Bond yields rose as dealers worried that increasing rates in Japan would make U.S. government securities more difficult to sell.

6   The Treasury announced that it would proceed with a $17.75 billion financing operation consisting of a 2-year, 11-month note; a 6-year, 11-month note; and a 19-year, 9-month bond.

7   Bond prices soared on strong foreign demand at the auction of U.S. Treasury bonds, given the realities of the Gramm-Rudman deficit reduction amendment. Federal Reserve Chairman Volcker also commented to reporters that inflation was under control.

U.S. TREASURY YIELDS
(Bond Equivalent Yields)

	Fed Funds	3-Month Bill	6-Month Bill	1-Year Bill	2-Year Note	3-Year Note	5-Year Note	7-Year Note	10-Year Note	30-Year Bond	Spread*
October											
1	8.26	7.26	7.56	7.94	8.83	9.25	9.69	10.13	10.29	10.55	3.30
2	7.97	7.25	7.62	7.95	8.84	9.23	9.69	10.15	10.30	10.59	3.34
3	7.90	7.20	7.64	7.97	8.84	9.26	9.69	10.17	10.32	10.59	3.39
4	7.73	7.21	7.63	7.97	8.84	9.26	9.73	10.20	10.36	10.61	3.40
7	7.80	7.31	7.69	8.07	8.97	9.36	9.83	10.29	10.42	10.66	3.35
8	7.70	7.39	7.75	8.06	8.96	9.35	9.81	10.25	10.36	10.63	3.24
9	8.32	7.42	7.75	8.05	8.97	9.35	9.82	10.27	10.37	10.64	3.22
10	8.28	7.46	7.78	8.08	8.96	9.35	9.82	10.26	10.35	10.61	3.15
11	7.94	7.42	7.75	8.05	8.96	9.35	9.82	10.25	10.34	10.61	3.19
15	8.16	7.44	7.75	8.06	8.94	9.33	9.79	10.20	10.30	10.56	3.12
16	7.98	7.44	7.73	8.02	8.89	9.27	9.73	10.13	10.25	10.52	3.08
17	7.99	7.42	7.69	7.99	8.85	9.21	9.67	10.08	10.21	10.47	3.05
18	8.00	7.43	7.69	7.97	8.81	9.20	9.62	10.04	10.17	10.44	3.01
21	8.15	7.44	7.73	7.98	8.83	9.21	9.63	10.05	10.18	10.44	3.00
22	8.11	7.39	7.70	7.98	8.80	9.17	9.60	10.00	10.12	10.39	3.00
23	8.71	7.46	7.78	8.02	8.84	9.21	9.62	10.01	10.14	10.39	2.94
24	8.22	7.49	7.85	8.09	8.90	9.22	9.64	10.01	10.15	10.41	2.92
25	7.87	7.48	7.81	8.07	8.88	9.25	9.67	10.06	10.21	10.47	2.99
28	7.86	7.44	7.79	8.08	8.91	9.32	9.75	10.16	10.28	10.53	3.09
29	7.73	7.44	7.72	8.01	8.82	9.19	9.61	10.01	10.11	10.37	2.93
30	7.80	7.42	7.67	7.91	8.68	9.02	9.45	9.79	9.97	10.26	2.84
31	8.08	7.42	7.67	7.92	8.70	9.06	9.47	9.82	10.01	10.28	2.86

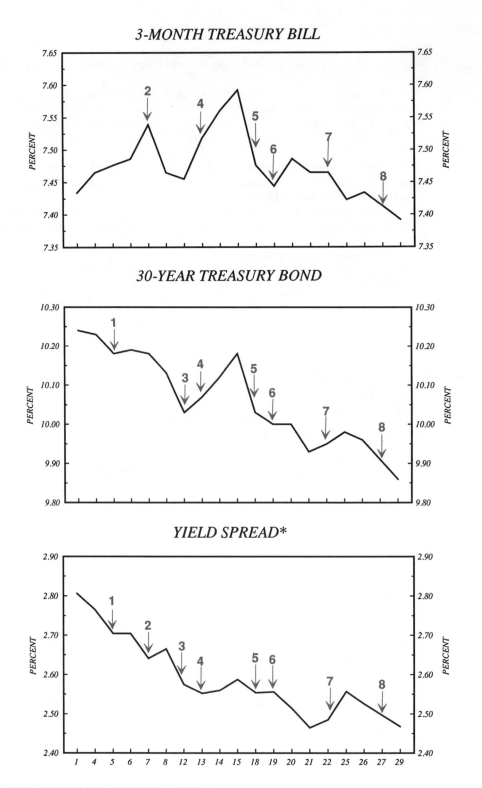

*NOTE: SPREAD=30-YEAR BOND MINUS 3-MONTH BILL

SELECTED MARKET FACTORS

1. Bond prices rose on speculation that oil prices would decline further in the wake of reduced OPEC discipline. This would enhance the inflation outlook.
2. Fed funds traded up to 8%, the high end of the trading range.
3. Bonds continued to rise on strong buying by many pension funds, insurance companies, banks, and mutual funds in the wake of a decline in oil, and a broader acceptance of the Gramm-Rudman amendment with its attempt to cut the budget deficit.
4. Rates rose as the government disclosed plans to sell $61 billion of new debt over the next two weeks as the debt limit problem was cleared with the passage of Gramm-Rudman amendment.
5. Optimism about interest rates grew in response to a lower fed funds rate and increased prospects for lower oil prices.
6. The Treasury sold $8.76 billion of new 3-year notes at an average annual yield of 8.74%.
7. Consumers cut spending by 0.9% during October, the largest decline in 25 years.
8. The Treasury's auction of 5-year notes drew aggressive bids in a favorable bond market environment.

U.S. TREASURY YIELDS
(Bond Equivalent Yields)

	Fed Funds	3-Month Bill	6-Month Bill	1-Year Bill	2-Year Note	3-Year Note	5-Year Note	7-Year Note	10-Year Note	30-Year Bond	Spread*
November											
1	8.32	7.43	7.67	7.91	8.70	9.04	9.45	9.79	9.98	10.24	2.81
4	8.33	7.47	7.70	7.95	8.71	9.04	9.44	9.80	9.98	10.23	2.77
5	8.29	7.48	7.70	7.93	8.69	9.02	9.39	9.75	9.93	10.18	2.70
6	8.42	7.49	7.70	7.91	8.67	9.01	9.38	9.75	9.93	10.19	2.70
7	8.18	7.54	7.74	7.92	8.67	9.00	9.38	9.74	9.91	10.18	2.64
8	7.87	7.47	7.65	7.82	8.57	8.91	9.30	9.67	9.84	10.13	2.67
12	8.03	7.46	7.63	7.81	8.53	8.85	9.20	9.53	9.74	10.03	2.57
13	7.97	7.52	7.68	7.88	8.58	8.92	9.28	9.61	9.78	10.07	2.55
14	7.95	7.56	7.75	7.91	8.63	8.98	9.33	9.67	9.84	10.12	2.56
15	8.58	7.59	7.76	7.94	8.66	9.00	9.39	9.72	9.92	10.18	2.59
18	7.81	7.48	7.67	7.83	8.51	8.82	9.22	9.54	9.72	10.03	2.55
19	7.29	7.44	7.65	7.83	8.52	8.75	9.20	9.54	9.73	10.00	2.56
20	8.12	7.49	7.69	7.87	8.54	8.78	9.22	9.53	9.72	10.00	2.51
21	8.04	7.47	7.68	7.84	8.51	8.75	9.17	9.48	9.58	9.93	2.47
22	7.41	7.47	7.68	7.86	8.52	8.79	9.22	9.55	9.66	9.95	2.48
25	7.94	7.42	7.67	7.87	8.52	8.78	9.23	9.55	9.68	9.98	2.56
26	7.90	7.43	7.66	7.90	8.53	8.78	9.24	9.55	9.68	9.96	2.53
27	7.88	7.41	7.65	7.86	8.52	8.72	9.12	9.51	9.64	9.91	2.50
29	8.54	7.39	7.64	7.85	8.46	8.70	9.07	9.47	9.59	9.86	2.47

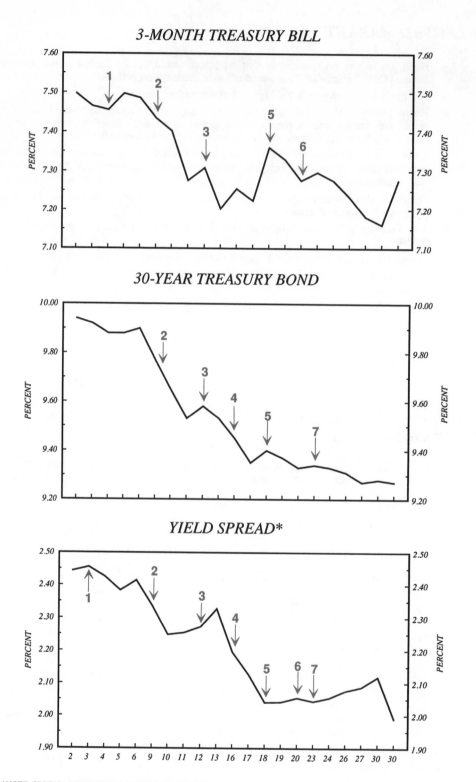

3-MONTH TREASURY BILL

30-YEAR TREASURY BOND

YIELD SPREAD*

*NOTE: SPREAD=30-YEAR BOND MINUS 3-MONTH BILL

SELECTED MARKET FACTORS

1   A decline in short-term rates, coupled with speculation that Congress would soon move to cut the budget deficit, sent bond prices higher. An unexpected decline in the funds rate from 8 1/2% to 8% last week also helped rally the short end of the curve.

2   OPEC decided to abandon a four-year effort to limit oil production, escalating the oil price war.

3   Retail sales gained 1.1% in November as promotions lifted automobile sales in a year-end inventory cleanup move.

4   Bonds surged after news that Henry Kaufman, chief economist at Salomon Brothers Inc., predicted that the Federal Reserve would cut its discount rate to 7% early next year.

5   Rates rose as fed funds traded between 8 1/8% and 9 1/4% most of the day.

6   Short-term rates retreated as fed funds eased.

7   Consumer spending fueled by automobile purchases rose 0.9% in November.

U.S. TREASURY YIELDS
(Bond Equivalent Yields)

December	Fed Funds	3-Month Bill	6-Month Bill	1-Year Bill	2-Year Note	3-Year Note	5-Year Note	7-Year Note	10-Year Note	30-Year Bond	Spread*
2	8.56	7.50	7.70	7.91	8.54	8.75	9.14	9.55	9.69	9.94	2.44
3	8.68	7.47	7.69	7.92	8.52	8.77	9.15	9.55	9.68	9.92	2.46
4	8.69	7.46	7.68	7.87	8.49	8.75	9.10	9.50	9.63	9.88	2.43
5	8.29	7.50	7.72	7.91	8.47	8.75	9.10	9.49	9.62	9.88	2.38
6	7.99	7.49	7.69	7.89	8.47	8.75	9.12	9.51	9.65	9.90	2.41
9	8.02	7.43	7.65	7.83	8.35	8.62	8.98	9.34	9.49	9.77	2.34
10	7.93	7.40	7.62	7.76	8.23	8.50	8.83	9.20	9.36	9.65	2.25
11	7.99	7.28	7.41	7.53	8.00	8.28	8.64	9.02	9.20	9.53	2.25
12	7.90	7.31	7.43	7.61	8.07	8.38	8.72	9.12	9.27	9.58	2.27
13	7.84	7.20	7.32	7.50	7.97	8.25	8.63	9.05	9.21	9.53	2.33
16	8.00	7.26	7.38	7.53	8.00	8.28	8.62	9.00	9.16	9.45	2.19
17	7.93	7.22	7.36	7.52	7.94	8.18	8.48	8.89	9.04	9.35	2.13
18	8.98	7.36	7.47	7.64	8.04	8.25	8.57	8.95	9.11	9.40	2.04
19	8.17	7.33	7.45	7.59	8.00	8.27	8.58	8.95	9.10	9.37	2.04
20	7.99	7.28	7.44	7.58	8.01	8.18	8.52	8.89	9.04	9.33	2.05
23	8.03	7.30	7.47	7.63	8.01	8.24	8.56	8.94	9.08	9.34	2.04
24	7.97	7.28	7.44	7.63	8.02	8.27	8.56	8.93	9.07	9.33	2.05
26	8.00	7.23	7.37	7.55	7.99	8.23	8.52	8.89	9.04	9.31	2.08
27	7.62	7.18	7.38	7.55	7.99	8.23	8.50	8.86	8.99	9.27	2.09
30	9.08	7.16	7.44	7.62	7.99	8.24	8.49	8.87	9.01	9.28	2.12
31	13.46	7.28	7.44	7.60	7.98	8.22	8.49	8.87	9.00	9.27	1.99

1986

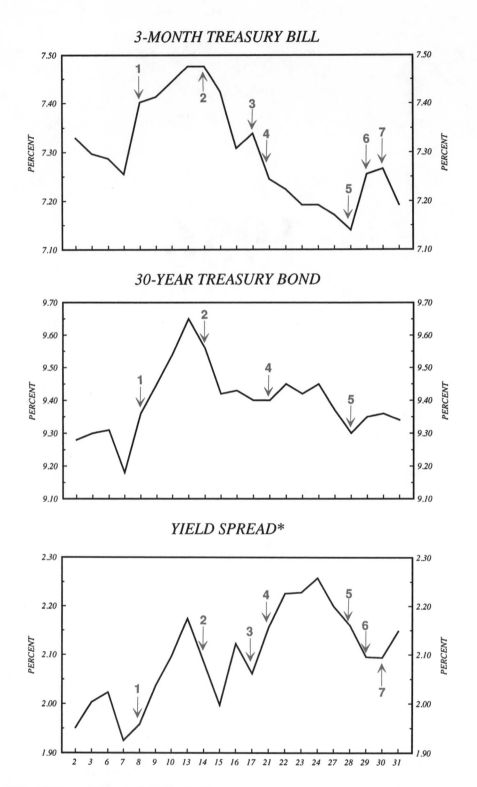

3-MONTH TREASURY BILL

30-YEAR TREASURY BOND

YIELD SPREAD*

*NOTE: SPREAD=30-YEAR BOND MINUS 3-MONTH BILL

SELECTED MARKET FACTORS

1 Total payroll employment rose by a surprising 320,000 workers in December, with the manufacturing sector alone accounting for a strong increase of 45,000 new jobs.

2 December retail sales increased by 1.9% in response to a rise in automobile sales, the result of a resumption of limited financing incentives by domestic manufacturers. At the same time, rumors circulated that a G-5 meeting, which took place on Sunday, January 19, concluded without any agreement reached on an international effort to lower rates.

3 New housing starts rose by 17.5% in December to a level of 1.84 million units, the highest start rate in eight months.

4 Spot market oil prices plunged for a fourth consecutive trading session, prompting reduced inflationary expectations.

5 The central bank of Japan executed a unilateral 50 basis point cut in its discount rate to 4 1/2%.

6 December leading indicators rose by a strong 0.9%, adding to evidence of a late fourth-quarter rebound in economic growth.

7 Sales of new single-family homes climbed by 1.7% in December, bringing the level of home sales 14.0% above the depressed October sales rate.

U.S. TREASURY YIELDS
(Bond Equivalent Yields)

January	Fed Funds	3-Month Bill	6-Month Bill	1-Year Bill	2-Year Note	3-Year Note	5-Year Note	7-Year Note	10-Year Note	30-Year Bond	Spread*
2	8.76	7.33	7.50	7.64	8.02	8.26	8.51	8.92	9.04	9.28	1.95
3	8.34	7.30	7.50	7.65	8.03	8.28	8.52	8.94	9.05	9.30	2.00
6	8.00	7.29	7.47	7.64	8.04	8.30	8.54	8.96	9.07	9.31	2.02
7	7.82	7.26	7.43	7.59	7.97	8.20	8.44	8.78	8.94	9.18	1.92
8	7.79	7.40	7.58	7.73	8.09	8.31	8.58	8.97	9.13	9.36	1.96
9	7.93	7.41	7.68	7.83	8.27	8.53	8.78	9.10	9.27	9.45	2.04
10	7.87	7.44	7.70	7.89	8.36	8.62	8.89	9.24	9.39	9.54	2.10
13	8.08	7.48	7.70	7.95	8.38	8.69	9.00	9.33	9.49	9.65	2.17
14	7.94	7.48	7.68	7.93	8.33	8.65	8.93	9.26	9.43	9.56	2.08
15	8.04	7.42	7.66	7.85	8.24	8.52	8.82	9.12	9.31	9.42	2.00
16	7.92	7.31	7.57	7.79	8.21	8.51	8.79	9.11	9.30	9.43	2.12
17	7.80	7.34	7.58	7.80	8.19	8.46	8.74	9.08	9.24	9.40	2.06
21	7.96	7.25	7.53	7.77	8.20	8.47	8.74	9.05	9.22	9.40	2.16
22	8.01	7.22	7.51	7.76	8.19	8.47	8.77	9.09	9.28	9.45	2.23
23	7.89	7.19	7.47	7.71	8.17	8.45	8.74	9.07	9.23	9.42	2.23
24	7.79	7.19	7.46	7.68	8.13	8.44	8.74	9.06	9.23	9.45	2.26
27	7.95	7.17	7.43	7.63	8.07	8.34	8.63	8.95	9.13	9.37	2.20
28	7.85	7.14	7.39	7.60	8.02	8.26	8.53	8.86	9.05	9.30	2.16
29	7.78	7.26	7.49	7.65	8.05	8.31	8.56	8.90	9.09	9.35	2.09
30	8.02	7.27	7.46	7.64	8.04	8.31	8.57	8.92	9.10	9.36	2.09
31	8.09	7.19	7.41	7.57	7.99	8.25	8.53	8.88	9.08	9.34	2.15

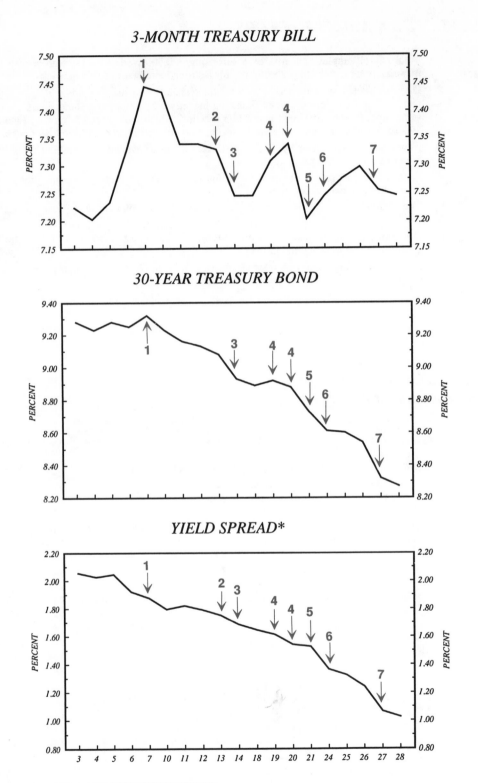

*NOTE: SPREAD=30-YEAR BOND MINUS 3-MONTH BILL

SELECTED MARKET FACTORS

1 The January payroll employment report revealed an exceptionally large 566,000 rise in the number of new jobs, including an additional 35,000 rise in manufacturing workers. On the same day, the panel of three judges who were reviewing the Gramm-Rudman legislation found the automatic deficit-cutting procedure to be unconstitutional; however, because of the importance of the issue, the decision was stayed pending appeal.

2 Retail sales rose by only 0.1% in January as total sales less autos contracted by 0.2%.

3 The minutes of the December FOMC meeting revealed that the Fed had eased monetary policy slightly, reflecting "concern that the level of economic activity continued to be inadequate."

4 Federal Reserve Chairman Volcker's Monetary Policy Report to Congress revealed that the FOMC viewed the sharp decline in the exchange value of the dollar and evidence of renewed economic growth as persuasive reasons not to cut in the discount rate at this stage.

5 Both personal income and personal consumption expenditures were much weaker than expected. During the month of January, personal income fell by 0.1%, while the Street had expected a 0.4% increase. At the same time, consumption expenditures fell by 0.4%, instead of the forecasted 0.4% gain called for by most analysts.

6 Short-term rates rose as a renewed decline in the exchange value of the dollar led to speculation that the Federal Reserve would not ease rates because of concern about a possible freefall in the dollar. At the long end, news of a possible OPEC move to stabilize oil prices prompted the bond market rally to stall.

7 The Federal Reserve executed customer repo on the first day of a reserve week, which fundamentally was a drain.

U.S. TREASURY YIELDS
(Bond Equivalent Yields)

	Fed Funds	3-Month Bill	6-Month Bill	1-Year Bill	2-Year Note	3-Year Note	5-Year Note	7-Year Note	10-Year Note	30-Year Bond	Spread*
February											
3	8.02	7.22	7.42	7.59	7.97	8.21	8.50	8.83	9.02	9.28	2.06
4	7.79	7.20	7.40	7.55	7.94	8.10	8.44	8.76	8.96	9.23	2.03
5	7.69	7.23	7.43	7.58	7.99	8.17	8.51	8.83	8.97	9.28	2.05
6	7.73	7.33	7.50	7.63	8.02	8.22	8.54	8.88	9.03	9.25	1.92
7	7.80	7.44	7.64	7.80	8.15	8.33	8.62	8.95	9.11	9.32	1.88
10	7.92	7.43	7.62	7.74	8.08	8.24	8.54	8.86	9.00	9.23	1.80
11	7.84	7.34	7.54	7.68	8.04	8.18	8.47	8.79	8.93	9.16	1.82
12	8.03	7.34	7.56	7.71	8.08	8.19	8.46	8.78	8.91	9.13	1.79
13	7.89	7.33	7.56	7.71	8.06	8.18	8.43	8.71	8.85	9.08	1.75
14	7.75	7.25	7.47	7.59	7.99	8.06	8.29	8.53	8.68	8.93	1.68
18	8.09	7.25	7.42	7.56	7.96	8.04	8.28	8.51	8.64	8.89	1.65
19	7.91	7.31	7.51	7.67	8.06	8.14	8.37	8.58	8.70	8.92	1.61
20	7.82	7.34	7.54	7.68	8.05	8.17	8.39	8.57	8.67	8.88	1.54
21	7.73	7.20	7.42	7.56	7.93	8.04	8.24	8.40	8.48	8.73	1.53
24	7.89	7.25	7.41	7.53	7.86	7.99	8.20	8.31	8.39	8.61	1.36
25	7.88	7.28	7.43	7.59	7.89	8.01	8.21	8.33	8.40	8.60	1.32
26	7.95	7.30	7.42	7.57	7.88	7.98	8.07	8.26	8.36	8.54	1.24
27	7.91	7.26	7.36	7.48	7.72	7.80	7.91	8.06	8.15	8.32	1.07
28	7.95	7.25	7.37	7.43	7.71	7.79	7.91	8.05	8.13	8.27	1.02

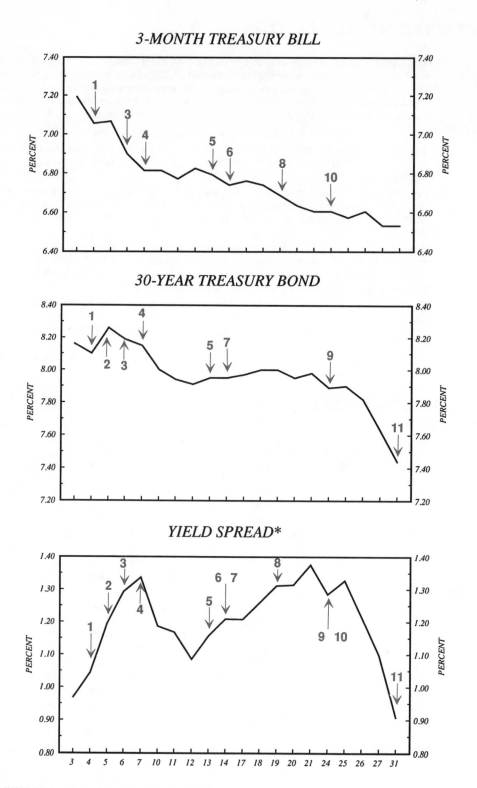

3-MONTH TREASURY BILL

30-YEAR TREASURY BOND

YIELD SPREAD*

*NOTE: SPREAD=30-YEAR BOND MINUS 3-MONTH BILL

SELECTED MARKET FACTORS

1 The Index of Leading Economic Indicators fell by 0.6% in January as new contracts and orders for plant and equipment declined sharply.

2 A flood of about $2 billion in new corporate debt issues were brought to market.

3 The Bundesbank cut its discount rate by 50 basis points from 4.0% to 3.5%.

4 A 50 basis point discount rate cut was announced by both the central bank of Japan and the Federal Reserve. The Japanese cut the discount rate to 4% while the Federal Reserve lowered its basic lending rate to 7%.

5 Despite the 0.1% decline recorded in retail sales, the market focused on the modest increase experienced in retail sales ex-autos.

6 Industrial production fell by 0.6% in February in response to a weakening in the manufacturing sector. The February decline in output follows a 0.6% average increase over the intervening period.

7 OPEC had its first meeting, beginning on Sunday, March 16, since Saudi Arabia declared an oil price war in January. Many non-OPEC oil producers also attended the meeting.

8 The OPEC meeting ended without any agreement being reached by the members of the cartel on production quotas. The members did agree in theory, however, to raise prices to $28-$29 a barrel.

9 The second revision to the fourth-quarter real GNP report reduced the pace of economic growth to +0.7% from a previously reported +1.5%.

10 Consumer prices fell by 0.4% in February as a combination of sharply declining energy and food prices offset a moderate rise in the underlying rate of retail price growth.

11 Crude oil futures prices closed at an 11-year low, below $11 a barrel, as Saudi Arabia suggested that the cartel cancel its meeting scheduled for April 15 since little progress had been made toward a production quota agreement.

U.S. TREASURY YIELDS
(Bond Equivalent Yields)

March	Fed Funds	3-Month Bill	6-Month Bill	1-Year Bill	2-Year Note	3-Year Note	5-Year Note	7-Year Note	10-Year Note	30-Year Bond	Spread*
3	7.93	7.19	7.30	7.35	7.55	7.62	7.76	7.92	7.99	8.16	0.97
4	7.76	7.06	7.11	7.23	7.38	7.44	7.55	7.84	7.93	8.10	1.04
5	7.77	7.07	7.16	7.30	7.54	7.63	7.76	8.02	8.12	8.26	1.19
6	7.66	6.90	7.02	7.14	7.38	7.47	7.68	7.90	8.04	8.19	1.29
7	7.39	6.81	6.93	7.07	7.29	7.37	7.56	7.80	7.96	8.15	1.34
10	7.42	6.81	6.87	7.01	7.16	7.24	7.41	7.63	7.76	8.00	1.19
11	7.53	6.77	6.88	7.03	7.15	7.22	7.35	7.58	7.70	7.94	1.17
12	7.88	6.83	6.91	7.04	7.17	7.25	7.37	7.57	7.68	7.91	1.09
13	7.56	6.79	6.95	7.07	7.21	7.31	7.46	7.65	7.75	7.95	1.16
14	7.39	6.74	6.88	7.00	7.18	7.27	7.40	7.62	7.72	7.95	1.21
17	7.60	6.76	6.92	7.03	7.22	7.27	7.42	7.68	7.77	7.97	1.21
18	7.55	6.74	6.90	7.03	7.23	7.29	7.48	7.76	7.83	8.00	1.26
19	7.38	6.69	6.88	7.02	7.17	7.30	7.46	7.72	7.82	8.00	1.31
20	7.25	6.64	6.82	7.00	7.17	7.29	7.45	7.69	7.78	7.95	1.31
21	7.17	6.61	6.80	6.98	7.19	7.28	7.47	7.70	7.80	7.98	1.38
24	7.24	6.61	6.78	6.92	7.11	7.22	7.40	7.62	7.70	7.89	1.28
25	7.35	6.57	6.76	6.93	7.12	7.23	7.39	7.62	7.70	7.90	1.33
26	7.41	6.61	6.74	6.92	7.11	7.19	7.36	7.47	7.64	7.82	1.21
27	7.42	6.53	6.62	6.79	7.04	7.13	7.28	7.35	7.49	7.63	1.10
31	8.06	6.53	6.57	6.72	6.92	7.02	7.19	7.21	7.39	7.44	0.91

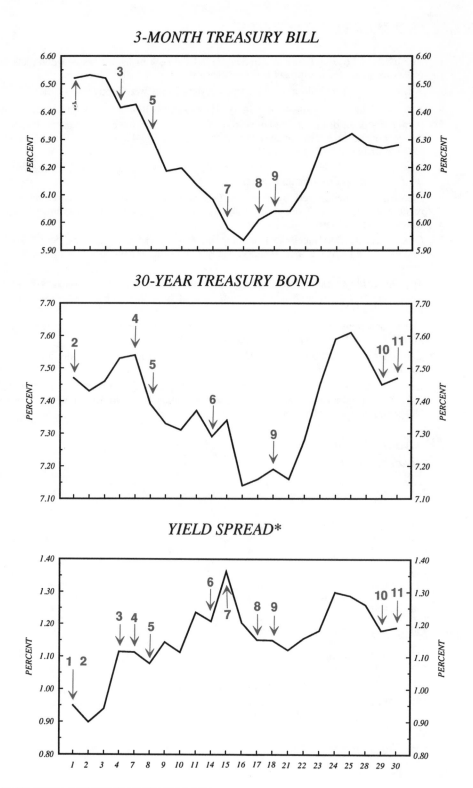

3-MONTH TREASURY BILL

30-YEAR TREASURY BOND

YIELD SPREAD*

*NOTE: SPREAD=30-YEAR BOND MINUS 3-MONTH BILL

SELECTED MARKET FACTORS

1   Construction expenditures rose by a surprisingly strong 1.2% for March as residential building responded to the gains recorded in housing starts since the beginning of the year.

2   During intra-day trading, the futures market price for oil fell below $10 a barrel before hints of a trip by Vice President Bush to Saudi Arabia began to circulate on the Street.

3   The civilian unemployment rate fell by 0.1% to 7.2% of the civilian labor force in March while manufacturing payroll fell by a sizable 47,000 jobs.

4   Vice President Bush warned Saudi Arabia that at some point the administration would consider the drop in oil prices a threat to national security.

5   Rumors of a second round of coordinated discount rate cuts circulated following the G-5 meeting in Washington.

6   President Reagan ordered an attack on Libya in retaliation for a terrorist bombing of a West German discoteque which killed an American soldier.

7   The March Index of Industrial Production fell by 0.5% following an even larger 0.7% drop in February.

8   As a result of a strong rebound in inventory accumulation, and over 4.0% growth in consumption expenditures, real GNP rose by 3.2% in the first quarter.

9   The Fed cut the discount rate by only 50 basis points to 6.5%. The Street had been expecting a 100 basis point cut. This move to lower rates was followed by a similar discount rate cut by Japan, but not by West Germany, which led to a drop in the dollar.

10   In response to strong growth in stock prices and real M2, the March Index of Leading Indicators rose by 0.5%. The Commerce Department also reported that home sales rose by 27.4% to 903,000, the highest selling rate since the series has been compiled.

11   The Treasury announced a record $27 billion refunding package, some $4 billion above the previous quarterly refunding. All of the extra new money was added to the 10- and 30-year offerings to make up for eliminating the 20-year bond cycle.

U.S. TREASURY YIELDS
(Bond Equivalent Yields)

	Fed Funds	3-Month Bill	6-Month Bill	1-Year Bill	2-Year Note	3-Year Note	5-Year Note	7-Year Note	10-Year Note	30-Year Bond	Spread*
April											
1	7.49	6.52	6.62	6.70	6.89	7.01	7.18	7.25	7.37	7.47	0.95
2	7.45	6.53	6.64	6.68	6.90	7.05	7.21	7.24	7.33	7.43	0.90
3	7.44	6.52	6.62	6.68	6.94	7.07	7.29	7.32	7.41	7.46	0.94
4	6.97	6.42	6.51	6.58	6.85	7.00	7.22	7.33	7.45	7.53	1.11
7	7.09	6.43	6.51	6.56	6.82	6.99	7.19	7.30	7.43	7.54	1.11
8	6.96	6.31	6.40	6.48	6.70	6.88	7.07	7.16	7.31	7.39	1.08
9	6.92	6.19	6.28	6.33	6.58	6.73	6.99	7.10	7.27	7.33	1.14
10	7.11	6.20	6.29	6.32	6.58	6.71	6.95	7.05	7.23	7.31	1.11
11	6.87	6.13	6.29	6.34	6.65	6.78	7.00	7.13	7.29	7.37	1.24
14	6.99	6.08	6.23	6.26	6.53	6.66	6.89	7.02	7.19	7.29	1.21
15	7.07	5.98	6.18	6.26	6.53	6.65	6.88	7.03	7.22	7.34	1.36
16	7.02	5.94	6.07	6.14	6.39	6.49	6.68	6.79	6.98	7.14	1.20
17	6.79	6.01	6.10	6.19	6.44	6.55	6.75	6.86	7.03	7.16	1.15
18	6.71	6.04	6.10	6.19	6.44	6.58	6.78	6.91	7.09	7.19	1.15
21	7.00	6.04	6.14	6.23	6.46	6.57	6.75	6.88	7.04	7.16	1.12
22	7.14	6.12	6.24	6.32	6.58	6.74	6.93	7.13	7.25	7.28	1.16
23	7.37	6.27	6.38	6.48	6.67	6.97	7.11	7.27	7.36	7.45	1.18
24	6.99	6.29	6.44	6.62	6.89	7.17	7.31	7.41	7.51	7.59	1.30
25	6.78	6.32	6.50	6.65	6.91	7.26	7.39	7.49	7.58	7.61	1.29
28	6.90	6.28	6.46	6.59	6.86	7.10	7.27	7.37	7.48	7.54	1.26
29	6.87	6.27	6.42	6.55	6.85	7.03	7.17	7.28	7.38	7.45	1.18
30	7.05	6.28	6.43	6.54	6.83	7.02	7.17	7.26	7.38	7.47	1.19

3-MONTH TREASURY BILL

30-YEAR TREASURY BOND

YIELD SPREAD*

*NOTE: SPREAD=30-YEAR BOND MINUS 3-MONTH BILL

SELECTED MARKET FACTORS

1 The April unemployment rate report turned out to be a negative for the bond market as the civilian jobless rate fell by 0.1% to 7.1% of the labor force. The 206,000 rise in total payroll employment also masked a third consecutive decline in manufacturing jobs.

2 At the economic summit in Tokyo, the finance ministers of the seven industrialized nations agreed to cooperate in formulating policy targets. The G-7 also agreed to meet regularly to apply "peer pressure" to each other's policy.

3 The Treasury auctioned $27 billion in new coupon securities as part of the May refinancing.

4 For the first time in the postwar era, the dollar traded below the 160 yen level at one point during the day.

5 April retail sales rose by a modest 0.5%, about half of the Street's anticipated increase. Moreover, retail sales net of automobile sales fell by 0.4% during the month.

6 Industrial production rose by a surprisingly strong 0.2% in April in response to strong automobile assemblies. The Street had been expecting an April report which would show a 0.2% decline. Furthermore, with the large Japanese holdings of the old long bond (9 1/4% of 2016), cash-future arbitrage traders began to experience substantial losses on their short cash positions.

7 The housing market showed additional strength in April, as new housing starts rose by 4.1% to 2.01 million units. Building permits also expanded by 2.7% in April.

8 As refiners struggled to build inventories of gasoline, spot and futures oil prices rose substantially. In fact, the futures price closed above $17 a barrel, the highest price since February.

9 A rumor circulated that Japan and West Germany were about to ease rates in order to stimulate their economies.

10 Although the Street was looking for an increase of 0.4%, the April durable goods order report recorded a 0.8% decrease.

11 A combination of financial variables and consumer new orders boosted the April Index of Leading Indicators to 1.5%, twice the size of the Street's expectation.

12 In response to higher prices received for hogs, lettuce, cattle, apples, and oranges, the Agricultural Price Index rose by 2.5% in May, the first major uptick in this series since December 1985.

U.S. TREASURY YIELDS
(Bond Equivalent Yields)

May	Fed Funds	3-Month Bill	6-Month Bill	1-Year Bill	2-Year Note	3-Year Note	5-Year Note	7-Year Note	10-Year Note	30-Year Bond	Spread*
1	7.13	6.29	6.42	6.55	6.85	7.07	7.20	7.30	7.45	7.54	1.25
2	6.86	6.33	6.42	6.57	6.88	7.11	7.23	7.35	7.51	7.62	1.29
5	6.88	6.24	6.38	6.51	6.82	7.04	7.17	7.28	7.45	7.49	1.25
6	6.73	6.23	6.36	6.48	6.82	6.96	7.16	7.30	7.46	7.50	1.27
7	6.74	6.22	6.35	6.49	6.83	6.98	7.21	7.37	7.43	7.53	1.31
8	6.84	6.22	6.33	6.45	6.78	6.93	7.17	7.32	7.40	7.36	1.14
9	6.78	6.23	6.36	6.51	6.85	7.01	7.25	7.41	7.48	7.37	1.14
12	6.92	6.31	6.43	6.61	6.98	7.14	7.41	7.57	7.67	7.41	1.10
13	6.85	6.27	6.38	6.61	7.00	7.18	7.46	7.59	7.63	7.42	1.15
14	6.82	6.27	6.34	6.56	7.00	7.17	7.48	7.62	7.66	7.43	1.16
15	7.00	6.35	6.44	6.65	7.16	7.37	7.67	7.80	7.79	7.50	1.15
16	6.80	6.40	6.56	6.80	7.32	7.56	7.89	7.99	7.99	7.64	1.24
19	6.89	6.39	6.56	6.80	7.28	7.48	7.87	7.97	7.98	7.68	1.30
20	6.86	6.42	6.55	6.75	7.23	7.46	7.80	7.85	7.88	7.58	1.16
21	6.96	6.39	6.50	6.72	7.20	7.43	7.76	7.86	7.90	7.58	1.20
22	6.87	6.39	6.55	6.73	7.20	7.45	7.76	7.85	7.88	7.50	1.12
23	6.79	6.36	6.53	6.70	7.19	7.43	7.73	7.82	7.84	7.45	1.09
27	6.98	6.34	6.51	6.67	7.14	7.36	7.65	7.72	7.73	7.41	1.07
28	6.97	6.38	6.55	6.72	7.17	7.37	7.55	7.72	7.73	7.45	1.08
29	6.84	6.49	6.68	6.87	7.35	7.55	7.78	7.98	7.99	7.66	1.17

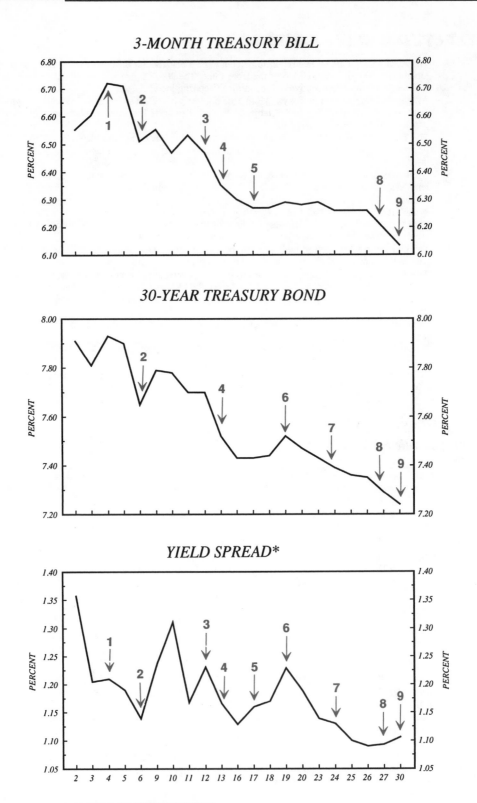

3-MONTH TREASURY BILL

30-YEAR TREASURY BOND

YIELD SPREAD*

*NOTE: SPREAD=30-YEAR BOND MINUS 3-MONTH BILL

SELECTED MARKET FACTORS

1   While attending the International Monetary Conference, Federal Reserve Chairman Volcker suggested that any change in the Fed's discount rate would depend on whether West Germany and Japan had already undertaken a similar rate reduction.

2   The civilian unemployment rate rose by a surprisingly large 0.2% in May to 7.3% of the workforce. At the same time, payroll employment in the manufacturing sector fell by 39,000 workers, the third such decline in this series. Total payroll employment rose by 149,000 as a result of strong job growth in the service sector.

3   In May, retail sales fell by 0.1% as sales excluding automobiles slid by 0.3%.

4   Industrial production tumbled by 0.6% in May, as reduced manufacturing and mining output offset a modest rise in electric utility production. The Street had been anticipating a more moderate 0.2% decline in May factory output.

5   In response to pressure from the Bundesbank, The Bank of France reduced its money market intervention rate from 7.25% to 7.0%. At the same time, the Commerce Department reported a 7.4% drop in May new housing starts.

6   Despite the 0.1% decline reported in personal income for May, consumption spending rose by a strong 0.9%.

7   According to the Economic Planning Agency in Japan, real GNP fell by a seasonally-adjusted annual rate of 2.1% over the January-to-March period. The first-quarter drop in growth was traced to the sudden impact of the yen, which had appreciated sharply relative to the dollar.

8   As a result of a pickup in imports, the May merchandise trade deficit increased from $12.1 billion in April to $14.2 billion. On a revised statistical month basis, however, the trade deficit rose to $14.3 billion.

9   The OPEC meeting in Yugoslavia, which began on June 25, ended with no agreement on a production quota that could boost prices. Estimates suggest that OPEC has been producing about 19 million barrels a day in the past few weeks, 2 million barrels more than necessary to boost prices.

U.S. TREASURY YIELDS
(Bonds Equivalent Yields)

	Fed Funds	3-Month Bill	6-Month Bill	1-Year Bill	2-Year Note	3-Year Note	5-Year Note	7-Year Note	10-Year Note	30-Year Bond	Spread*
June											
2	7.05	6.55	6.78	7.00	7.50	7.77	8.05	8.28	8.32	7.91	1.36
3	7.10	6.61	6.77	7.01	7.49	7.76	7.99	8.15	8.19	7.81	1.20
4	7.16	6.72	6.89	7.08	7.63	7.86	8.17	8.30	8.39	7.93	1.21
5	6.99	6.71	6.83	7.05	7.54	7.83	8.10	8.22	8.31	7.90	1.19
6	6.85	6.51	6.68	6.84	7.27	7.49	7.78	7.87	7.95	7.65	1.14
9	7.00	6.55	6.73	6.90	7.39	7.67	7.94	8.06	8.13	7.79	1.24
10	6.87	6.47	6.70	6.89	7.38	7.63	7.92	8.02	8.07	7.78	1.31
11	6.84	6.53	6.75	6.93	7.39	7.63	7.90	7.99	8.01	7.70	1.17
12	6.90	6.47	6.69	6.88	7.31	7.58	7.83	7.91	7.98	7.70	1.23
13	6.84	6.35	6.55	6.66	7.15	7.36	7.57	7.66	7.73	7.52	1.17
16	6.95	6.30	6.51	6.63	7.10	7.25	7.47	7.58	7.63	7.43	1.13
17	6.83	6.27	6.46	6.58	7.08	7.26	7.45	7.56	7.63	7.43	1.16
18	6.87	6.27	6.44	6.57	7.01	7.21	7.41	7.54	7.57	7.44	1.17
19	6.88	6.29	6.50	6.66	7.10	7.27	7.49	7.66	7.69	7.52	1.23
20	6.83	6.28	6.46	6.60	7.06	7.26	7.45	7.61	7.60	7.47	1.19
23	6.91	6.29	6.47	6.60	7.03	7.24	7.42	7.55	7.55	7.43	1.14
24	6.88	6.26	6.37	6.57	6.98	7.19	7.35	7.47	7.47	7.39	1.13
25	6.84	6.26	6.37	6.53	6.91	7.12	7.31	7.36	7.42	7.36	1.10
26	6.85	6.26	6.34	6.52	6.91	7.08	7.29	7.37	7.42	7.35	1.09
27	6.82	6.20	6.27	6.47	6.84	7.06	7.27	7.35	7.38	7.29	1.09
30	7.72	6.13	6.22	6.41	6.81	7.00	7.23	7.29	7.35	7.24	1.11

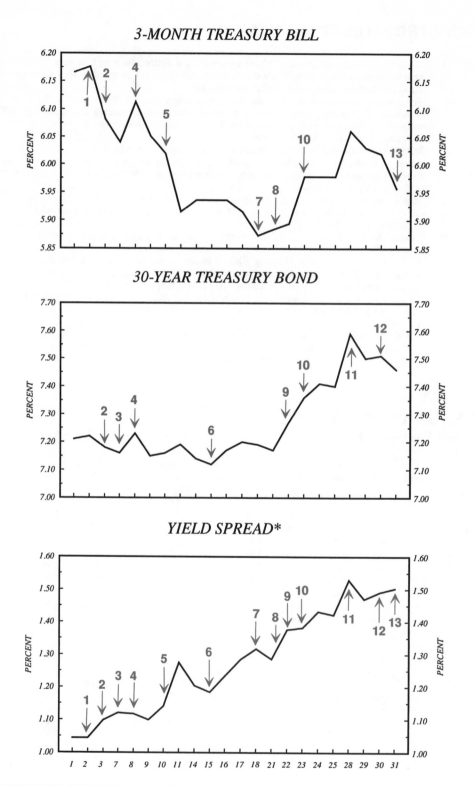

3-MONTH TREASURY BILL

30-YEAR TREASURY BOND

YIELD SPREAD*

*NOTE: SPREAD=30-YEAR BOND MINUS 3-MONTH BILL

SELECTED MARKET FACTORS

1. Despite widespread speculation about a possible easing in West German money market rates, the Bundesbank voted to maintain the 3 1/2% discount rate which has been in place since March.
2. A strike at AT&T and ALCOA resulted in a surprisingly large 89,000 drop in payroll jobs in June.
3. The Supreme Court ruled that the automatic trigger mechanism of Gramm-Rudman was unconstitutional since it violated the doctrine of separation of powers.
4. A *Washington Post* story quoted several governors of the Federal Reserve who suggested that a further easing in monetary policy was unnecessary.
5. The Fed cut the discount rate to 6.0%, citing a pattern of relatively sluggish domestic economic growth and excess capacity in the industrialized world. This move was the first unilateral change in policy since the G-5 meeting last September.
6. Retail sales rose by 0.2% in June, half the growth expected by the Street.
7. Following a drop of almost 8.0% in May, housing starts declined by an additional 0.8% in June due to a recent backup in mortgage rates to 11.02% from 10.47% in May.
8. Federal Reserve Chairman Volcker indicated that the Federal Reserve would ignore above-target M1 growth in favor of a more flexible monetary policy approach which would be aimed at maintaining economic growth.
9. The Commerce Department estimated that the economy expanded by only 1.1% in the second quarter after growing by an upward revised 3.8% earlier in the year.
10. Although personal income rose by a weak 0.1% in June, personal consumption expanded by 0.6% following a 0.9% increase in May.
11. A sizable 1.77% drop in the dollar relative to the yen caused an increase of bearish sentiment in the bond market.
12. The Treasury's announced August refunding package of $28 billion was some $2 billion smaller than most Street estimates.
13. Factory orders fell by a surprising 0.3% in June as a small 0.1% increase in durable goods orders was outstripped by a 0.7% drop in non-durable goods orders.

U.S. TREASURY YIELDS
(Bond Equivalent Yields)

July	Fed Funds	3-Month Bill	6-Month Bill	1-Year Bill	2-Year Note	3-Year Note	5-Year Note	7-Year Note	10-Year Note	30-Year Bond	Spread*
1	6.97	6.17	6.24	6.39	6.80	7.00	7.23	7.31	7.37	7.21	1.04
2	7.12	6.18	6.22	6.38	6.81	7.02	7.23	7.31	7.37	7.22	1.04
3	6.87	6.08	6.11	6.26	6.71	6.92	7.15	7.23	7.31	7.18	1.10
7	6.93	6.04	6.10	6.26	6.70	6.92	7.14	7.24	7.31	7.16	1.12
8	6.88	6.11	6.24	6.41	6.84	7.05	7.26	7.37	7.44	7.23	1.12
9	6.80	6.05	6.16	6.31	6.73	6.93	7.14	7.25	7.31	7.15	1.10
10	6.78	6.02	6.15	6.29	6.73	6.91	7.12	7.24	7.31	7.16	1.14
11	6.47	5.92	6.07	6.17	6.60	6.81	7.00	7.23	7.30	7.19	1.28
14	6.48	5.94	6.08	6.18	6.58	6.78	6.97	7.16	7.25	7.14	1.20
15	6.39	5.94	6.06	6.17	6.56	6.74	6.91	7.08	7.16	7.12	1.18
16	6.54	5.94	6.09	6.20	6.59	6.72	6.90	7.11	7.20	7.17	1.23
17	6.50	5.92	6.08	6.21	6.61	6.73	6.91	7.11	7.18	7.20	1.29
18	6.38	5.87	6.04	6.15	6.56	6.69	6.88	7.07	7.16	7.19	1.32
21	6.48	5.88	6.04	6.14	6.56	6.69	6.88	7.05	7.14	7.17	1.29
22	6.39	5.89	6.05	6.20	6.60	6.75	6.93	7.10	7.20	7.27	1.38
23	6.41	5.98	6.14	6.29	6.63	6.87	7.04	7.21	7.29	7.36	1.38
24	6.33	5.98	6.14	6.30	6.67	6.91	7.12	7.26	7.35	7.41	1.43
25	6.30	5.98	6.15	6.32	6.67	6.87	7.09	7.25	7.33	7.40	1.42
28	6.42	6.06	6.21	6.39	6.76	7.01	7.23	7.42	7.53	7.59	1.53
29	6.31	6.03	6.14	6.33	6.71	6.93	7.13	7.31	7.41	7.50	1.47
30	6.26	6.02	6.13	6.30	6.67	6.90	7.10	7.30	7.41	7.51	1.49
31	6.35	5.96	6.06	6.20	6.57	6.81	7.02	7.22	7.34	7.46	1.50

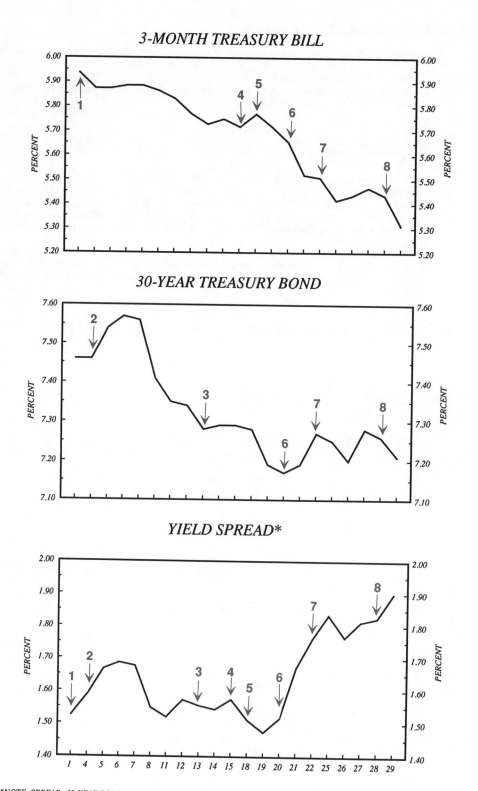

3-MONTH TREASURY BILL

30-YEAR TREASURY BOND

YIELD SPREAD*

*NOTE: SPREAD=30-YEAR BOND MINUS 3-MONTH BILL

SELECTED MARKET FACTORS

1   In July, payroll employment rose by 389,000 workers as 170,000 strikers returned to work. Net of the returning strikers, total payroll employment rose by a weak 219,000, and manufacturing employment fell by about 63,000 workers.

2   In a major political victory for Iran, OPEC approved a two-month production quota. Under the new agreement, total daily OPEC production will be held at 16.8 million barrels per day beginning in September, compared to about 21.0 million barrels currently.

3   Retail sales rose by 0.1% in July as a result of strong sales activity in the furniture and building materials categories. The major factor which biased down the retail number was a 1.7% drop in automotive dealer sales.

4   Industrial production remained in a slump during July as mining and utility output continued to slide. On the other hand, manufacturing held steady in response to a third consecutive drop in consumer goods production.

5   After incorporating additional data, the Commerce Department revised downward its estimate of real second-quarter GNP to only +0.6% from a preliminary +1.1% report. Despite the decline in overall growth, final sales accelerated to +3.8% from a preliminary +3.9%. Stronger consumption and producer durable goods purchases accounted for the upward correction to final sales.

6   The Federal Reserve announced a 50 basis point cut in the discount rate to 5.5%, on the day following the most recent FOMC meeting, citing weak economic growth and stress in the financial system.

7   According to an advanced report, new orders for durable goods rose by 4.3% in July—well above the Street's estimate of a 0.5% increase. The July surge in orders was the result of a 46.6% jump in defense capital goods orders and a sharp rise in new orders for aircraft.

8   Reports circulated in the markets that both the Bundesbank and the central bank of Japan were about to cut rates in order to reduce the sharp downward pressure on the dollar in the foreign exchange markets.

U.S. TREASURY YIELDS
(Bond Equivalent Yields)

August	Fed Funds	3-Month Bill	6-Month Bill	1-Year Bill	2-Year Note	3-Year Note	5-Year Note	7-Year Note	10-Year Note	30-Year Bond	Spread*
1	6.38	5.94	6.04	6.15	6.56	6.81	7.02	7.22	7.34	7.46	1.52
4	6.38	5.87	6.00	6.13	6.56	6.80	7.01	7.22	7.33	7.46	1.59
5	6.35	5.87	6.02	6.16	6.58	6.74	7.07	7.27	7.39	7.54	1.67
6	6.28	5.88	6.04	6.20	6.61	6.78	7.13	7.35	7.47	7.57	1.69
7	6.33	5.88	6.04	6.19	6.61	6.76	7.10	7.31	7.45	7.56	1.68
8	6.36	5.86	6.01	6.12	6.54	6.68	6.97	7.16	7.30	7.41	1.55
11	6.40	5.83	5.95	6.08	6.51	6.64	6.90	7.12	7.25	7.35	1.52
12	6.28	5.77	5.83	6.03	6.46	6.60	6.89	7.09	7.23	7.34	1.57
13	6.09	5.73	5.79	5.97	6.37	6.51	6.83	7.03	7.15	7.28	1.55
14	6.29	5.75	5.80	6.00	6.39	6.51	6.89	7.02	7.16	7.29	1.54
15	6.47	5.72	5.78	5.98	6.36	6.49	6.83	7.02	7.14	7.29	1.57
18	6.41	5.77	5.81	5.98	6.37	6.50	6.83	7.01	7.14	7.28	1.51
19	6.32	5.72	5.81	5.89	6.29	6.38	6.70	6.89	7.02	7.19	1.47
20	6.24	5.65	5.78	5.85	6.17	6.34	6.65	6.83	7.00	7.17	1.52
21	5.94	5.52	5.63	5.74	6.08	6.24	6.62	6.78	6.96	7.19	1.67
22	5.86	5.51	5.66	5.78	6.14	6.31	6.68	6.88	7.07	7.27	1.76
25	5.90	5.42	5.62	5.72	6.10	6.29	6.65	6.86	7.06	7.25	1.84
26	5.83	5.44	5.54	5.68	6.02	6.22	6.63	6.75	6.97	7.20	1.77
27	5.86	5.47	5.56	5.73	6.12	6.32	6.53	6.85	7.06	7.28	1.81
28	5.87	5.44	5.53	5.68	6.07	6.28	6.52	6.83	7.04	7.26	1.83
29	5.77	5.31	5.38	5.52	5.94	6.13	6.40	6.75	6.95	7.21	1.90

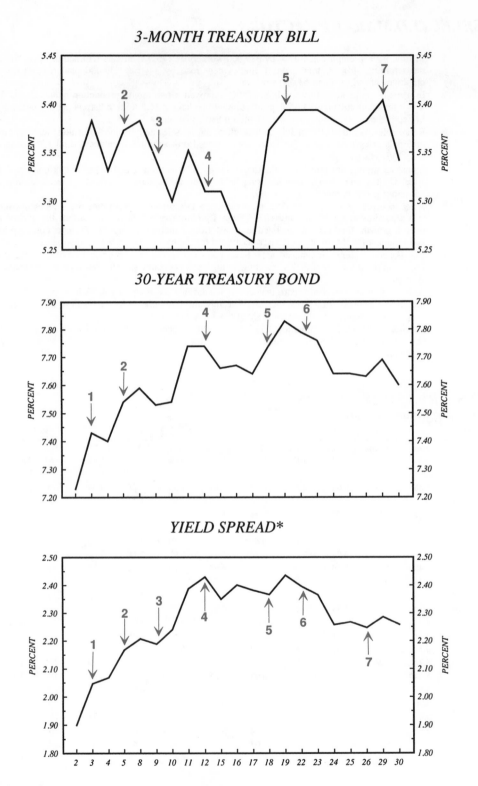

3-MONTH TREASURY BILL

30-YEAR TREASURY BOND

YIELD SPREAD*

*NOTE: SPREAD=30-YEAR BOND MINUS 3-MONTH BILL

SELECTED MARKET FACTORS

1   The bond market responded negatively to an unexpected surge in the price of some commodities, especially precious metal prices. For example, gold prices in the September COMEX contract soared more than $18.00 an ounce to close at $405.70.

2   Payroll employment rose by a strong 202,000 in August, although the Street had been expecting only 145,000 new workers. The manufacturing employment sector also rose by 19,000, representing the first increase since the beginning of the year.

3   Rumors circulated in the market that the Bundesbank would lower rates at the Central Committee meeting scheduled for September 10; however, this discount rate cut never materialized.

4   Despite record financing incentives, retail sales rose by a surprisingly modest 0.8% in August. Furthermore, net of autos, the retail sales report showed that consumer spending was unchanged.

5   The dollar fell below 2.00 Deutsche marks, the lowest level recorded since 1981, as Treasury Secretary Baker intensified his campaign to encourage other industrialized countries to stimulate their economies.

6   Following intense speculation about the exchange value of the dollar, Secretary Baker announced to the G-5 meeting that he would no longer publicly talk down the dollar.

7   The trade balance improved by almost $5 billion in August to $13.3 billion in response to a sharp drop in manufactured imports. The biggest drop in factory imports was a decline in foreign car shipments. Relative to the Street's expectation, the trade deficit improved by an additional $2 billion.

U.S. TREASURY YIELDS
(Bond Equivalent Yields)

September	Fed Funds	3-Month Bill	6-Month Bill	1-Year Bill	2-Year Note	3-Year Note	5-Year Note	7-Year Note	10-Year Note	30-Year Bond	Spread*
2	5.94	5.33	5.40	5.59	5.99	6.19	6.45	6.81	7.03	7.23	1.90
3	5.92	5.38	5.50	5.68	6.14	6.35	6.64	7.01	7.20	7.43	2.05
4	5.83	5.33	5.47	5.63	6.11	6.34	6.63	6.98	7.15	7.40	2.07
5	5.75	5.37	5.53	5.72	6.25	6.50	6.81	7.14	7.32	7.54	2.17
8	5.86	5.38	5.57	5.78	6.30	6.59	6.89	7.23	7.38	7.59	2.21
9	5.83	5.34	5.56	5.77	6.30	6.58	6.88	7.20	7.35	7.53	2.19
10	6.00	5.30	5.54	5.74	6.27	6.54	6.85	7.20	7.35	7.54	2.24
11	5.88	5.35	5.65	5.84	6.43	6.73	7.07	7.41	7.57	7.74	2.39
12	5.86	5.31	5.61	5.80	6.43	6.74	7.09	7.48	7.63	7.74	2.43
15	5.97	5.31	5.57	5.77	6.39	6.69	7.00	7.36	7.53	7.66	2.35
16	5.88	5.27	5.55	5.76	6.38	6.66	6.99	7.35	7.53	7.67	2.40
17	5.82	5.26	5.54	5.77	6.37	6.64	6.93	7.28	7.46	7.64	2.38
18	5.84	5.37	5.65	5.87	6.47	6.75	7.02	7.41	7.62	7.74	2.37
19	5.80	5.39	5.67	5.86	6.52	6.81	7.10	7.50	7.67	7.83	2.44
22	5.89	5.39	5.63	5.82	6.49	6.77	7.06	7.44	7.62	7.79	2.40
23	5.75	5.39	5.64	5.83	6.46	6.77	7.03	7.40	7.58	7.76	2.37
24	5.76	5.38	5.57	5.78	6.37	6.66	6.94	7.29	7.48	7.64	2.26
25	5.91	5.37	5.58	5.78	6.37	6.66	6.94	7.32	7.47	7.64	2.27
26	5.90	5.38	5.60	5.79	6.39	6.71	6.96	7.32	7.47	7.63	2.25
29	6.03	5.40	5.63	5.86	6.46	6.76	7.04	7.39	7.54	7.69	2.29
30	6.90	5.34	5.62	5.82	6.38	6.68	6.98	7.31	7.45	7.60	2.26

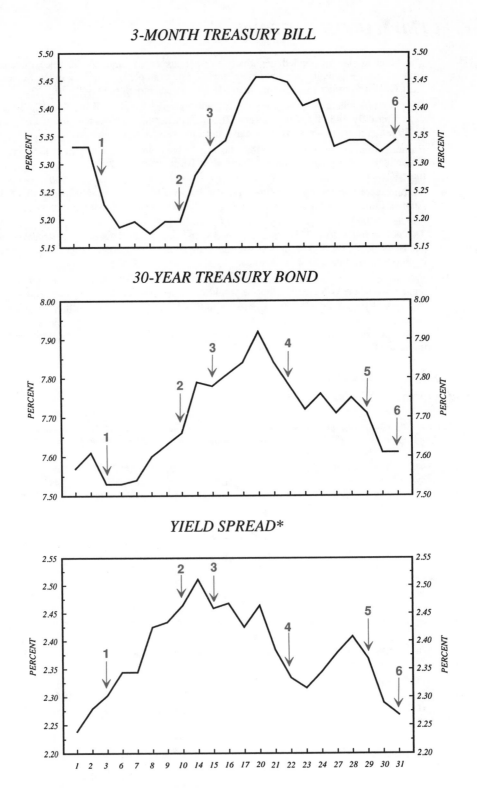

3-MONTH TREASURY BILL

30-YEAR TREASURY BOND

YIELD SPREAD*

*NOTE: SPREAD=30-YEAR BOND MINUS 3-MONTH BILL

SELECTED MARKET FACTORS

1 Details of the September unemployment rate report indicated more slack in the labor market than generally anticipated by the Street. The civilian unemployment rate backed up by 0.25% to 7.0% of the labor force, while payroll employment also expanded by a mere 107,000 new jobs.

2 In response to a temporary increase in energy prices, the September PPI for finished goods expanded by a strong 0.4%. Excluding energy, however, the PPI rose by a more modest 0.1% in September.

3 Retail sales in September, reflecting a 19.5% leap in automobile sales, rose by 4.6% over August. With the September increase, the level of sales activity is 7.5% higher than the previous year. On the other hand, without auto sales, retail sales rose by only 0.1% in September.

4 The exchange value of the dollar improved for the second consecutive day following the Commerce Department's release of a 2.4% preliminary third-quarter GNP estimate. At the same time, news from Geneva indicated that Iran had engineered an extension of the current 17 million barrel a day OPEC production agreement.

5 Although the Treasury announced a large $29 billion quarterly refunding package, the composition of the financing was perceived as a positive by the market. Specifically, the bulk of the additional $1 billion borrowing incorporated in the refunding was raised in the shorter maturity issues.

6 Japan cut its discount rate by 50 basis points from 3.5% to 3.0%. At the same time, the Reagan administration pledged to refrain from foreign currency trading to boost the value of the yen. This new accord between the U.S. and Japan was made public in a joint statement by Secretary Baker and the Japanese Finance Minister Miyazawa.

U.S. TREASURY YIELDS
(Bond Equivalent Yields)

October	Fed Funds	3-Month Bill	6-Month Bill	1-Year Bill	2-Year Note	3-Year Note	5-Year Note	7-Year Note	10-Year Note	30-Year Bond	Spread*
1	5.99	5.33	5.61	5.82	6.36	6.65	6.93	7.26	7.41	7.57	2.24
2	5.94	5.33	5.61	5.83	6.38	6.68	6.95	7.31	7.45	7.61	2.28
3	5.79	5.23	5.39	5.60	6.16	6.46	6.74	7.14	7.31	7.53	2.30
6	5.78	5.19	5.37	5.58	6.14	6.42	6.71	7.11	7.28	7.53	2.34
7	5.56	5.20	5.29	5.57	6.13	6.42	6.71	7.09	7.28	7.54	2.34
8	5.57	5.18	5.25	5.55	6.11	6.41	6.71	7.12	7.31	7.60	2.43
9	5.84	5.20	5.26	5.57	6.15	6.43	6.73	7.14	7.33	7.63	2.43
10	5.78	5.20	5.34	5.59	6.16	6.45	6.73	7.18	7.36	7.66	2.46
14	5.95	5.28	5.38	5.69	6.26	6.54	6.82	7.29	7.49	7.79	2.51
15	5.93	5.32	5.50	5.70	6.27	6.58	6.87	7.32	7.51	7.78	2.46
16	5.89	5.34	5.51	5.72	6.29	6.58	6.87	7.34	7.53	7.81	2.47
17	5.84	5.42	5.60	5.81	6.38	6.67	6.94	7.38	7.57	7.84	2.43
20	5.91	5.46	5.65	5.88	6.47	6.78	7.05	7.50	7.66	7.92	2.46
21	5.86	5.46	5.63	5.83	6.40	6.67	6.96	7.39	7.57	7.84	2.38
22	6.17	5.45	5.60	5.82	6.34	6.64	6.91	7.33	7.49	7.78	2.33
23	5.94	5.40	5.55	5.79	6.31	6.56	6.82	7.25	7.43	7.72	2.32
24	5.83	5.42	5.56	5.79	6.35	6.64	6.86	7.28	7.47	7.76	2.34
27	5.90	5.33	5.53	5.76	6.32	6.60	6.82	7.26	7.42	7.71	2.38
28	5.85	5.34	5.49	5.79	6.34	6.62	6.85	7.21	7.45	7.75	2.41
29	5.88	5.34	5.48	5.75	6.32	6.59	6.82	7.19	7.41	7.71	2.37
30	5.88	5.32	5.46	5.69	6.24	6.52	6.75	7.08	7.31	7.61	2.29
31	5.93	5.34	5.50	5.73	6.26	6.51	6.76	7.10	7.34	7.61	2.27

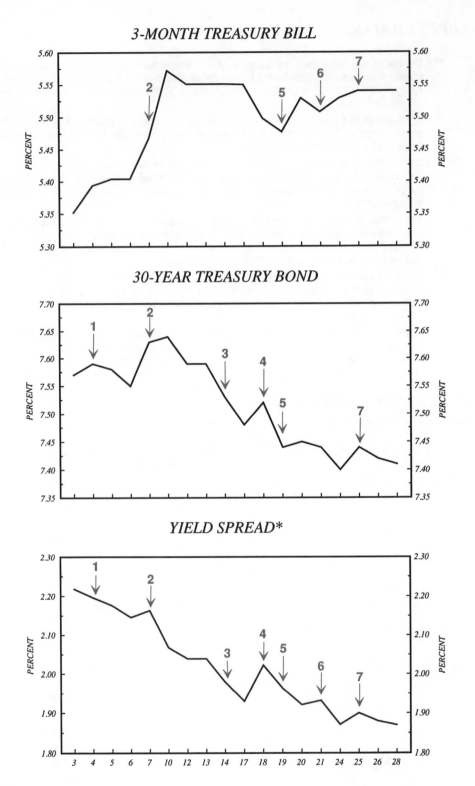

3-MONTH TREASURY BILL

30-YEAR TREASURY BOND

YIELD SPREAD*

*NOTE: SPREAD=30-YEAR BOND MINUS 3-MONTH BILL

SELECTED MARKET FACTORS

1   Despite several close political races in the 1986 elections, the Republicans lost control of the Senate and the Democrats increased their majority in the House of Representatives.

2   The minutes of the September FOMC meeting showed that the Committee had voted for an unchanged policy, but was more likely to tighten than to ease monetary policy. The FOMC's concern centered around strong money growth, a surge in precious metals prices, a speculative drop in the dollar, and a backup in bond yields which reflected increased inflationary expectations.

3   In response to a sharp drop in domestic automobile sales following the end of financing incentives, retail sales fell by 5.0% in November. Net of the volatile auto component, the underlying trend in sales also remained weak, expanding by only 0.2%.

4   The insider trading scandal ballooned as the S.E.C. probed into Drexel's involvement in the high-yield bond market scandal involving Ivan Boesky.

5   Both housing starts and building permits declined in October. New starts fell 0.2% to only 1.65 million units, the fifth decline in the past six months. For the fourth consecutive month, building permits slipped, bringing the level to 1.56 million units, down 2.9% from September.

6   In a surprising leak of information, key monetary policy officers have indicated that the bond market overreacted to the minutes of the September FOMC meeting.

7   With non-defense capital goods orders down 7.4% and defense orders down 43.1%, the advance October report indicated that total durable goods orders had dropped by 6.0%.

U.S. TREASURY YIELDS
(Bond Equivalent Yields)

	Fed Funds	3-Month Bill	6-Month Bill	1-Year Bill	2-Year Note	3-Year Note	5-Year Note	7-Year Note	10-Year Note	30-Year Bond	Spread*
November											
3	6.00	5.35	5.50	5.71	6.21	6.49	6.71	7.06	7.29	7.57	2.22
4	5.94	5.39	5.55	5.72	6.23	6.41	6.71	7.07	7.31	7.59	2.20
5	6.55	5.40	5.58	5.75	6.26	6.45	6.72	7.09	7.24	7.58	2.18
6	6.07	5.40	5.61	5.79	6.29	6.49	6.79	7.16	7.32	7.55	2.15
7	5.94	5.47	5.65	5.85	6.35	6.55	6.86	7.24	7.40	7.63	2.16
10	5.99	5.57	5.75	5.92	6.42	6.59	6.89	7.23	7.38	7.64	2.07
12	5.99	5.55	5.75	5.89	6.38	6.56	6.87	7.20	7.35	7.59	2.04
13	5.94	5.55	5.70	5.87	6.35	6.53	6.83	7.17	7.33	7.59	2.04
14	5.89	5.55	5.69	5.86	6.33	6.50	6.81	7.13	7.29	7.53	1.98
17	6.14	5.55	5.69	5.84	6.32	6.47	6.77	7.06	7.22	7.48	1.93
18	6.02	5.50	5.64	5.81	6.32	6.47	6.79	7.09	7.27	7.52	2.02
19	7.13	5.48	5.60	5.73	6.21	6.42	6.73	7.02	7.19	7.44	1.96
20	6.16	5.53	5.65	5.82	6.26	6.45	6.74	7.04	7.19	7.45	1.92
21	5.96	5.51	5.63	5.75	6.21	6.40	6.72	7.01	7.17	7.44	1.93
24	5.98	5.53	5.64	5.75	6.19	6.37	6.69	6.95	7.11	7.40	1.87
25	5.98	5.54	5.66	5.77	6.23	6.40	6.66	7.00	7.15	7.44	1.90
26	5.99	5.54	5.65	5.78	6.21	6.39	6.65	7.00	7.15	7.42	1.88
28	6.03	5.54	5.65	5.76	6.21	6.38	6.65	7.00	7.15	7.41	1.87

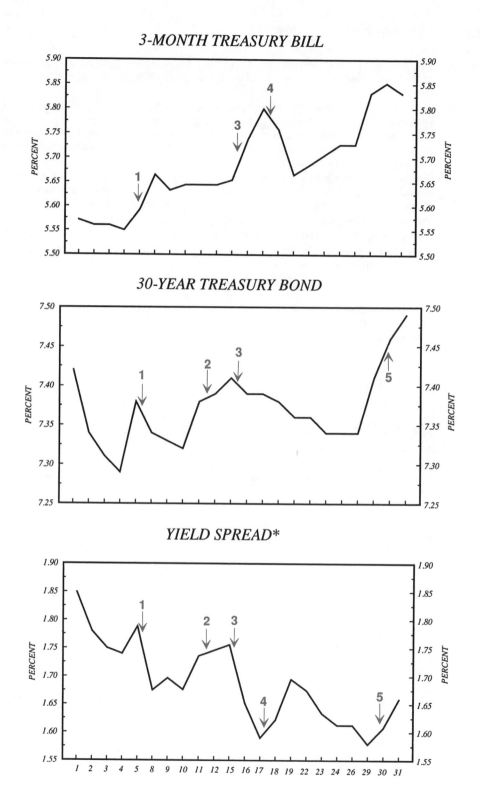

3-MONTH TREASURY BILL

30-YEAR TREASURY BOND

YIELD SPREAD*

*NOTE: SPREAD=30-YEAR BOND MINUS 3-MONTH BILL

SELECTED MARKET FACTORS

1 The level of non-farm payroll employment rose by a surprisingly strong 249,000 new jobs in November, up 89,000 from most Street estimates. Moreover, manufacturing employment increased by 30,000 workers even as the work week lengthened to 40.9 hours.

2 In a show of unity that had not existed in many years, OPEC appeared headed for a steep production cut aimed at raising oil prices to $18 a barrel.

3 Following the strong November payroll employment report, the level of industrial production rose by a sizable 0.6% in the month. In fact, all major component output series recorded substantial advances in November.

4 Reflecting quarter-end pressures—specifically the corporate tax data—fed funds averaged 7.46% for the final day of the early December period. Fed funds traded in a wide 6.0 % to 8 1/4% range during the course of the day.

5 The foreign exchange value of the dollar fell to a 1986 low of 1.9550 against the Deutsche mark, on Friday, December 26, in Japan. The previous low had been 1.9580 Deutsche marks to the dollar.

U.S. TREASURY YIELDS
(Bond Equivalent Yields)

	Fed Funds	3-Month Bill	6-Month Bill	1-Year Bill	2-Year Note	3-Year Note	5-Year Note	7-Year Note	10-Year Note	30-Year Bond	Spread*
December											
1	6.38	5.57	5.69	5.82	6.25	6.43	6.69	7.02	7.18	7.42	1.85
2	6.54	5.56	5.68	5.80	6.22	6.37	6.61	6.91	7.08	7.34	1.78
3	6.72	5.56	5.66	5.75	6.17	6.35	6.58	6.89	7.06	7.31	1.75
4	6.14	5.55	5.63	5.73	6.15	6.30	6.53	6.85	7.01	7.29	1.74
5	5.94	5.59	5.69	5.81	6.24	6.38	6.65	6.96	7.12	7.38	1.79
8	6.02	5.67	5.75	5.83	6.24	6.39	6.61	6.92	7.10	7.34	1.67
9	5.95	5.63	5.72	5.82	6.21	6.36	6.60	6.91	7.07	7.33	1.70
10	5.86	5.64	5.71	5.82	6.19	6.35	6.58	6.90	7.05	7.32	1.68
11	5.86	5.64	5.72	5.83	6.24	6.39	6.64	6.95	7.12	7.38	1.74
12	5.93	5.64	5.73	5.84	6.24	6.40	6.66	6.98	7.13	7.39	1.75
15	6.53	5.65	5.82	5.88	6.29	6.45	6.69	7.00	7.15	7.41	1.76
16	6.48	5.74	5.82	5.88	6.29	6.44	6.67	6.97	7.12	7.39	1.65
17	7.46	5.80	5.85	5.93	6.31	6.46	6.68	6.98	7.12	7.39	1.59
18	6.44	5.76	5.83	5.90	6.31	6.46	6.69	6.98	7.11	7.38	1.62
19	6.22	5.67	5.82	5.89	6.29	6.46	6.69	6.98	7.10	7.36	1.70
22	6.48	5.69	5.84	5.91	6.30	6.45	6.69	6.98	7.10	7.36	1.68
23	6.39	5.71	5.85	5.94	6.30	6.45	6.68	6.95	7.08	7.34	1.63
24	6.23	5.73	5.83	5.92	6.30	6.45	6.68	6.96	7.07	7.34	1.61
26	6.42	5.73	5.82	5.91	6.30	6.47	6.69	6.96	7.08	7.34	1.61
29	8.38	5.83	5.95	6.02	6.37	6.53	6.78	7.06	7.17	7.41	1.58
30	16.17	5.85	5.93	6.06	6.42	6.59	6.82	7.09	7.23	7.46	1.61
31	14.35	5.83	5.87	5.95	6.35	6.56	6.81	7.09	7.23	7.49	1.66

1987

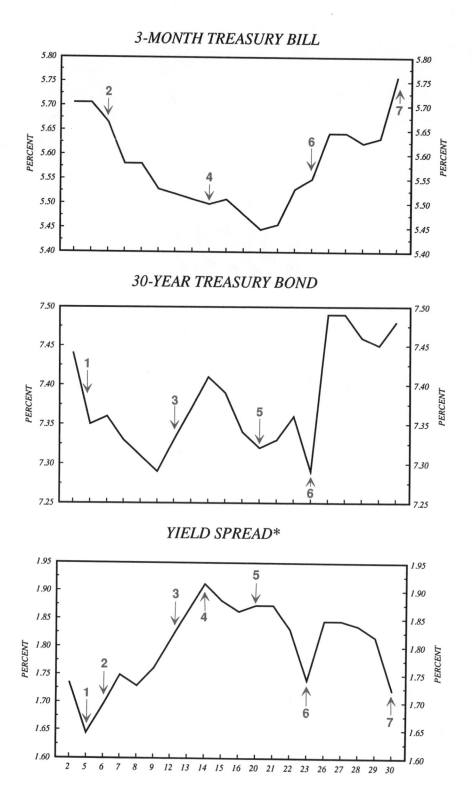

3-MONTH TREASURY BILL

30-YEAR TREASURY BOND

YIELD SPREAD*

*NOTE: SPREAD=30-YEAR BOND MINUS 3-MONTH BILL

SELECTED MARKET FACTORS

1 The exchange value of the dollar firmed early in January in response to fear of central bank intervention to support the currency following the dollar's recent weakness.

2 As quarter-end statement date pressures diminished, the effective fed funds rate began to return to the Federal Reserve's target of a 5 7/8% average rate.

3 Following a 3% appreciation in the Deutsche mark within the European Monetary System, the dollar resumed its decline which began in late December 1986.

4 The effective fed funds rate drifted down to a low of 5.89%, the lowest rate on overnight money since the middle of the fourth quarter when the insider trading problem disrupted the high-yield market.

5 The Bundesbank cut the discount rate by 50 basis points to 3% and the Lombard rate to 5%. At the same time, however, reserve requirements were raised.

6 Personal consumption expenditures rose by 2.0% in December on strong auto sales, causing speculation about an upward revision to the preliminary 1.7% rise in real GNP.

7 The Federal Reserve's unwillingness to execute system repo over the weekend with reserves trading at 6 3/8% resulted in increased market speculation about a possible policy tightening by the Fed to a 6 1/4% funds rate.

U.S. TREASURY YIELDS
(Bond Equivalent Yields)

January	Fed Funds	3-Month Bill	6-Month Bill	1-Year Bill	2-Year Note	3-Year Note	5-Year Note	7-Year Note	10-Year Note	30-Year Bond	Spread*
2	6.46	5.71	5.80	5.86	6.30	6.48	6.75	7.03	7.18	7.44	1.73
5	6.86	5.71	5.79	5.85	6.24	6.41	6.67	6.95	7.08	7.35	1.64
6	6.56	5.67	5.77	5.85	6.25	6.42	6.67	6.93	7.08	7.36	1.70
7	6.20	5.58	5.71	5.78	6.22	6.37	6.65	6.90	7.05	7.33	1.75
8	5.98	5.58	5.68	5.78	6.20	6.36	6.60	6.89	7.04	7.31	1.73
9	5.93	5.53	5.68	5.76	6.19	6.34	6.58	6.86	7.01	7.29	1.76
12	6.22	5.52	5.67	5.76	6.20	6.37	6.61	6.90	7.05	7.33	1.81
13	6.19	5.51	5.65	5.78	6.22	6.40	6.64	6.94	7.10	7.37	1.86
14	5.89	5.50	5.64	5.78	6.24	6.42	6.67	6.95	7.11	7.41	1.91
15	6.01	5.51	5.64	5.78	6.22	6.41	6.64	6.92	7.08	7.39	1.88
16	5.97	5.48	5.61	5.72	6.22	6.37	6.60	6.87	7.03	7.34	1.86
20	6.13	5.45	5.55	5.65	6.17	6.34	6.57	6.84	7.01	7.32	1.87
21	6.07	5.46	5.53	5.70	6.17	6.36	6.57	6.84	7.01	7.33	1.87
22	6.08	5.53	5.56	5.70	6.17	6.38	6.57	6.85	7.03	7.36	1.83
23	6.02	5.55	5.56	5.70	6.20	6.38	6.59	6.89	7.06	7.29	1.74
26	6.14	5.64	5.66	5.79	6.26	6.45	6.67	6.97	7.17	7.49	1.85
27	6.15	5.64	5.68	5.81	6.24	6.46	6.66	6.97	7.16	7.49	1.85
28	6.50	5.62	5.66	5.79	6.24	6.43	6.63	6.93	7.13	7.46	1.84
29	6.22	5.63	5.69	5.80	6.24	6.45	6.65	6.95	7.13	7.45	1.82
30	6.28	5.76	5.83	5.93	6.33	6.51	6.71	6.99	7.18	7.48	1.72

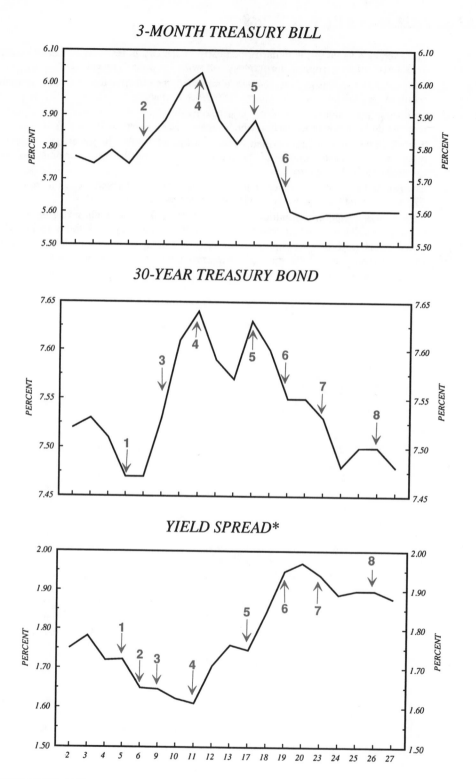

3-MONTH TREASURY BILL

30-YEAR TREASURY BOND

YIELD SPREAD*

*NOTE: SPREAD=30-YEAR BOND MINUS 3-MONTH BILL

SELECTED MARKET FACTORS

1 Despite apparent currency risk, foreign participation in the refunding bond auction was somewhat stronger than expected.

2 The January payroll employment report showed a 448,00 rise in new jobs, a figure substantially larger than anticipated. This increase was considered by some analysts to be a confirmation of an outright acceleration in growth.

3 As rumors of a G-5 currency agreement proved false, the dollar fell 4% from intra-day highs against major European currencies, ending a three-day rally.

4 With fed funds around 6 1/2%, and the absence of open market interventions as a rate protest, speculation about a Fed tightening in support of the dollar reached a peak.

5 Concluding the Treasury's February refunding operation, about $29 billion in new notes and bonds settled.

6 In talking to reporters after his Humphrey-Hawkins testimony, Chairman Volcker made it clear that recent reserve market pressures were not the result of a policy change. The same day, Japan had cut its discount rate by 50 basis points to 2 1/2%, and Brazil declared a moratorium on interest payments owed to its foreign creditors.

7 On February 22, the finance ministers of the United States and major economic allies agreed in Paris to stabilize exchange rates around their current rates.

8 The Tower Commission Report indicated that President Reagan had traded arms for hostages.

U.S. TREASURY YIELDS
(Bond Equivalent Yields)

	Fed Funds	3-Month Bill	6-Month Bill	1-Year Bill	2-Year Note	3-Year Note	5-Year Note	7-Year Note	10-Year Note	30-Year Bond	Spread*
February											
2	6.30	5.77	5.84	5.93	6.36	6.55	6.75	7.04	7.23	7.52	1.75
3	6.20	5.75	5.83	5.92	6.38	6.53	6.77	7.06	7.25	7.53	1.78
4	5.97	5.79	5.86	5.93	6.38	6.53	6.76	7.05	7.23	7.51	1.72
5	5.95	5.75	5.83	5.87	6.33	6.50	6.70	7.01	7.20	7.47	1.72
6	6.07	5.82	5.92	5.93	6.38	6.53	6.73	7.01	7.19	7.47	1.65
9	6.29	5.88	5.98	5.99	6.45	6.60	6.79	7.07	7.25	7.53	1.65
10	6.33	5.99	6.06	6.08	6.49	6.65	6.89	7.16	7.33	7.61	1.62
11	6.17	6.03	6.10	6.11	6.58	6.74	6.96	7.20	7.37	7.64	1.61
12	6.22	5.88	5.96	6.03	6.47	6.65	6.92	7.13	7.31	7.59	1.71
13	6.10	5.81	5.92	6.05	6.43	6.59	6.83	7.10	7.28	7.57	1.76
17	6.59	5.88	5.98	6.09	6.48	6.64	6.87	7.14	7.33	7.63	1.75
18	6.25	5.76	5.87	6.02	6.43	6.59	6.84	7.11	7.30	7.60	1.84
19	6.00	5.60	5.62	5.90	6.33	6.53	6.76	7.04	7.23	7.55	1.95
20	5.92	5.58	5.67	5.89	6.33	6.51	6.78	7.05	7.24	7.55	1.97
23	6.06	5.59	5.69	5.88	6.35	6.52	6.78	7.04	7.23	7.53	1.94
24	5.95	5.59	5.66	5.88	6.32	6.49	6.75	7.00	7.18	7.48	1.89
25	5.89	5.60	5.64	5.91	6.37	6.53	6.72	7.01	7.21	7.50	1.90
26	5.97	5.60	5.65	5.91	6.35	6.53	6.74	7.01	7.21	7.50	1.90
27	6.02	5.60	5.68	5.90	6.35	6.51	6.71	7.00	7.19	7.48	1.88

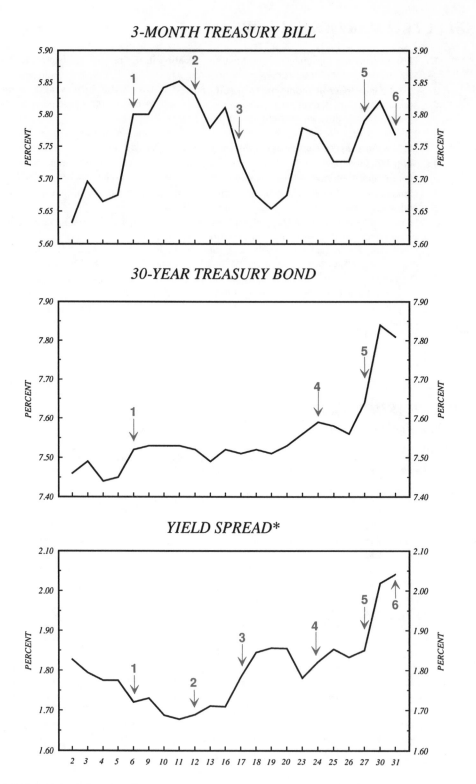

*NOTE: SPREAD=30-YEAR BOND MINUS 3-MONTH BILL

SELECTED MARKET FACTORS

1 For the second consecutive month, payroll employment growth was well above the 250,000 rate that prevailed throughout most of 1986. In fact, February employment was up by 337,000 workers, with manufacturing up 50,000 workers.

2 Retail sales rose by 4.1% in February after a pronounced 7.4% drop in the previous month. The month-to-month swing in sales was attributed to changes in the automobile industry.

3 Following a surprising three-day term system repo, the fed funds rate temporarily dropped below 6%.

4 After the U.S. exchange rate fell below 150 yen, the G-6 central banks began a significant coordinated intervention to attempt to stabilize the dollar.

5 The Reagan administration's plan to impose stiff tarrifs on Japanese consumer electronic imports sparked fears of an outright trade war, which caused a speculative collapse in the dollar.

6 Citing the high cost of funds, Citibank and Chase Manhattan banks raised their prime lending rates from 7 1/2% to 7 3/4%. This marked the first increase in the prime lending rate since mid-1984.

U.S. TREASURY YIELDS
(Bond Equivalent Yields)

	Fed Funds	3-Month Bill	6-Month Bill	1-Year Bill	2-Year Note	3-Year Note	5-Year Note	7-Year Note	10-Year Note	30-Year Bond	Spread*
March											
2	6.18	5.63	5.68	5.92	6.34	6.50	6.69	6.97	7.17	7.46	1.83
3	6.22	5.70	5.80	5.96	6.37	6.52	6.72	7.01	7.21	7.49	1.79
4	6.01	5.67	5.77	5.90	6.32	6.48	6.66	6.95	7.14	7.44	1.78
5	5.99	5.68	5.77	5.91	6.35	6.51	6.69	6.97	7.16	7.45	1.78
6	6.00	5.80	5.91	6.02	6.42	6.58	6.77	7.04	7.23	7.52	1.72
9	6.21	5.80	5.93	6.04	6.43	6.56	6.78	7.04	7.23	7.53	1.73
10	6.25	5.84	5.90	6.09	6.44	6.57	6.78	7.05	7.23	7.53	1.69
11	6.32	5.85	5.88	6.09	6.44	6.57	6.78	7.05	7.23	7.53	1.68
12	6.14	5.83	5.87	6.09	6.43	6.56	6.78	7.05	7.22	7.52	1.69
13	6.05	5.78	5.86	6.01	6.39	6.52	6.75	7.01	7.19	7.49	1.71
16	6.25	5.81	5.88	6.04	6.41	6.55	6.77	7.04	7.22	7.52	1.71
17	6.05	5.73	5.81	6.00	6.42	6.54	6.75	7.03	7.20	7.51	1.78
18	5.97	5.68	5.75	5.99	6.40	6.54	6.76	7.04	7.21	7.52	1.84
19	6.06	5.65	5.73	5.95	6.38	6.51	6.75	7.02	7.21	7.51	1.86
20	6.09	5.68	5.79	5.98	6.40	6.53	6.77	7.04	7.22	7.53	1.86
23	6.21	5.78	5.87	6.03	6.42	6.59	6.80	7.07	7.25	7.56	1.78
24	6.14	5.77	5.83	6.06	6.44	6.63	6.82	7.09	7.27	7.59	1.82
25	6.28	5.73	5.83	6.07	6.46	6.64	6.84	7.10	7.26	7.58	1.85
26	6.21	5.73	5.84	6.06	6.42	6.61	6.81	7.03	7.24	7.56	1.83
27	6.15	5.79	5.91	6.14	6.49	6.69	6.89	7.12	7.33	7.64	1.85
30	6.33	5.82	6.01	6.23	6.63	6.85	7.07	7.33	7.54	7.84	2.02
31	6.23	5.77	5.99	6.15	6.54	6.79	7.02	7.29	7.51	7.81	2.04

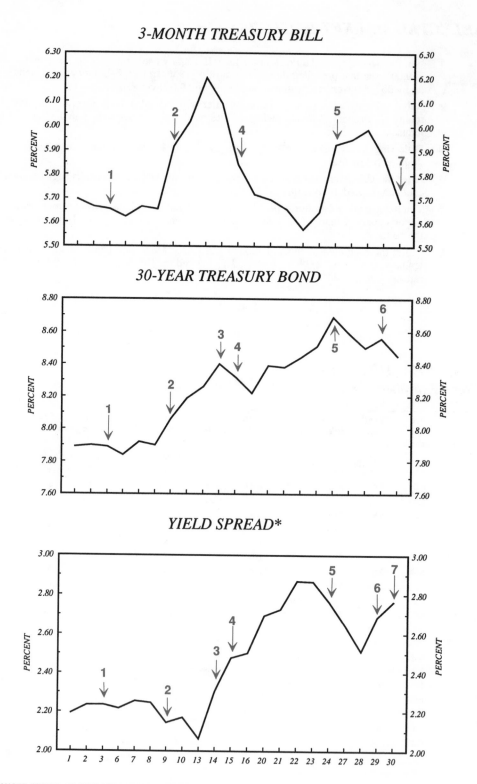

*NOTE: SPREAD=30-YEAR BOND MINUS 3-MONTH BILL

SELECTED MARKET FACTORS

1. Despite Street estimates of a pickup in economic activity, payroll employment rose by a marginal 164,000 workers in March following a 101,000 downward revision to February job growth.

2. The dollar plunged to a postwar low against the yen as currency traders paid little attention to the results of the Washington meeting of key international finance ministers. The movement in the dollar was generally perceived as a factor that would force the Fed to tighten policy.

3. According to Commerce Department data, a $5 billion surge in imports offset a $2.2 billion rise in exports, pushing the trade deficit for February to $15 billion.

4. Treasury Secretary Baker spoke out forcefully in support of the dollar for the first time, commenting that a further decline in the dollar would be counter-productive.

5. The dollar fell to the lowest level in thirty-five years against the yen, carried along by the momentum of the previous day's trading in New York.

6. The controversial trade retaliation amendment supported by Rep. Gephardt passed the House by a razor-thin margin of 218 to 214 votes.

7. In testimony before a panel of the House Banking Committee, Chairman Volcker indicated that the Fed had "snugged" reserve market conditions in response to the latest collapse in the dollar. At the same time, during a crisis summit in Washington, D.C., Prime Minister Nakasone announced Japan's intention to lower short-term rates to stimulate domestic growth.

U.S. TREASURY YIELDS
(Bond Equivalent Yields)

April	Fed Funds	3-Month Bill	6-Month Bill	1-Year Bill	2-Year Note	3-Year Note	5-Year Note	7-Year Note	10-Year Note	30-Year Bond	Spread*
1	6.22	5.70	6.01	6.21	6.65	6.90	7.12	7.39	7.59	7.89	2.19
2	6.14	5.67	6.01	6.18	6.63	6.90	7.12	7.39	7.59	7.90	2.24
3	5.99	5.65	5.96	6.14	6.62	6.88	7.10	7.39	7.59	7.89	2.24
6	6.20	5.62	5.93	6.10	6.57	6.83	7.06	7.34	7.54	7.84	2.22
7	6.17	5.67	5.93	6.15	6.59	6.89	7.14	7.42	7.62	7.92	2.26
8	6.45	5.65	5.93	6.17	6.59	6.89	7.14	7.41	7.61	7.90	2.25
9	6.27	5.92	6.05	6.33	6.74	7.01	7.30	7.58	7.78	8.06	2.15
10	6.35	6.02	6.25	6.56	6.97	7.27	7.55	7.79	7.98	8.19	2.17
13	6.56	6.20	6.39	6.69	7.08	7.42	7.68	7.90	8.07	8.26	2.06
14	6.55	6.09	6.40	6.73	7.19	7.54	7.83	8.05	8.28	8.40	2.31
15	6.45	5.84	6.22	6.57	7.02	7.38	7.67	7.90	8.10	8.32	2.48
16	6.26	5.72	6.11	6.41	6.90	7.24	7.55	7.81	8.03	8.22	2.50
20	6.21	5.70	6.29	6.61	7.06	7.45	7.72	8.00	8.20	8.39	2.69
21	6.42	5.65	6.18	6.52	7.09	7.44	7.71	7.99	8.19	8.38	2.73
22	6.78	5.57	6.16	6.66	7.23	7.51	7.77	8.05	8.24	8.44	2.87
23	6.42	5.64	6.08	6.72	7.36	7.64	7.92	8.17	8.39	8.51	2.87
24	6.29	5.93	6.27	6.84	7.48	7.79	8.05	8.31	8.47	8.69	2.76
27	6.57	5.95	6.35	6.88	7.50	7.77	7.97	8.20	8.37	8.59	2.64
28	6.75	5.99	6.40	6.75	7.43	7.68	7.91	8.12	8.28	8.50	2.51
29	6.87	5.87	6.39	6.75	7.43	7.71	7.93	8.18	8.35	8.56	2.69
30	7.63	5.69	6.23	6.62	7.38	7.63	7.82	8.07	8.21	8.45	2.76

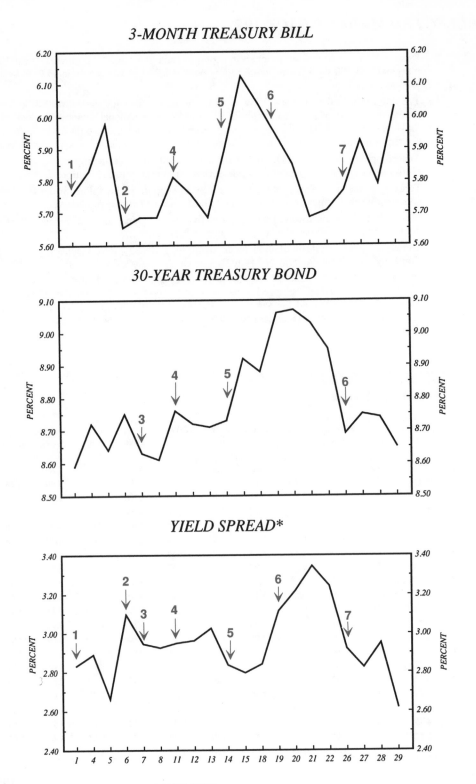

*NOTE: SPREAD=30-YEAR BOND MINUS 3-MONTH BILL

SELECTED MARKET FACTORS

1   Most banks increased the prime rate from 7 3/4% to 8.0% in response to Chairman Volcker's announcement that the Federal Reserve had "snugged" reserve market conditions.

2   Although Federal Reserve Vice Chairman Johnson supported the recent monetary policy tightening, he did not consider the decline of the dollar to be inflationary—especially when contrasted with the excessively strict nature of international monetary policies.

3   Substantial foreign participation accompanied the final stage of the May refunding operation.

4   Commodity price gains, which ranged across most raw materials markets, resulted in one of the largest single-day advances in the Commodity Reserach Bureau Futures Index (+2.7% or 6.17 points).

5   Speculation about an imminent discount rate increase intensified when the exchange value of the dollar failed to improve following a 12.9% increase in merchandise exports, which prompted a $1.5 billion narrowing in the trade deficit.

6   Citicorp's announcement of a $3 billion increase in its loan-loss reserve is a major departure from the general strategy for renegotiating foreign loans.

7   At the same time that the dollar staged its biggest one-day rally this year, rising 2.2% against the yen, commodity prices moved lower.

U.S. TREASURY YIELDS
(Bond Equivalent Yields)

May	Fed Funds	3-Month Bill	6-Month Bill	1-Year Bill	2-Year Note	3-Year Note	5-Year Note	7-Year Note	10-Year Note	30-Year Bond	Spread*
1	7.67	5.76	6.25	6.78	7.47	7.75	7.98	8.23	8.39	8.59	2.83
4	7.00	5.83	6.30	6.92	7.61	7.88	8.12	8.35	8.52	8.72	2.89
5	6.86	5.98	6.40	6.90	7.60	7.84	8.08	8.30	8.45	8.64	2.66
6	6.61	5.65	6.04	6.85	7.62	7.92	8.15	8.39	8.54	8.75	3.10
7	6.84	5.69	6.04	6.87	7.60	7.88	8.08	8.34	8.50	8.63	2.95
8	6.72	5.69	6.11	6.84	7.57	7.81	8.04	8.28	8.43	8.61	2.93
11	6.84	5.81	6.14	6.92	7.66	7.93	8.19	8.43	8.57	8.76	2.95
12	6.75	5.76	6.09	6.92	7.68	7.94	8.19	8.41	8.55	8.72	2.96
13	6.67	5.69	6.10	7.00	7.68	7.95	8.18	8.42	8.55	8.71	3.03
14	6.75	5.89	6.23	7.02	7.66	7.95	8.20	8.42	8.57	8.73	2.84
15	6.84	6.12	6.54	7.27	7.95	8.21	8.45	8.67	8.80	8.92	2.80
18	6.88	6.04	6.57	7.24	7.93	8.19	8.42	8.60	8.73	8.88	2.84
19	6.67	5.95	6.56	7.30	7.99	8.27	8.55	8.76	8.89	9.06	3.11
20	6.60	5.85	6.51	7.23	8.05	8.35	8.61	8.79	8.92	9.07	3.22
21	6.77	5.69	6.40	7.12	8.06	8.32	8.55	8.74	8.87	9.03	3.34
22	6.72	5.71	6.42	7.10	7.97	8.23	8.49	8.66	8.78	8.95	3.24
26	6.97	5.77	6.40	6.96	7.79	8.01	8.23	8.40	8.55	8.69	2.92
27	6.97	5.93	6.50	7.01	7.84	8.06	8.28	8.47	8.60	8.75	2.83
28	6.80	5.79	6.49	6.94	7.81	8.04	8.25	8.44	8.56	8.74	2.95
29	6.63	6.03	6.44	6.88	7.69	7.94	8.15	8.35	8.49	8.65	2.62

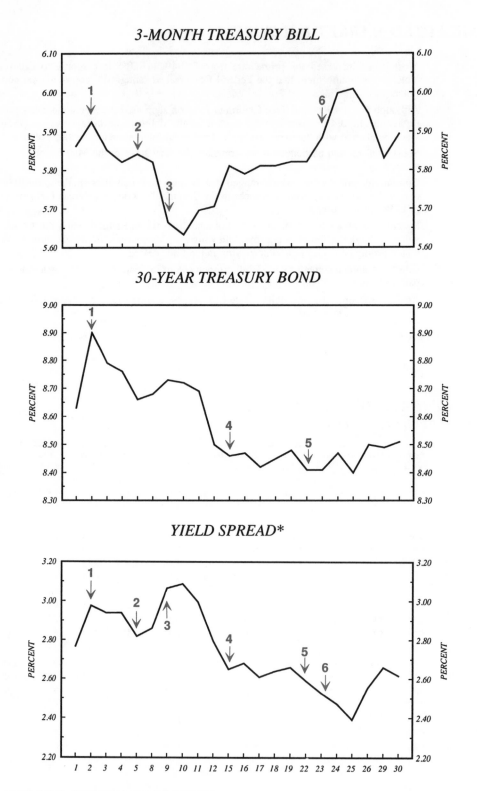

NOTE: SPREAD=30-YEAR BOND MINUS 3-MONTH BILL

SELECTED MARKET FACTORS

1 Paul Volcker, Chairman of the Federal Reserve Board for eight years, resigned. The Reagan administration nominated Alan Greenspan to succeed Volcker.

2 Following strong increases in employment during the first four months of the year, May payroll figures revealed a relatively weak 123,000 gain in new jobs. This weak growth in employment resulted from a decelerating service sector.

3 As depositors lost confidence in the state's embattled savings and loan associations, Texas thrifts began to search for funds to meet accelerating withdrawals.

4 Despite sharply rising food commodity prices and Texas crude closing above $20 per barrel, an improved foreign exchange value of the dollar—the result of stable currency talk by Japan—sent bond prices higher.

5 A firmer dollar and widespread precipitation in the farm belt battered most commodity markets, resulting in one of the steepest one-day declines in the widely watched commodity price gauge. In fact, the Commodity Research Bureau Index plunged 6.46 points to 223.06.

6 The Texas thrift crisis and record high June cash balances suggested several end-of-quarter pressures in the reserve market; however, this situation was avoided because of aggressive Fed market intervention.

U.S. TREASURY YIELDS
(Bond Equivalent Yields)

	Fed Funds	3-Month Bill	6-Month Bill	1-Year Bill	2-Year Note	3-Year Note	5-Year Note	7-Year Note	10-Year Note	30-Year Bond	Spread*
June											
1	6.74	5.86	6.43	6.88	7.67	7.91	8.08	8.30	8.45	8.63	2.77
2	6.56	5.93	6.43	6.98	7.85	8.10	8.31	8.58	8.72	8.90	2.98
3	6.58	5.85	6.38	6.91	7.78	8.06	8.25	8.50	8.64	8.79	2.94
4	6.74	5.82	6.37	6.87	7.76	8.00	8.20	8.45	8.58	8.76	2.94
5	6.70	5.84	6.28	6.90	7.66	7.92	8.11	8.36	8.50	8.66	2.82
8	6.75	5.82	6.18	6.90	7.68	7.95	8.14	8.41	8.53	8.68	2.86
9	6.68	5.67	6.16	6.83	7.71	7.97	8.18	8.43	8.56	8.73	3.07
10	6.63	5.63	6.12	6.76	7.68	7.91	8.15	8.45	8.56	8.72	3.09
11	6.73	5.70	6.18	6.78	7.66	7.91	8.13	8.41	8.52	8.69	2.99
12	6.71	5.71	6.13	6.71	7.51	7.73	7.90	8.19	8.32	8.50	2.79
15	6.85	5.81	6.21	6.73	7.47	7.68	7.89	8.16	8.28	8.46	2.65
16	6.74	5.79	6.23	6.74	7.47	7.70	7.89	8.16	8.28	8.47	2.68
17	6.80	5.81	6.21	6.72	7.42	7.64	7.83	8.10	8.23	8.42	2.61
18	6.81	5.81	6.16	6.73	7.44	7.67	7.87	8.13	8.27	8.45	2.64
19	6.76	5.82	6.19	6.72	7.45	7.69	7.89	8.17	8.30	8.48	2.66
22	6.83	5.82	6.19	6.69	7.42	7.64	7.83	8.09	8.23	8.41	2.59
23	6.84	5.88	6.29	6.75	7.45	7.66	7.85	8.10	8.23	8.41	2.53
24	6.75	6.00	6.37	6.83	7.54	7.77	7.94	8.19	8.31	8.47	2.47
25	6.81	6.01	6.37	6.77	7.47	7.72	7.91	8.10	8.25	8.40	2.39
26	6.72	5.95	6.41	6.80	7.56	7.82	8.02	8.23	8.37	8.50	2.55
29	6.68	5.83	6.29	6.73	7.48	7.77	7.97	8.20	8.34	8.49	2.66
30	6.56	5.89	6.18	6.77	7.48	7.76	8.02	8.24	8.38	8.51	2.62

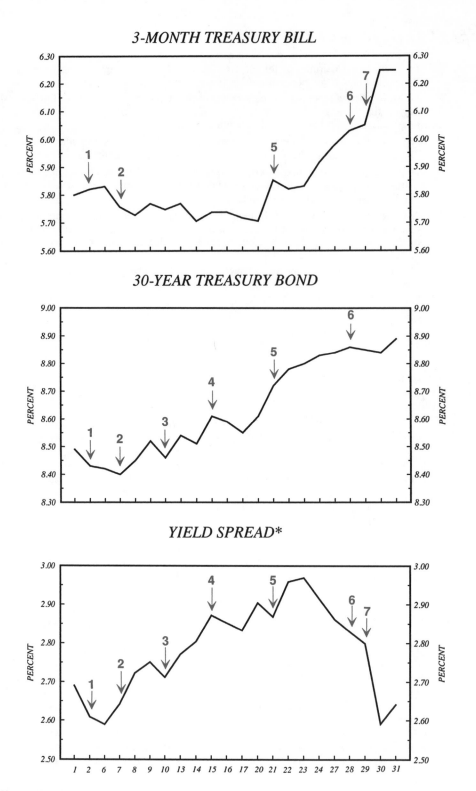

3-MONTH TREASURY BILL

30-YEAR TREASURY BOND

YIELD SPREAD*

*NOTE: SPREAD=30-YEAR BOND MINUS 3-MONTH BILL

SELECTED MARKET FACTORS

1. Following the lead of reduced service sector employment, total payroll employment expanded by a somewhat lethargic 116,00 workers in June. Despite a third consecutive month of deceleration in employment, the unemployment rate fell to just 6.1% of the labor force.

2. Responding to favorable testimony from Colonel Oliver North, the dollar surged past 150 yen for the first time in three and a half months. A level of 150 had previously been considered a key technical resistance on the dollar.

3. Although the Street had anticipated a pronounced 0.7% rise in wholesale prices, and considering the prospect of a weak July figure, the reported June rise of only 0.2% was a temporary positive for the bond market.

4. The trade deficit widened to $14.4 billion in June, reflecting higher prices for imported goods and an uptick in oil imports. Increased tension in the Persian Gulf pushed U.S. crude oil prices above $21.00 per barrel.

5. During his semi-annual Humphrey-Hawkins testimony, Federal Reserve Chairman Volcker squelched market speculation about a Fed "de-snugging" by revealing that the program had remained essentially unchanged since May. At the same time, the Senate passed a sweeping trade bill with a number of protectionist measures.

6. Persian Gulf tension lifted oil prices to their largest one-day rise in five years. Specifically, September crude rose 85 cents to a price of $21.32 per barrel.

7. A short-term debt limit extension cleared the way for $59 billion in gross short-term financing which had been delayed since Friday, July 17.

U.S. TREASURY YIELDS
(Bond Equivalent Yields)

July	Fed Funds	3-Month Bill	6-Month Bill	1-Year Bill	2-Year Note	3-Year Note	5-Year Note	7-Year Note	10-Year Note	30-Year Bond	Spread*
1	6.07	5.80	6.07	6.69	7.44	7.72	7.96	8.22	8.36	8.49	2.69
2	6.68	5.82	6.01	6.66	7.38	7.64	7.90	8.14	8.30	8.43	2.61
6	6.73	5.83	6.05	6.67	7.38	7.66	7.90	8.13	8.29	8.42	2.59
7	6.72	5.76	5.83	6.63	7.36	7.63	7.90	8.10	8.28	8.40	2.64
8	6.59	5.73	5.67	6.62	7.35	7.65	7.90	8.13	8.32	8.45	2.72
9	6.62	5.77	5.75	6.64	7.38	7.68	7.95	8.19	8.37	8.52	2.75
10	6.54	5.75	5.68	6.51	7.32	7.62	7.88	8.13	8.32	8.46	2.71
13	6.62	5.77	5.76	6.51	7.36	7.66	7.93	8.18	8.38	8.54	2.77
14	6.40	5.71	5.76	6.50	7.32	7.61	7.89	8.15	8.33	8.51	2.80
15	6.38	5.74	5.82	6.57	7.37	7.69	7.97	8.25	8.43	8.61	2.87
16	6.56	5.74	5.81	6.54	7.34	7.66	7.95	8.21	8.41	8.59	2.85
17	6.56	5.72	5.85	6.55	7.34	7.64	7.92	8.16	8.36	8.55	2.83
20	6.66	5.71	5.86	6.58	7.38	7.68	7.96	8.22	8.41	8.61	2.90
21	6.58	5.85	6.06	6.69	7.45	7.75	8.03	8.30	8.49	8.72	2.87
22	6.52	5.82	6.09	6.73	7.47	7.78	8.05	8.35	8.54	8.78	2.96
23	6.60	5.83	6.13	6.74	7.46	7.79	8.08	8.37	8.56	8.80	2.97
24	6.62	5.92	6.26	6.82	7.53	7.84	8.12	8.40	8.58	8.83	2.92
27	6.64	5.98	6.30	6.84	7.59	7.87	8.15	8.42	8.60	8.84	2.86
28	6.58	6.03	6.36	6.86	7.61	7.90	8.17	8.44	8.62	8.86	2.83
29	6.70	6.05	6.37	6.91	7.64	7.87	8.16	8.44	8.61	8.85	2.80
30	6.72	6.25	6.42	6.88	7.63	7.94	8.20	8.45	8.61	8.84	2.59
31	6.75	6.25	6.43	6.89	7.63	7.95	8.21	8.48	8.66	8.89	2.64

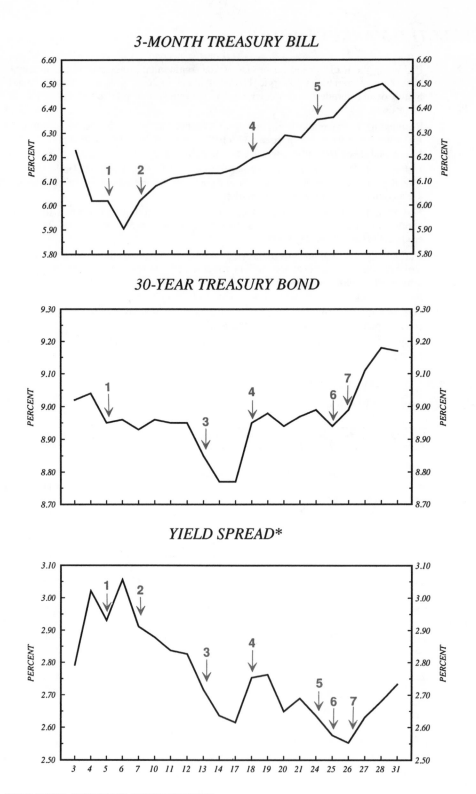

3-MONTH TREASURY BILL

30-YEAR TREASURY BOND

*YIELD SPREAD**

*NOTE: SPREAD=30-YEAR BOND MINUS 3-MONTH BILL

SELECTED MARKET FACTORS

1 World oil prices tumbled amidst indications of increased U.S. supplies and an uneasy calm in the Persian Gulf region.

2 Non-farm payroll employment in the United States rose by an unexpectedly strong 304,000 workers as manufacturing industries added 70,000 new jobs.

3 While bond prices declined for the seventh day in eight trading sessions, Japanese interest in the Treasury's new 30-year bond precipitated a market rally.

4 The dollar plunged by nearly 2.0% against the yen, and 1.4% against the Deutsche mark. This was an apparent delayed response to a $1.7 billion widening in the June trade deficit. This currency move resulted from the Fed's change to a back-filling operating style from the recent tendency to front-load the add.

5 Personal consumption expenditures rose by 0.9% in both the June and July reports, suggesting that retail activity had begun to accelerate after two quarters of weakness. Consumer strength implied increased import demand and a need for a tighter monetary policy.

6 Although the trade deficit deteriorated substantially in June, the U.S. Trade Representative, Clayton Yeutter said the administration did not want to see a further depreciation in the dollar.

7 In an abrupt reversal, world oil prices surged as traders scrambled to cover short positions amidst signs that OPEC would attempt to restrain above-quota production. In addition, hostilities increased in the Persian Gulf as Iraq resumed attacks on Iranian shipping boats.

U.S. TREASURY YIELDS
(Bonds Equivalent Yields)

August	Fed Funds	3-Month Bill	6-Month Bill	1-Year Bill	2-Year Note	3-Year Note	5-Year Note	7-Year Note	10-Year Note	30-Year Bond	Spread*
3	6.82	6.23	6.46	7.01	7.72	8.08	8.34	8.62	8.81	9.02	2.79
4	6.76	6.02	6.40	7.01	7.72	8.07	8.34	8.62	8.81	9.04	3.02
5	6.68	6.02	6.34	6.90	7.65	7.99	8.26	8.52	8.71	8.95	2.93
6	6.62	5.90	6.33	6.91	7.65	7.99	8.28	8.54	8.73	8.96	3.06
7	6.57	6.02	6.36	6.97	7.69	7.99	8.27	8.52	8.70	8.93	2.91
10	6.58	6.08	6.40	6.98	7.71	8.03	8.29	8.55	8.74	8.96	2.88
11	6.47	6.11	6.35	6.94	7.69	7.94	8.26	8.54	8.73	8.95	2.84
12	6.65	6.12	6.30	6.92	7.67	7.94	8.27	8.54	8.72	8.95	2.83
13	6.67	6.13	6.28	6.89	7.64	7.90	8.21	8.47	8.63	8.85	2.72
14	6.75	6.13	6.32	6.91	7.62	7.86	8.18	8.43	8.58	8.77	2.64
17	6.91	6.16	6.30	6.93	7.62	7.86	8.17	8.41	8.56	8.77	2.61
18	6.70	6.20	6.47	6.98	7.71	7.97	8.31	8.57	8.73	8.95	2.75
19	6.66	6.22	6.49	7.04	7.76	8.02	8.34	8.60	8.77	8.98	2.76
20	6.63	6.29	6.53	7.07	7.77	8.02	8.35	8.58	8.74	8.94	2.65
21	6.62	6.28	6.53	7.04	7.79	8.05	8.35	8.60	8.77	8.97	2.69
24	6.77	6.35	6.58	7.07	7.81	8.06	8.34	8.61	8.78	8.99	2.64
25	6.85	6.36	6.47	7.08	7.79	8.02	8.32	8.56	8.73	8.94	2.58
26	7.24	6.44	6.47	7.15	7.87	8.09	8.36	8.61	8.79	8.99	2.55
27	6.90	6.48	6.55	7.24	7.95	8.21	8.48	8.75	8.92	9.11	2.63
28	6.84	6.50	6.64	7.26	8.01	8.27	8.54	8.84	9.02	9.18	2.68
31	6.95	6.44	6.60	7.23	7.97	8.27	8.52	8.83	9.00	9.17	2.73

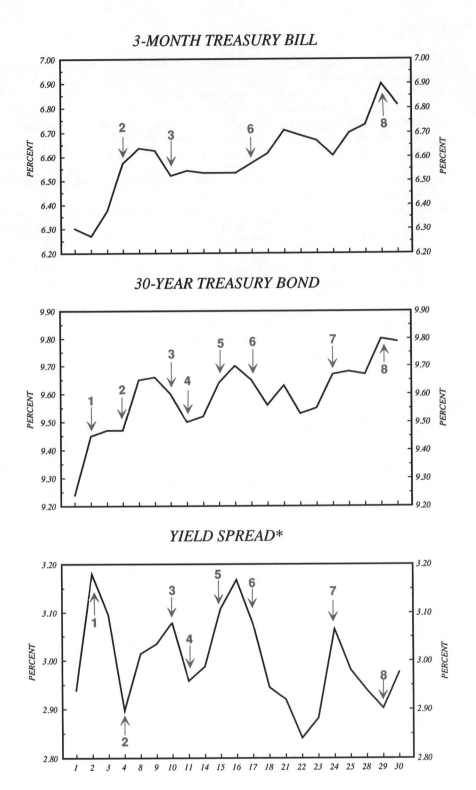

*NOTE: SPREAD=30-YEAR BOND MINUS 3-MONTH BILL

SELECTED MARKET FACTORS

1   Despite aggressive central bank intervention, the foreign exchange value of the dollar declined 5% to 142 yen and 4% to 1.79 Deutsche marks. This weakening in the dollar began with the June trade deficit report released August 14.

2   The Federal Reserve raised the discount rate by 50 basis points to 6.0%, citing inflation concerns, as evidenced by higher bond yields.

3   The Japanese Trade Ministry announced that during August the Japanese trade surplus with the U.S. narrowed to $5.15 billion from $7.56 billion a year earlier, marking the fourth consecutive month of year-over-year decline in this trade measure.

4   Responding to a surprisingly large 1.3% drop in wholesale food prices, the August PPI was unchanged, marking the best inflation performance of 1987.

5   Morning newspapers highlighted the lobbying in Congress by the Reagan administration against the proposed Gramm-Rudman "fix."

6   Technical pressures in the market for reserves brought about by the September corporate tax date began to influence short-term rates. At the same time, the House-Senate Conference Committee settled their differences over the revised Gramm-Rudman procedure.

7   News of a prime lending rate increase by several Japanese long-term credit banks resulted in widespread speculation about an outright monetary policy tightening by the central bank of Japan. These rumors were quickly denied by Japanese officials.

8   Technical pressures in the banking system associated with the quarter-end-bank statement date pushed the funds rate well above target, and touched off speculation about a second round of monetary policy tightening. Concerns about a possible Fed tightening coincided with rumors of a move to restrict credit growth by the central bank of Japan.

U.S. TREASURY YIELDS
(Bond Equivalent Yields)

	Fed Funds	3-Month Bill	6-Month Bill	1-Year Bill	2-Year Note	3-Year Note	5-Year Note	7-Year Note	10-Year Note	30-Year Bond	Spread*
September											
1	6.84	6.30	6.60	7.30	7.98	8.29	8.57	8.87	9.05	9.24	2.94
2	6.77	6.27	6.65	7.40	8.15	8.46	8.77	9.10	9.28	9.45	3.18
3	6.84	6.38	6.60	7.50	8.19	8.48	8.77	9.10	9.29	9.47	3.10
4	6.85	6.57	6.86	7.63	8.26	8.56	8.82	9.12	9.30	9.47	2.90
8	7.15	6.64	6.88	7.78	8.46	8.75	9.02	9.34	9.50	9.65	3.01
9	7.23	6.63	7.02	7.75	8.43	8.74	9.00	9.35	9.48	9.66	3.03
10	7.19	6.52	6.68	7.67	8.36	8.69	8.95	9.26	9.42	9.60	3.08
11	7.13	6.54	6.78	7.66	8.31	8.62	8.88	9.19	9.33	9.50	2.96
14	7.24	6.53	6.84	7.67	8.26	8.56	8.87	9.17	9.34	9.52	2.99
15	7.42	6.53	6.99	7.66	8.30	8.63	8.95	9.29	9.44	9.64	3.11
16	7.26	6.53	7.02	7.66	8.35	8.70	9.00	9.35	9.52	9.70	3.17
17	7.09	6.57	7.01	7.65	8.34	8.69	8.98	9.32	9.48	9.65	3.08
18	7.05	6.62	7.01	7.62	8.30	8.63	8.91	9.22	9.38	9.56	2.95
21	7.32	6.71	7.09	7.68	8.33	8.67	8.94	9.28	9.45	9.63	2.92
22	7.54	6.69	7.08	7.67	8.31	8.64	8.91	9.20	9.37	9.53	2.84
23	7.74	6.67	7.07	7.66	8.31	8.66	8.92	9.24	9.40	9.55	2.88
24	7.35	6.61	7.15	7.74	8.42	8.77	9.03	9.36	9.51	9.67	3.06
25	7.27	6.70	7.21	7.77	8.48	8.80	9.06	9.37	9.53	9.68	2.98
28	7.48	6.73	7.24	7.76	8.48	8.78	9.07	9.38	9.52	9.67	2.94
29	7.90	6.90	7.28	7.88	8.60	8.92	9.17	9.49	9.64	9.80	2.90
30	8.38	6.81	7.17	7.92	8.60	8.93	9.21	9.50	9.63	9.79	2.98

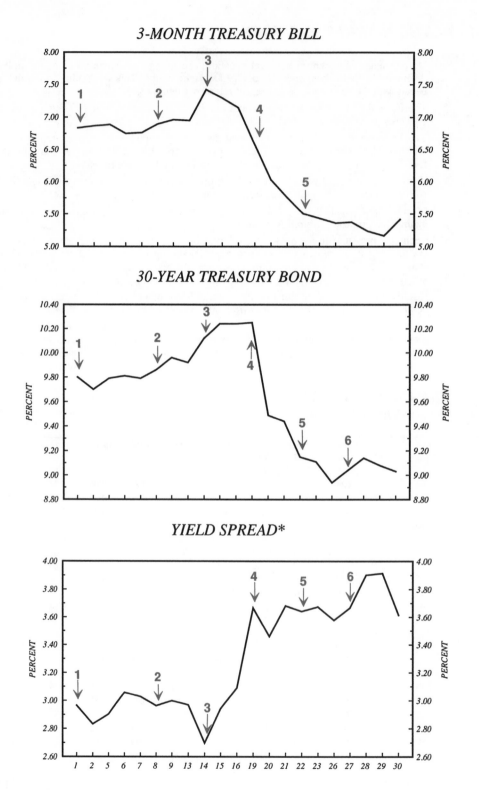

*NOTE: SPREAD=30-YEAR BOND MINUS 3-MONTH BILL

SELECTED MARKET FACTORS

1   According to reserve data for the first week of the October 7 statement period, the Fed forced the banking system into a slight reserve deficiency as strong economic data continued to be received.

2   In response to growing speculation about a discount rate increase, sources close to Chairman Greenspan indicated that recent prime lending rate increases were not a signal of potentially higher rates.

3   An unusually large deterioration was recorded in the trade deficit for July, and the August trade improvement was less than anticipated. In fact, a 4.2% drop in imports was almost completely offset by a 3.7% slide in exports, and resulted in a $15.7 billion August trade shortfall.

4   The Dow Jones Industrial Average plummeted an astonishing 508.32 points, or 22.6% to 1738.42. The one-day drop far exceeded the 12.8% decline on the famous day of October 29, 1929, generally considered the day that ushered in the Great Depression.

5   Most money center banks cut their prime lending rate following pronounced improvement in the fixed income markets.

6   The dollar tumbled to an eight-year low relative to the Deutsche mark, and a five-year low against the British pound as speculation continued about a reduced target for the dollar relative to the G-5 currencies.

U.S. TREASURY YIELDS
(Bond Equivalent Yields)

	Fed Funds	3-Month Bill	6-Month Bill	1-Year Bill	2-Year Note	3-Year Note	5-Year Note	7-Year Note	10-Year Note	30-Year Bond	Spread*
October											
1	7.71	6.84	7.16	7.94	8.62	8.93	9.22	9.53	9.66	9.80	2.97
2	7.42	6.87	7.19	7.92	8.61	8.91	9.20	9.48	9.60	9.70	2.83
5	7.45	6.89	7.21	8.00	8.66	8.97	9.28	9.57	9.69	9.79	2.90
6	7.32	6.75	7.32	8.01	8.73	9.03	9.32	9.60	9.72	9.81	3.06
7	7.30	6.76	7.31	8.00	8.73	9.02	9.31	9.55	9.71	9.79	3.03
8	7.55	6.90	7.65	8.24	9.03	9.20	9.49	9.73	9.86	9.86	2.96
9	7.58	6.96	7.72	8.25	9.01	9.30	9.56	9.81	9.94	9.96	3.00
13	7.65	6.95	7.67	8.17	8.94	9.22	9.51	9.76	9.90	9.92	2.97
14	7.59	7.42	7.96	8.35	9.14	9.44	9.75	9.99	10.13	10.12	2.70
15	7.76	7.30	8.08	8.42	9.23	9.52	9.82	10.05	10.18	10.24	2.94
16	7.55	7.15	7.99	8.38	9.22	9.52	9.84	10.08	10.23	10.24	3.09
19	7.61	6.58	7.49	7.98	8.93	9.32	9.70	10.00	10.15	10.25	3.67
20	7.07	6.03	6.64	7.15	8.09	8.53	8.93	9.23	9.40	9.49	3.46
21	6.47	5.76	6.49	7.03	7.90	8.44	8.80	9.17	9.30	9.44	3.68
22	7.14	5.51	6.28	7.02	7.76	8.19	8.52	8.86	8.97	9.15	3.64
23	7.00	5.44	6.27	6.93	7.76	8.20	8.55	8.88	8.98	9.11	3.68
26	7.24	5.36	6.21	6.73	7.57	7.98	8.33	8.65	8.80	8.94	3.58
27	7.14	5.37	6.28	6.81	7.66	8.06	8.42	8.73	8.92	9.04	3.67
28	6.72	5.24	6.16	6.72	7.65	8.05	8.43	8.79	9.01	9.14	3.90
29	6.76	5.17	6.06	6.66	7.53	7.95	8.33	8.68	8.89	9.08	3.92
30	6.62	5.42	6.25	6.75	7.58	8.00	8.37	8.69	8.88	9.03	3.61

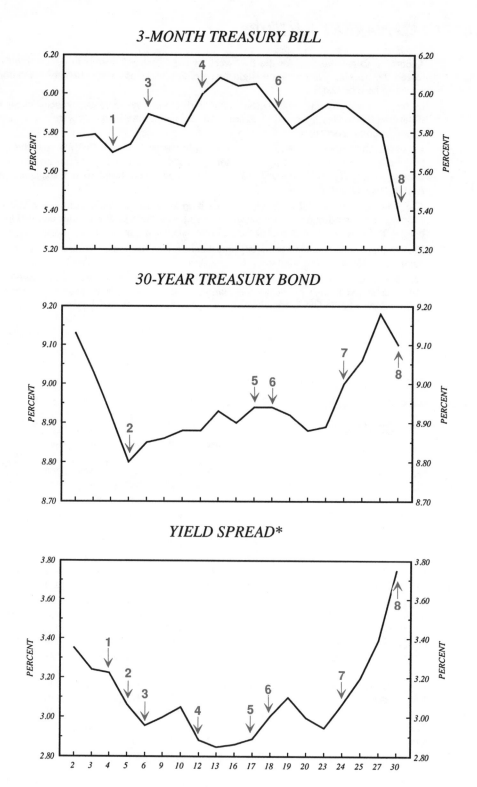

3-MONTH TREASURY BILL

30-YEAR TREASURY BOND

YIELD SPREAD*

*NOTE: SPREAD=30-YEAR BOND MINUS 3-MONTH BILL

SELECTED MARKET FACTORS

1 Because of the close operating correlation between the Dutch and the West German central banks, the 25 basis point reduction in the Dutch discount rate raised hopes of a Bundesbank easing.

2 Domestic commercial banks cut the prime lending rate from 9.0% to 8.75% citing reduced cost of funds.

3 Gains in both goods-producing and service-producing jobs resulted in a 549,000 rise in October payroll employment. The Street had anticipated a 230,000 increase in jobs.

4 With financial market uncertainties lessening in the post-October 19 period, the Fed appeared to move to constrain the flow of liquidity to the banking system, causing a backup in the funds rate.

5 In an article "Japanese Buy Fewer Debt Issues, Clouding Outlook for Interest Rates," *The Wall Street Journal* cited contract basis data which indicated a substantial drop in foreign net purchases to only $2.0 billion — in comparison to June's figures of $12.3 billion.

6 Total housing starts slipped by 8.2% in October to only 1.513 million units — a clear response to a 7.0% drop in single-family starts, and an 11.3% tumble in multi-family starts.

7 Reflecting higher prices, particularly for copper, the Commodity Research Bureau Futures Index breached 232, the closing price on October 17, and ended the day at 234.08. As such, the Commodity Research Bureau completely reversed the downdraft in inflation speculation created by the stock market drop.

8 Stock prices plunged, pulled down by continued sharp declines in the dollar. The Dow Jones Industrial Average fell 76.93 points, its eighth largest point loss, closing at 1833.55.

U.S. TREASURY YIELDS
(Bond Equivalent Yields)

	Fed Funds	3-Month Bill	6-Month Bill	1-Year Bill	2-Year Note	3-Year Note	5-Year Note	7-Year Note	10-Year Note	30-Year Bond	Spread*
November											
2	6.64	5.78	6.54	6.98	7.72	8.09	8.44	8.78	8.98	9.13	3.35
3	6.06	5.79	6.36	6.87	7.67	8.02	8.38	8.72	8.91	9.03	3.24
4	5.69	5.70	6.30	6.83	7.60	7.97	8.30	8.66	8.85	8.92	3.22
5	6.57	5.74	6.29	6.76	7.50	7.81	8.18	8.54	8.72	8.80	3.06
6	6.70	5.89	6.38	6.90	7.62	7.92	8.28	8.62	8.76	8.85	2.96
9	6.82	5.86	6.47	6.92	7.64	7.95	8.30	8.63	8.78	8.86	3.00
10	6.63	5.83	6.47	6.89	7.61	7.91	8.27	8.62	8.79	8.88	3.05
12	6.72	6.00	6.56	6.96	7.67	7.96	8.27	8.64	8.80	8.88	2.88
13	6.80	6.08	6.70	7.07	7.75	8.01	8.34	8.67	8.84	8.93	2.85
16	7.11	6.04	6.70	7.13	7.78	8.02	8.34	8.66	8.82	8.90	2.86
17	6.72	6.05	6.56	7.06	7.73	7.99	8.38	8.70	8.86	8.94	2.89
18	6.46	5.94	6.54	7.02	7.74	7.99	8.38	8.68	8.85	8.94	3.00
19	6.82	5.82	6.46	6.98	7.69	7.95	8.34	8.65	8.83	8.92	3.10
20	6.74	5.88	6.53	6.88	7.66	7.93	8.32	8.61	8.79	8.88	3.00
23	6.89	5.95	6.54	6.96	7.67	7.95	8.34	8.62	8.80	8.89	2.94
24	6.77	5.94	6.33	6.97	7.73	7.99	8.35	8.72	8.89	9.00	3.06
25	6.73	5.86	6.46	7.03	7.78	8.06	8.41	8.80	8.98	9.06	3.20
27	6.76	5.79	6.50	7.12	7.87	8.20	8.55	8.94	9.11	9.18	3.39
30	7.19	5.35	6.38	7.00	7.73	8.05	8.43	8.82	8.99	9.10	3.75

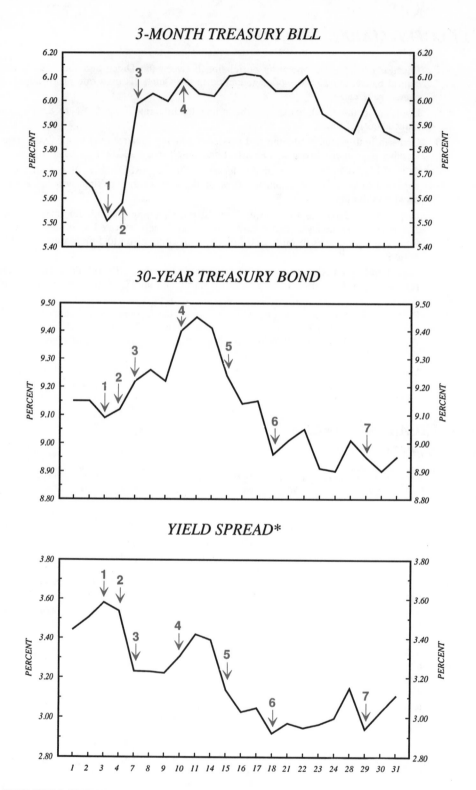

3-MONTH TREASURY BILL

30-YEAR TREASURY BOND

YIELD SPREAD*

*NOTE: SPREAD=30-YEAR BOND MINUS 3-MONTH BILL

SELECTED MARKET FACTORS

1 The Bundesbank cut its discount rate by 50 basis points from 3.0% to 2.5% as part of its role in a coordinated European move to lower rates to support the exchange value of the dollar.

2 Following a surprising 536,000 rise in payroll employment in October, November's 274,000 increase in new jobs provided strong evidence of an economic uptrend, despite the collapse in stock prices.

3 A *Wall Street Journal* article cited unnamed administration sources as saying, "In the wake of European economic concessions, the U.S. is making a significant shift in its international emphasis on supporting the exchange value of the dollar."

4 Reflecting a 12.3% surge in the dollar value of imports, the U.S. merchandise trade deficit widened by $3.5 billion to a record $17.6 billion.

5 The Organization of Petroleum Exporting Countries (OPEC) reached a flimsy price and production accord for 1988 that is unlikely to forestall a widely predicted slide in oil prices.

6 Federal Reserve Board Chairman Greenspan stated that the October widening of the trade deficit was "an aberration" that probably was reversed in November.

7 Under the Mexican debt-for-loan swap, the Treasury will raise some $2 billion through long-term non-cancellable financing during the first quarter. This source of financing has been viewed as a partial substitute for the February bond offering.

U.S. TREASURY YIELDS
(Bond Equivalent Yields)

December	Fed Funds	3-Month Bill	6-Month Bill	1-Year Bill	2-Year Note	3-Year Note	5-Year Note	7-Year Note	10-Year Note	30-Year Bond	Spread*
1	7.04	5.71	6.48	7.05	7.77	8.07	8.44	8.84	9.01	9.15	3.44
2	7.00	5.64	6.47	7.03	7.79	8.07	8.43	8.83	9.01	9.15	3.51
3	6.99	5.51	6.43	7.01	7.72	8.01	8.35	8.76	8.94	9.09	3.58
4	6.82	5.58	6.43	7.00	7.72	8.00	8.35	8.76	8.94	9.12	3.54
7	6.93	5.99	6.75	7.20	7.86	8.16	8.48	8.90	9.07	9.22	3.23
8	6.79	6.03	6.74	7.21	7.88	8.15	8.49	8.91	9.09	9.26	3.23
9	6.72	6.00	6.70	7.18	7.88	8.15	8.47	8.88	9.05	9.22	3.22
10	6.83	6.09	6.78	7.32	8.00	8.29	8.63	9.05	9.23	9.40	3.31
11	6.81	6.03	6.78	7.30	8.02	8.31	8.65	9.08	9.28	9.45	3.42
14	6.78	6.02	6.81	7.30	8.01	8.31	8.63	9.06	9.23	9.41	3.39
15	6.51	6.10	6.74	7.22	7.92	8.20	8.54	8.93	9.09	9.24	3.14
16	5.52	6.11	6.70	7.21	7.89	8.15	8.46	8.82	9.00	9.14	3.03
17	6.67	6.10	6.75	7.27	7.89	8.15	8.47	8.85	9.03	9.15	3.05
18	6.75	6.04	6.69	7.16	7.82	8.06	8.39	8.74	8.89	8.96	2.92
21	6.85	6.04	6.77	7.18	7.84	8.09	8.38	8.74	8.88	9.01	2.97
22	6.77	6.10	6.79	7.24	7.91	8.17	8.48	8.80	8.95	9.05	2.95
23	6.74	5.95	6.71	7.18	7.83	8.10	8.40	8.67	8.83	8.91	2.96
24	6.70	5.90	6.70	7.17	7.83	8.10	8.37	8.67	8.82	8.90	3.00
28	6.91	5.86	6.70	7.20	7.91	8.16	8.46	8.77	8.93	9.01	3.15
29	7.21	6.01	6.60	7.19	7.86	8.11	8.41	8.70	8.85	8.95	2.94
30	6.77	5.87	6.47	7.09	7.75	7.99	8.32	8.61	8.78	8.90	3.03
31	6.89	5.84	6.46	7.10	7.77	8.04	8.33	8.67	8.83	8.95	3.11

1988

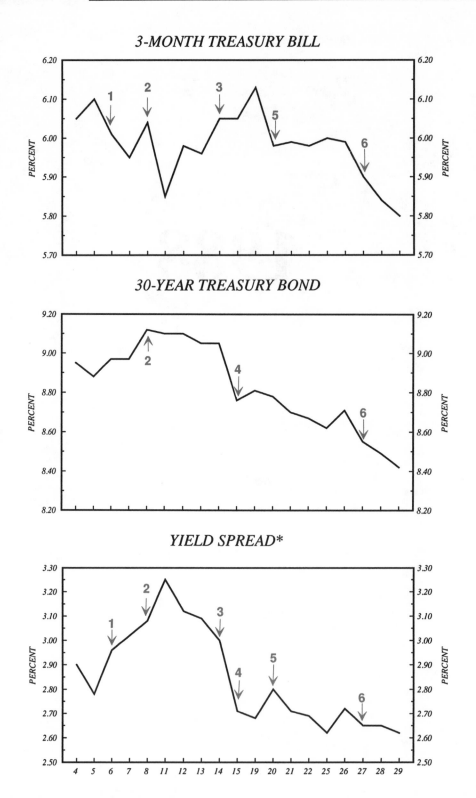

3-MONTH TREASURY BILL

30-YEAR TREASURY BOND

YIELD SPREAD*

*NOTE: SPREAD=30-YEAR BOND MINUS 3-MONTH BILL

SELECTED MARKET FACTORS

1 Coordinated central bank intervention in the currency markets not only helped to halt the fall of the dollar, but also reduced upward pressures on short rates.

2 Following large increases in both October and November, payroll employment rose by a solid 346,000 workers in December. High employment also produced a decline in the unemployment rate.

3 A 2.4% rise in automobile sales in December contributed significantly to the 0.7% gain recorded in total retail sales. Excluding the auto component, retail sales were up only 0.1% during the month.

4 The U.S. dollar improved by nearly 4.0% relative to the yen in response to a 24.9% drop in the trade deficit in November — down $4.4 billion to $13.22 billion.

5 With single-family starts down 7.8% and multi-family starts down 3.4%, the outlook for new building permits declined by 8.8% in December.

6 A $58.3 billion accumulation in business inventories during the fourth quarter prompted speculation about a production slowdown, which could combine with weak consumer demand and decelerating exports to produce a recession.

U.S. TREASURY YIELDS
(Bond Equivalent Yields)

	Fed Funds	3-Month Bill	6-Month Bill	1-Year Bill	2-Year Note	3-Year Note	5-Year Note	7-Year Note	10-Year Note	30-Year Bond	Spread*
January											
4	7.30	6.05	6.57	7.15	7.77	8.03	8.35	8.69	8.83	8.95	2.90
5	7.34	6.10	6.66	7.11	7.76	7.99	8.29	8.62	8.76	8.88	2.78
6	6.94	6.01	6.66	7.14	7.79	8.03	8.37	8.68	8.82	8.97	2.96
7	6.91	5.95	6.65	7.13	7.79	8.03	8.35	8.66	8.83	8.97	3.02
8	6.80	6.04	6.75	7.24	7.92	8.16	8.48	8.80	8.97	9.12	3.08
11	6.89	5.85	6.64	7.15	7.80	8.05	8.41	8.74	8.94	9.10	3.25
12	6.75	5.98	6.62	7.15	7.80	8.04	8.39	8.73	8.93	9.10	3.12
13	6.72	5.96	6.57	7.14	7.76	8.01	8.36	8.67	8.87	9.05	3.09
14	6.86	6.05	6.58	7.16	7.76	8.01	8.36	8.67	8.86	9.05	3.00
15	6.89	6.05	6.53	6.98	7.61	7.83	8.13	8.42	8.60	8.76	2.71
19	6.96	6.13	6.64	7.01	7.66	7.87	8.16	8.45	8.65	8.81	2.68
20	6.86	5.98	6.54	6.93	7.59	7.82	8.11	8.41	8.61	8.78	2.80
21	6.67	5.99	6.51	6,84	7.52	7.77	8.04	8.32	8.53	8.70	2.71
22	6.57	5.98	6.48	6.82	7.51	7.73	8.01	8.29	8.49	8.67	2.69
25	6.86	6.00	6.48	6.82	7.49	7.72	7.99	8.26	8.45	8.62	2.62
26	6.78	5.99	6.48	6.87	7.56	7.80	8.08	8.35	8.54	8.71	2.72
27	6.57	5.90	6.36	6.77	7.37	7.63	7.91	8.18	8.38	8.55	2.65
28	6.73	5.84	6.34	6.72	7.29	7.54	7.83	8.12	8.33	8.49	2.65
29	6.79	5.80	6.30	6.66	7.22	7.48	7.76	8.06	8.26	8.42	2.62

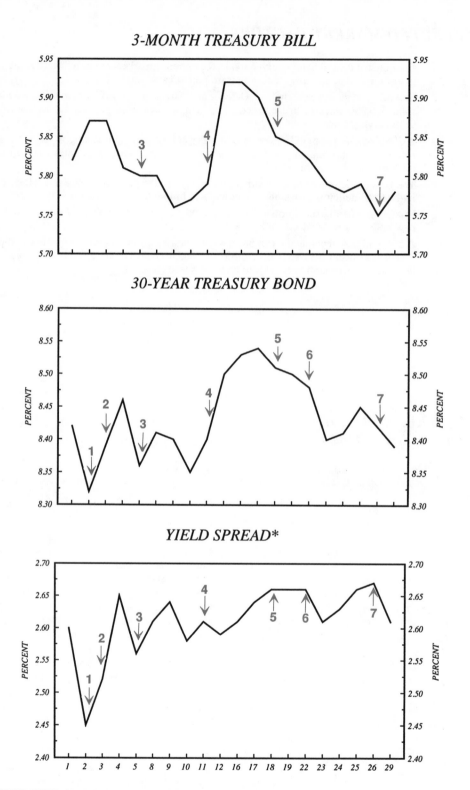

3-MONTH TREASURY BILL

30-YEAR TREASURY BOND

YIELD SPREAD*

*NOTE: SPREAD=30-YEAR BOND MINUS 3-MONTH BILL

SELECTED MARKET FACTORS

1　The combination of a 6.2% drop in new single-family home sales and a third consecutive monthly decline in the Index of Leading Indicators produced widespread speculation about an easing in monetary policy in response to a recession bias in the economy.

2　Bond prices fell as investors accorded a lukewarm reception to the Treasury 10- and 30-year offerings.

3　Despite strong employment growth in the fourth quarter, a drop in construction and mining, combined with a deceleration in service jobs, produced a modest 107,000 rise in January payroll employment.

4　Reports of a 0.5% rise in January retail sales and a 0.7% upward revision to December's sales pace offset an unanticipated $1 billion improvement in the trade deficit. On the following day, a 0.4% rise in the PPI for January contributed further to the market's deterioration.

5　As part of the annual benchmarking of the monetary aggregates, the Fed began to release weekly data on M2 and M3, prompting renewed talk of an easing and speculation on reborn monetarism at the Federal Reserve Board of Governors in light of weak 1987 money growth.

6　After reaching a peak of over $17.70 a barrel, West Texas Intermediate Crude fell to approximately $16.00 a barrel following renewed signs of OPEC over-production. This downward move in oil also correlated with the drop in the CRB Futures Index to a four-month low.

7　Speaking at a conference sponsored by the Cato Institute, Federal Reserve Board Governor Manual Johnson commented that the central bank should use the interest rate yield curve, the value of the dollar, and commodity prices as substitutes for money in gauging the effects of policy.

U.S. TREASURY YIELDS
(Bond Equivalent Yields)

	Fed Funds	3-Month Bill	6-Month Bill	1-Year Bill	2-Year Note	3-Year Note	5-Year Note	7-Year Note	10-Year Note	30-Year Bond	Spread*
February											
1	6.96	5.82	6.35	6.68	7.22	7.50	7.78	8.07	8.26	8.42	2.60
2	6.78	5.87	6.37	6.67	7.21	7.38	7.70	7.98	8.18	8.32	2.45
3	6.55	5.87	6.38	6.69	7.24	7.44	7.76	8.05	8.21	8.39	2.52
4	6.57	5.81	6.33	6.67	7.24	7.44	7.76	8.07	8.24	8.46	2.65
5	6.58	5.80	6.23	6.55	7.10	7.32	7.64	7.95	8.12	8.36	2.56
8	6.58	5.80	6.21	6.59	7.16	7.37	7.70	8.01	8.19	8.41	2.61
9	6.04	5.76	6.11	6.55	7.12	7.34	7.65	7.98	8.16	8.40	2.64
10	5.72	5.77	6.09	6.53	7.07	7.28	7.59	7.92	8.11	8.35	2.58
11	6.50	5.79	6.15	6.61	7.12	7.31	7.64	7.97	8.16	8.40	2.61
12	6.59	5.92	6.29	6.68	7.22	7.42	7.77	8.09	8.28	8.50	2.59
16	6.90	5.92	6.32	6.73	7.26	7.45	7.79	8.12	8.31	8.53	2.61
17	6.79	5.90	6.26	6.72	7.24	7.42	7.80	8.12	8.32	8.54	2.64
18	6.65	5.85	6.25	6.67	7.23	7.41	7.78	8.08	8.28	8.51	2.66
19	6.66	5.84	6.22	6.67	7.21	7.39	7.77	8.08	8.26	8.50	2.66
22	6.77	5.82	6.19	6.65	7.20	7.38	7.75	8.05	8.24	8.48	2.66
23	6.63	5.79	6.05	6.60	7.16	7.33	7.69	7.97	8.17	8.40	2.61
24	6.43	5.78	6.02	6.61	7.15	7.34	7.69	7.98	8.18	8.41	2.63
25	6.60	5.79	6.05	6.66	7.17	7.37	7.68	8.01	8.23	8.45	2.66
26	6.56	5.75	6.02	6.64	7.16	7.35	7.67	7.97	8.18	8.42	2.67
29	6.67	5.78	6.04	6.63	7.13	7.33	7.64	7.95	8.16	8.39	2.61

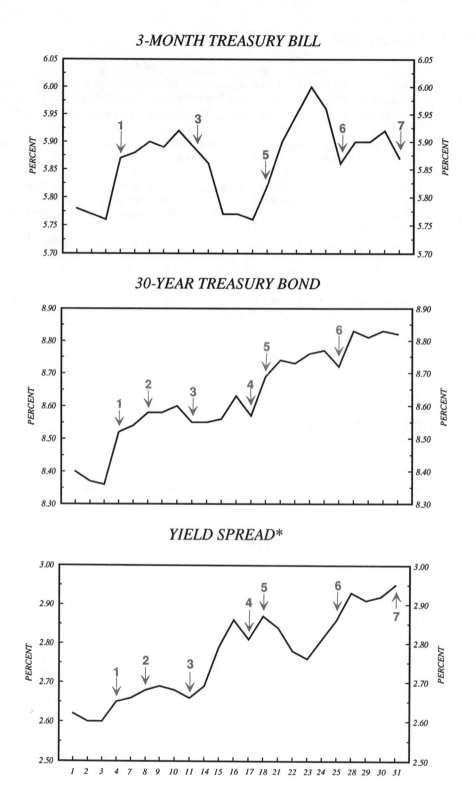

3-MONTH TREASURY BILL

30-YEAR TREASURY BOND

YIELD SPREAD*

*NOTE: SPREAD=30-YEAR BOND MINUS 3-MONTH BILL

SELECTED MARKET FACTORS

1   In response to a 223,000 increase in goods-producing employment, payroll employment expanded by a huge 531,000 new jobs in February. The dominant factor on the goods-producing side was a rebound in construction employment while strong gains in retail jobs produced a 201,000 rise in service-producing employment.

2   Some $625 million in new corporate issues were brought to market including a $400 million Eastman Kodak deal.

3   Despite a 0.6% February rise in retail sales, a 0.7% downward revision to January, from +0.5% to -0.2%, produced a net sales decline over the two-month period. At the same time, a drop in both food and energy prices resulted in a 0.2% drop in the price of finished wholesale goods.

4   A slightly larger drop in exports than in imports prompted a moderate widening in the trade deficit from $12.2 billion to $12.4 billion.

5   The Federal Reserve "Tan Book" released in advance of the March 29 FOMC meeting stated that "without exception" all regions reported continued growth, which was built on strong export demand in manufacturing.

6   With fed funds below 6 9/16%, the lack of Federal Reserve open market intervention to drain reserves eased market concern about a monetary policy tightening that had been building since Chairman Greenspan's testimony before the Joint Economic Committee on March 15.

7   Considering the First Republic situation, end-of-quarter bank statement date pressures were more moderate than expected.

U.S. TREASURY YIELDS
(Bond Equivalent Yields)

March	Fed Funds	3-Month Bill	6-Month Bill	1-Year Bill	2-Year Note	3-Year Note	5-Year Note	7-Year Note	10-Year Note	30-Year Bond	Spread*
1	6.66	5.78	6.13	6.61	7.11	7.30	7.61	7.95	8.15	8.40	2.62
2	6.62	5.77	6.11	6.59	7.07	7.29	7.59	7.92	8.13	8.37	2.60
3	6.58	5.76	6.11	6.60	7.08	7.29	7.59	7.90	8.12	8.36	2.60
4	6.51	5.87	6.24	6.72	7.20	7.45	7.74	8.06	8.28	8.52	2.65
7	6.51	5.88	6.23	6.74	7.22	7.44	7.77	8.08	8.30	8.54	2.66
8	6.36	5.90	6.14	6.75	7.25	7.45	7.79	8.11	8.33	8.58	2.68
9	6.59	5.89	6.11	6.72	7.22	7.45	7.76	8.11	8.32	8.58	2.69
10	6.70	5.92	6.11	6.76	7.25	7.48	7.81	8.15	8.35	8.60	2.68
11	6.60	5.89	6.10	6.63	7.20	7.43	7.76	8.11	8.29	8.55	2.66
14	6.70	5.86	6.10	6.64	7.20	7.42	7.76	8.11	8.29	8.55	2.69
15	6.60	5.77	6.02	6.62	7.19	7.42	7.76	8.11	8.30	8.56	2.79
16	6.48	5.77	6.05	6.67	7.24	7.47	7.81	8.18	8.36	8.63	2.86
17	6.47	5.76	5.96	6.58	7.17	7.41	7.76	8.12	8.30	8.57	2.81
18	6.45	5.82	6.09	6.64	7.23	7.46	7.81	8.23	8.41	8.69	2.87
21	6.45	5.90	6.15	6.73	7.32	7.56	7.91	8.29	8.47	8.74	2.84
22	6.46	5.95	6.22	6.73	7.33	7.58	7.91	8.29	8.46	8.73	2.78
23	6.83	6.00	6.29	6.80	7.39	7.61	7.95	8.32	8.47	8.76	2.76
24	6.66	5.96	6.32	6.83	7.46	7.66	8.01	8.35	8.51	8.77	2.81
25	6.60	5.86	6.26	6.76	7.41	7.61	7.95	8.31	8.47	8.72	2.86
28	6.64	5.90	6.28	6.79	7.42	7.66	8.03	8.42	8.58	8.83	2.93
29	6.57	5.90	6.32	6.79	7.42	7.66	8.03	8.39	8.56	8.81	2.91
30	6.66	5.92	6.33	6.79	7.42	7.65	8.03	8.40	8.57	8.83	2.92
31	6.83	5.87	6.32	6.76	7.41	7.66	8.04	8.40	8.57	8.82	2.95

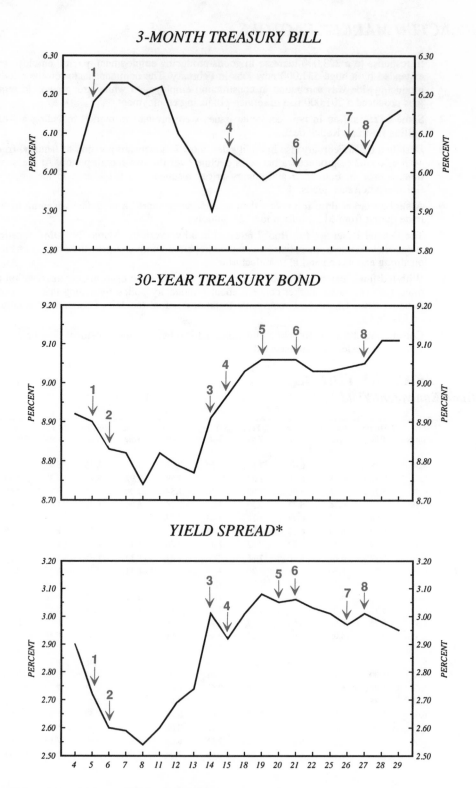

3-MONTH TREASURY BILL

30-YEAR TREASURY BOND

*YIELD SPREAD**

*NOTE: SPREAD=30-YEAR BOND MINUS 3-MONTH BILL

SELECTED MARKET FACTORS

1   With the second week of the April 6 statement period estimated to be a large $3.2 billion add, the absence of Federal Reserve intervention, with fed funds at 6 3/4%, caused speculation about an imminent policy tightening.

2   Bond and stock prices rose sharply in response to an unconfirmed report from Tokyo that the G-7 would reaffirm a 125 yen lower bound for the dollar at the upcoming Washington meeting.

3   A 7.5% surge in imports offset a 5.5% rise in exports, producing a wider $13.8 billion trade shortfall. This number resulted in a 1 1/2% point drop in bond prices and a 101.46 drop in stock prices.

4   March PPI rose by 0.6% as apparel prices moved 20% higher, producing a slight acceleration in the excluding food and energy wholesale price report (+0.4% vs. +0.3%).

5   A rebound in consumer food prices combined with a sharp acceleration in the underlying rate of consumer price inflation to create a 0.5% rise in the CPI.

6   Virtually discounting a Presidential veto threat, the House overwhelmingly approved a huge trade bill, which is designed to force the U.S. to take a more active role in opening up foreign markets. The bill was approved by a vote of 312 to 107.

7   The report of a 2.3% rise in first-quarter real GNP increased concern about the need for a Fed tightening as consumption spending rose by 3.8% and the trade deficit improved by a mere $3.6 billion.

8   The Senate passed the trade bill by a vote of 63 to 36, just short of the two-thirds majority that is necessary to override a Presidential veto.

U.S. TREASURY YIELDS
(Bond Equivalent Yields)

April	Fed Funds	3-Month Bill	6-Month Bill	1-Year Bill	2-Year Note	3-Year Note	5-Year Note	7-Year Note	10-Year Note	30-Year Bond	Spread*
4	6.71	6.02	6.51	7.00	7.58	7.81	8.19	8.53	8.68	8.92	2.90
5	6.83	6.18	6.50	7.04	7.60	7.84	8.18	8.52	8.67	8.90	2.72
6	7.30	6.23	6.47	7.04	7.57	7.79	8.13	8.47	8.61	8.83	2.60
7	6.93	6.23	6.48	7.04	7.54	7.77	8.12	8.46	8.60	8.82	2.59
8	6.84	6.20	6.47	6.95	7.47	7.69	8.05	8.37	8.52	8.74	2.54
11	6.83	6.22	6.51	6.96	7.50	7.73	8.10	8.44	8.59	8.82	2.60
12	6.75	6.10	6.41	6.89	7.49	7.71	8.09	8.40	8.57	8.79	2.69
13	6.67	6.03	6.34	6.83	7.45	7.67	8.05	8.36	8.56	8.77	2.74
14	6.74	5.90	6.34	6.89	7.56	7.79	8.15	8.48	8.67	8.91	3.01
15	6.87	6.05	6.51	7.03	7.60	7.85	8.20	8.53	8.74	8.97	2.92
18	6.84	6.02	6.48	7.05	7.60	7.88	8.25	8.60	8.81	9.03	3.01
19	6.85	5.98	6.49	7.03	7.57	7.87	8.24	8.59	8.81	9.06	3.08
20	7.49	6.01	6.54	7.04	7.65	7.90	8.27	8.61	8.83	9.06	3.05
21	6.95	6.00	6.52	7.02	7.64	7.90	8.26	8.58	8.82	9.06	3.06
22	6.81	6.00	6.52	7.02	7.64	7.87	8.23	8.56	8.78	9.03	3.03
25	6.90	6.02	6.53	7.04	7.64	7.87	8.23	8.55	8.78	9.03	3.01
26	6.81	6.07	6.55	7.02	7.64	7.87	8.24	8.57	8.80	9.04	2.97
27	6.83	6.04	6.52	7.03	7.63	7.89	8.25	8.57	8.80	9.05	3.01
28	7.10	6.13	6.62	7.10	7.69	7.97	8.32	8.64	8.86	9.11	2.98
29	6.98	6.16	6.66	7.14	7.73	7.98	8.33	8.65	8.87	9.11	2.95

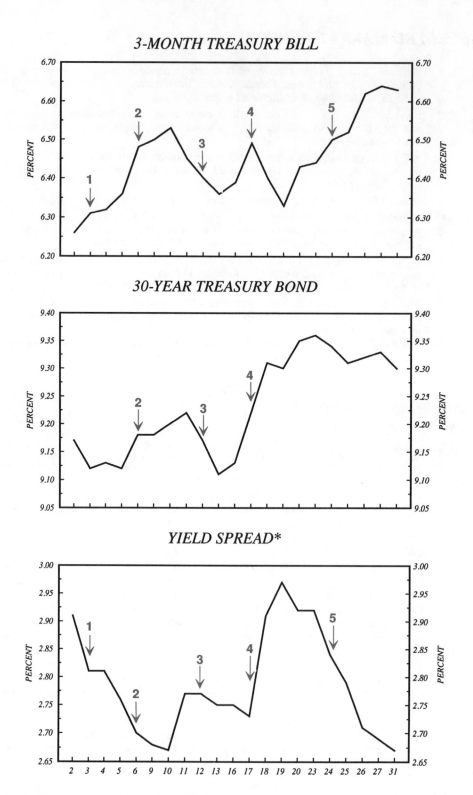

3-MONTH TREASURY BILL

30-YEAR TREASURY BOND

YIELD SPREAD*

*NOTE: SPREAD=30-YEAR BOND MINUS 3-MONTH BILL

SELECTED MARKET FACTORS

1 In a written response to questions from the Senate Banking Committee, Federal Reserve Chairman Greenspan stated that monetary policy must ensure that improvement in trade would not result in higher inflation.

2 Payroll employment rose by a lower than expected 174,000 workers, despite a sizable 44,000 jump in factory jobs, a lengthening in the factory workweek, and a 0.2% drop in the civilian unemployment rate to 5.4% of the labor force.

3 A combination of an accommodative reserve policy and weak retail sales were favorable for the market. The $349 million adjustment borrowing number for the May 18 reserve week confirmed that only a limited tightening in policy had taken place, while the 0.8% drop in consumer activity was surprisingly weak.

4 The Commodity Research Bureau Futures Index broke through a five-month high of 240% of its 1977 base as hot weather caused a rise in the price of most grains.

5 With non-defense capital goods orders rising by 1.4% — the first gain in two months — the market's concern over the rate of growth increased with a 0.8% rise in durable goods orders. These concerns were intensified further two days later when the first-quarter real GNP report was revised upward from a preliminary 2.3% estimate to 3.9%.

U.S. TREASURY YIELDS
(Bond Equivalent Yields)

	Fed Funds	3-Month Bill	6-Month Bill	1-Year Bill	2-Year Note	3-Year Note	5-Year Note	7-Year Note	10-Year Note	30-Year Bond	Spread*
May											
2	6.86	6.26	6.76	7.21	7.78	8.03	8.39	8.70	8.94	9.17	2.91
3	6.60	6.31	6.71	7.20	7.77	8.01	8.35	8.67	8.89	9.12	2.81
4	6.24	6.32	6.69	7.20	7.77	8.03	8.35	8.67	8.90	9.13	2.81
5	6.86	6.36	6.68	7.22	7.79	8.06	8.39	8.70	8.92	9.12	2.76
6	6.88	6.48	6.82	7.31	7.87	8.17	8.48	8.79	9.01	9.18	2.70
9	7.12	6.50	6.87	7.34	7.95	8.20	8.50	8.81	9.03	9.18	2.68
10	7.32	6.53	6.80	7.37	8.00	8.23	8.55	8.86	9.07	9.20	2.67
11	7.20	6.45	6.77	7.33	7.95	8.21	8.55	8.86	9.05	9.22	2.77
12	7.10	6.40	6.74	7.31	7.95	8.18	8.55	8.86	9.04	9.17	2.77
13	7.14	6.36	6.74	7.28	7.90	8.14	8.51	8.82	9.00	9.11	2.75
16	7.30	6.39	6.75	7.32	7.93	8.16	8.52	8.83	9.01	9.13	2.75
17	6.98	6.49	6.87	7.38	7.99	8.25	8.64	8.92	9.12	9.22	2.73
18	6.45	6.40	6.86	7.39	8.04	8.28	8.68	9.00	9.19	9.31	2.91
19	7.04	6.33	6.88	7.45	8.04	8.28	8.67	8.99	9.18	9.30	2.97
20	7.15	6.43	6.90	7.45	8.08	8.32	8.70	9.02	9.22	9.35	2.92
23	7.21	6.44	6.96	7.52	8.12	8.36	8.74	9.05	9.23	9.36	2.92
24	7.07	6.50	7.04	7.52	8.14	8.36	8.73	9.03	9.22	9.34	2.84
25	7.19	6.52	7.11	7.58	8.17	8.37	8.73	9.03	9.20	9.31	2.79
26	7.49	6.62	7.17	7.65	8.23	8.43	8.72	9.04	9.21	9.32	2.71
27	7.42	6.64	7.17	7.65	8.23	8.46	8.75	9.06	9.24	9.33	2.69
31	7.48	6.63	7.18	7.66	8.21	8.44	8.73	9.03	9.20	9.30	2.67

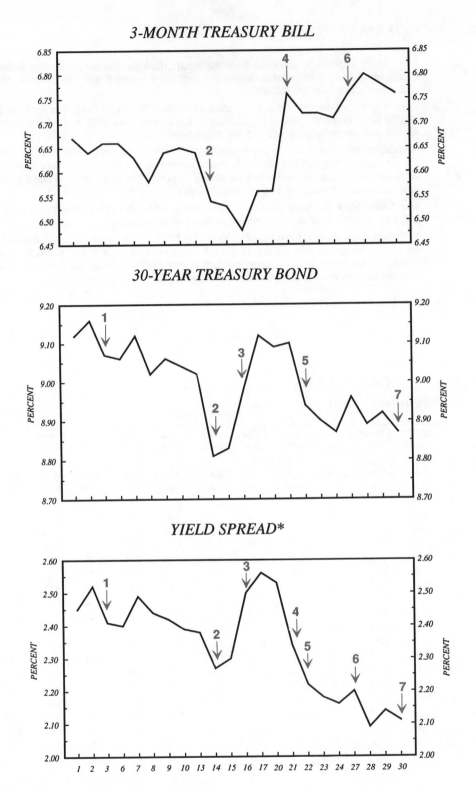

3-MONTH TREASURY BILL

30-YEAR TREASURY BOND

YIELD SPREAD*

*NOTE: SPREAD=30-YEAR BOND MINUS 3-MONTH BILL

SELECTED MARKET FACTORS

1   The civilian unemployment rate rose by 0.2% to 5.6% of the labor force as the household employment measure contracted sharply in May.

2   In response to a steep 6.4% decline in imports, the trade gap narrowed to a seasonally-adjusted $9.89 billion from a deficit total of $11.7 billion in March, and $14.4 billion in February. This figure represents the smallest trade gap since December 1984.

3   A weak dollar and another surge in commodity prices caused renewed speculation that both the Fed and West Germany were planning an imminent tightening to combat inflation.

4   The Bundesbank increased the one-month repo rate by 25 basis points to calm inflation fears in West Germany. Central bank officials stressed, however, that the move was not designed to halt the appreciation in the dollar.

5   Because there was no central bank intervention to slow the rise of the dollar, U.S. currency closed up 2.0% against the Yen (128.93), and 1.5% against the Deutsche mark (1.755).

6   European analysts speculated about a West German discount rate increase (+50 basis points to 5.0%) which was executed on June 30 in response to both strong domestic demand and a weak currency.

7   The price of West Texas Intermediate reached its own milestone, closing at a low for the year at $15.16 a barrel, down 27 cents in continued concern about OPEC overproduction.

U.S. TREASURY YIELDS
(Bond Equivalent Yields)

	Fed Funds	3-Month Bill	6-Month Bill	1-Year Bill	2-Year Note	3-Year Note	5-Year Note	7-Year Note	10-Year Note	30-Year Bond	Spread*
June											
1	7.24	6.67	7.12	7.58	8.09	8.32	8.57	8.88	9.03	9.12	2.45
2	7.37	6.64	7.14	7.62	8.13	8.34	8.60	8.91	9.07	9.16	2.52
3	7.34	6.66	7.05	7.51	8.06	8.24	8.52	8.81	8.97	9.07	2.41
6	7.45	6.66	7.04	7.51	8.04	8.23	8.51	8.81	8.97	9.06	2.40
7	7.38	6.63	7.03	7.52	8.04	8.25	8.54	8.85	9.02	9.12	2.49
8	7.37	6.58	6.95	7.41	7.96	8.17	8.46	8.77	8.92	9.02	2.44
9	7.32	6.64	6.97	7.43	7.97	8.19	8.50	8.80	8.96	9.06	2.42
10	7.34	6.65	6.97	7.43	7.99	8.18	8.47	8.77	8.92	9.04	2.39
13	7.52	6.64	6.97	7.43	7.98	8.17	8.45	8.75	8.91	9.02	2.38
14	7.39	6.54	6.87	7.29	7.80	7.98	8.25	8.55	8.69	8.81	2.27
15	7.75	6.53	6.84	7.32	7.84	8.02	8.29	8.58	8.71	8.83	2.30
16	7.51	6.48	6.92	7.42	7.96	8.17	8.46	8.76	8.89	8.98	2.50
17	7.54	6.56	7.03	7.54	8.10	8.30	8.58	8.88	9.02	9.12	2.56
20	7.62	6.56	7.09	7.57	8.14	8.32	8.59	8.88	9.02	9.09	2.53
21	7.57	6.76	7.20	7.60	8.15	8.34	8.61	8.90	9.03	9.10	2.34
22	7.46	6.72	7.13	7.50	8.04	8.22	8.49	8.77	8.90	8.94	2.22
23	7.55	6.72	7.09	7.50	8.05	8.22	8.47	8.74	8.88	8.90	2.18
24	7.56	6.71	7.08	7.48	8.03	8.21	8.45	8.72	8.85	8.87	2.16
27	7.61	6.76	7.15	7.55	8.10	8.27	8.54	8.81	8.94	8.96	2.20
28	7.68	6.80	7.06	7.53	8.05	8.24	8.48	8.75	8.87	8.89	2.09
29	7.87	6.78	7.05	7.53	8.03	8.21	8.47	8.75	8.88	8.92	2.14
30	8.27	6.76	7.04	7.50	8.02	8.18	8.41	8.70	8.82	8.87	2.11

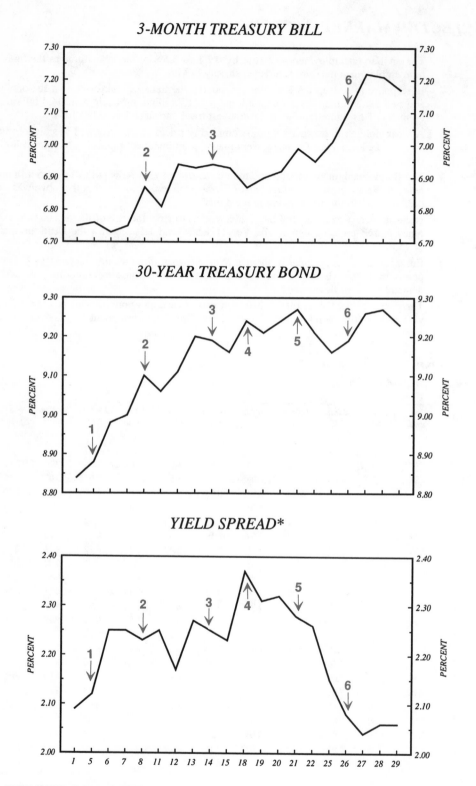

3-MONTH TREASURY BILL

30-YEAR TREASURY BOND

YIELD SPREAD*

*NOTE: SPREAD=30-YEAR BOND MINUS 3-MONTH BILL

SELECTED MARKET FACTORS

1   The National Association of Purchasing Manager's Composite Index indicated an expanding economy. With the index value at a near-term peak of 59.3%, up 4.2% from May, the economy entered the third-quarter on an uptrend.

2   Payroll employment rose by a surprisingly strong 346,000 workers in June, while manufacturing added 45,000 new jobs.

3   In his mid-year review of monetary policy, Federal Reserve Chairman Greenspan affirmed that monetary policy makers would be willing to err on the side of a restrictive stance because the economy was close to the threshold of capacity and unemployment.

4   Iran agreed to accept a United Nations' cease-fire resolution designed to end the bitter war with Iraq.

5   Following a week where major central banks cut short the dollar's recent surge, currency traders have concluded that governments are willing to tolerate much wider trading bands than previously assumed.

6   A surge in aircraft and military orders produced an 8.8% rise in the preliminary report on durable goods. A day later, the Commerce Department released a +3.1% second-quarter real GNP figure and a +4.1% implicit price deflator.

U.S. TREASURY YIELDS

(Bond Equivalent Yields)

July	Fed Funds	3-Month Bill	6-Month Bill	1-Year Bill	2-Year Note	3-Year Note	5-Year Note	7-Year Note	10-Year Note	30-Year Bond	Spread*
1	7.75	6.75	7.13	7.49	7.98	8.14	8.38	8.65	8.77	8.84	2.09
5	7.75	6.76	7.03	7.53	8.04	8.18	8.42	8.70	8.82	8.88	2.12
6	7.67	6.73	7.01	7.55	8.07	8.22	8.47	8.76	8.91	8.98	2.25
7	7.66	6.75	7.09	7.60	8.13	8.28	8.52	8.81	8.95	9.00	2.25
8	7.54	6.87	7.34	7.78	8.25	8.41	8.64	8.92	9.04	9.10	2.23
11	7.59	6.81	7.29	7.76	8.25	8.40	8.62	8.90	9.02	9.06	2.25
12	7.51	6.94	7.34	7.76	8.27	8.45	8.68	8.95	9.08	9.11	2.17
13	7.78	6.93	7.34	7.76	8.27	8.46	8.69	8.97	9.12	9.20	2.27
14	7.80	6.94	7.38	7.82	8.33	8.50	8.70	8.97	9.12	9.19	2.25
15	7.87	6.93	7.42	7.82	8.31	8.46	8.67	8.92	9.08	9.16	2.23
18	7.89	6.87	7.43	7.82	8.35	8.52	8.73	8.99	9.15	9.24	2.37
19	7.79	6.90	7.42	7.76	8.32	8.48	8.70	8.95	9.10	9.21	2.31
20	7.74	6.92	7.42	7.75	8.31	8.49	8.70	8.96	9.11	9.24	2.32
21	7.85	6.99	7.47	7.83	8.39	8.55	8.75	9.00	9.16	9.27	2.28
22	7.87	6.95	7.40	7.78	8.35	8.50	8.71	8.96	9.11	9.21	2.26
25	7.89	7.01	7.43	7.79	8.34	8.50	8.69	8.93	9.07	9.16	2.15
26	7.82	7.11	7.45	7.80	8.35	8.52	8.72	8.94	9.09	9.19	2.08
27	7.42	7.22	7.54	7.88	8.44	8.60	8.77	8.98	9.14	9.26	2.04
28	7.88	7.21	7.52	7.89	8.44	8.62	8.79	9.02	9.16	9.27	2.06
29	7.84	7.17	7.50	7.90	8.39	8.57	8.75	8.98	9.12	9.23	2.06

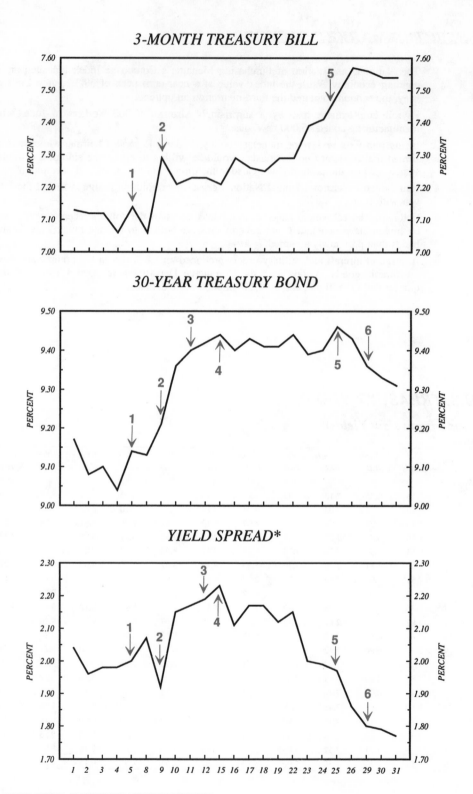

*NOTE: SPREAD=30-YEAR BOND MINUS 3-MONTH BILL

SELECTED MARKET FACTORS

1   Details of the July payroll employment report indicated that the pace of economic growth was accelerating as manufacturing jobs increased by 68,000 workers, and the factory work week held steady at 41.1 hours.

2   The Federal Reserve boosted the discount rate from 6.0% to 6.50%, citing growth inflation pressures, and a widening spread between the discount rate and the fed funds rate.

3   In response to a significant acceleration in the underlying rate of wholesale price growth, the PPI for finished goods climbed by 0.6% in July.

4   Industrial production rose by 0.8% in July as a 1.0% surge in business equipment output pushed manufacturing output up by 0.8%.

5   The Bundesbank raised its discount rate by 50 basis points to 3.50%, emphasizing the strong desire of West German policy makers to keep the mark from improving further relative to the dollar.

6   Japanese stock prices tumbled by 299.81 points (or 1.08%) following the concerted move by European central bankers to boost rates following the tightening executed by West Germany.

U.S. TREASURY YIELDS
(Bond Equivalent Yields)

	Fed Funds	3-Month Bill	6-Month Bill	1-Year Bill	2-Year Note	3-Year Note	5-Year Note	7-Year Note	10-Year Note	30-Year Bond	Spread*
August											
1	7.91	7.13	7.49	7.89	8.36	8.53	8.70	8.94	9.07	9.17	2.04
2	7.81	7.12	7.49	7.85	8.32	8.49	8.63	8.87	9.00	9.08	1.96
3	7.73	7.12	7.45	7.84	8.34	8.51	8.64	8.89	9.04	9.10	1.98
4	7.75	7.06	7.43	7.83	8.31	8.46	8.61	8.84	8.99	9.04	1.98
5	7.74	7.14	7.62	8.03	8.47	8.62	8.78	8.98	9.12	9.14	2.00
8	7.78	7.06	7.62	8.04	8.48	8.63	8.79	8.96	9.12	9.13	2.07
9	7.73	7.29	7.79	8.16	8.59	8.72	8.88	9.04	9.20	9.21	1.92
10	7.80	7.21	7.80	8.17	8.64	8.81	9.00	9.18	9.30	9.36	2.15
11	8.15	7.23	7.84	8.25	8.68	8.82	9.02	9.22	9.35	9.40	2.17
12	8.14	7.23	7.84	8.23	8.68	8.82	9.03	9.23	9.36	9.42	2.19
15	8.41	7.21	7.84	8.25	8.70	8.82	9.04	9.24	9.37	9.44	2.23
16	8.22	7.29	7.94	8.28	8.72	8.84	9.03	9.21	9.35	9.40	2.11
17	8.11	7.26	7.94	8.28	8.74	8.86	9.06	9.24	9.38	9.43	2.18
18	8.14	7.25	7.93	8.27	8.74	8.86	9.05	9.21	9.35	9.41	2.17
19	8.09	7.29	7.93	8.27	8.74	8.86	9.05	9.21	9.35	9.41	2.12
22	8.05	7.29	7.94	8.27	8.76	8.89	9.09	9.24	9.37	9.44	2.15
23	7.89	7.39	7.87	8.25	8.71	8.85	9.04	9.19	9.32	9.39	2.00
24	7.82	7.41	7.86	8.25	8.73	8.85	9.02	9.21	9.34	9.40	1.99
25	8.21	7.49	7.87	8.31	8.78	8.92	9.08	9.28	9.41	9.46	1.97
26	8.16	7.57	7.88	8.32	8.78	8.92	9.07	9.26	9.38	9.43	1.86
29	8.16	7.56	7.87	8.30	8.75	8.86	9.00	9.19	9.30	9.36	1.80
30	8.08	7.54	7.90	8.30	8.73	8.86	8.98	9.16	9.27	9.33	1.79
31	8.14	7.54	7.89	8.28	8.71	8.83	8.95	9.13	9.25	9.31	1.77

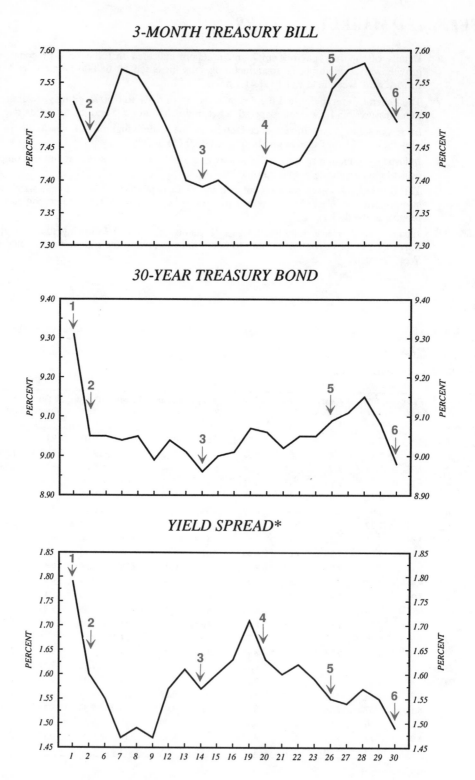

3-MONTH TREASURY BILL

30-YEAR TREASURY BOND

YIELD SPREAD*

*NOTE: SPREAD=30-YEAR BOND MINUS 3-MONTH BILL

SELECTED MARKET FACTORS

1 The Nikkei stock index plummeted 431.69 points, closing at 26,934.64 — the first close below 27,000 since May 28, and the second largest one-day drop this year.

2 Unusually hot weather during the peak summer period was considered to be the cause of a relatively modest payroll employment increase. Specifically, employment rose by only 219,000 jobs after an 83,000 downward revision to the July employment increase.

3 A sharp 8.9% across-the-board drop in merchandise imports prompted a sizable improvement in the trade deficit, which helped the dollar to continue moving higher in the face of strong central bank intervention.

4 Corporate tax receipts began to drain reserves from the banking system, which caused a technical dislocation of reserves.

5 The latest G-7 communique was exceptionally vague, causing speculation about the central bank's tolerance for a higher dollar.

6 Oil traded below $18 per barrel for the first time since May 1986 as OPEC's continued overproduction prompted Saudi Arabia to abdicate its role temporarily as swing producer. The National Association of Purchasing Managers indicated that the composite index had declined by 1.4% to 54.8% in July, marking the lowest rate in this indicator in six months.

U.S. TREASURY YIELDS
(Bond Equivalent Yields)

September	Fed Funds	3-Month Bill	6-Month Bill	1-Year Bill	2-Year Note	3-Year Note	5-Year Note	7-Year Note	10-Year Note	30-Year Bond	Spread*
1	8.27	7.52	7.89	8.24	8.68	8.82	8.95	9.14	9.25	9.31	1.79
2	8.27	7.46	7.79	8.06	8.45	8.58	8.70	8.87	9.00	9.05	1.60
6	7.98	7.50	7.80	8.08	8.47	8.58	8.70	8.88	8.99	9.05	1.55
7	7.74	7.57	7.81	8.09	8.45	8.57	8.69	8.87	8.99	9.04	1.47
8	8.13	7.56	7.82	8.10	8.45	8.58	8.69	8.88	8.99	9.05	1.49
9	8.13	7.52	7.81	8.07	8.42	8.52	8.62	8.82	8.93	8.99	1.47
12	8.17	7.47	7.79	8.08	8.44	8.55	8.66	8.85	8.97	9.04	1.57
13	8.11	7.40	7.79	8.02	8.40	8.52	8.65	8.83	8.94	9.01	1.61
14	8.09	7.39	7.74	7.95	8.36	8.47	8.59	8.77	8.88	8.96	1.57
15	8.24	7.40	7.77	7.98	8.39	8.51	8.63	8.80	8.91	9.00	1.60
16	8.08	7.38	7.76	8.02	8.40	8.53	8.65	8.82	8.93	9.01	1.63
19	8.05	7.36	7.78	8.05	8.44	8.55	8.69	8.86	8.97	9.07	1.71
20	8.06	7.43	7.77	8.07	8.45	8.56	8.68	8.86	8.97	9.06	1.63
21	8.63	7.42	7.76	8.05	8.40	8.51	8.64	8.82	8.93	9.02	1.60
22	8.28	7.43	7.78	8.09	8.44	8.54	8.67	8.85	8.95	9.05	1.62
23	8.21	7.47	7.84	8.09	8.47	8.56	8.69	8.86	8.97	9.05	1.59
26	8.27	7.54	7.89	8.17	8.52	8.61	8.73	8.90	9.00	9.09	1.55
27	8.26	7.57	7.96	8.21	8.55	8.66	8.77	8.94	9.04	9.11	1.54
28	8.25	7.58	7.97	8.23	8.59	8.69	8.81	8.97	9.06	9.15	1.57
29	8.39	7.53	7.89	8.18	8.53	8.63	8.73	8.89	8.98	9.08	1.55
30	8.54	7.49	7.86	8.13	8.43	8.52	8.61	8.78	8.87	8.98	1.49

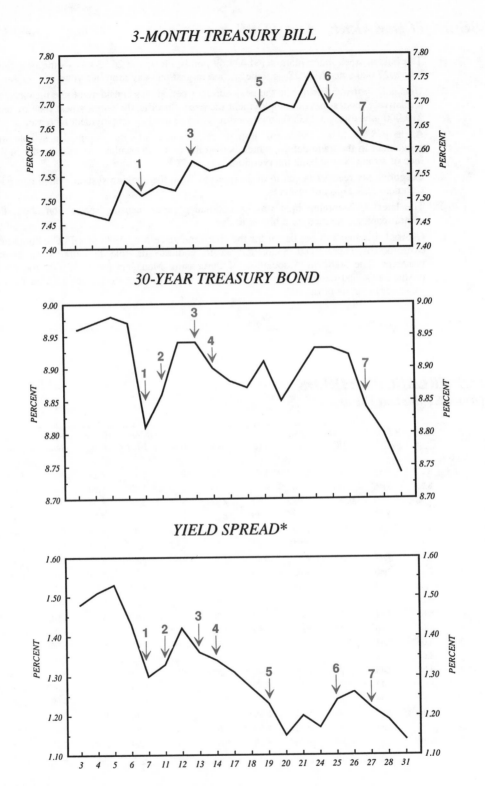

3-MONTH TREASURY BILL

30-YEAR TREASURY BOND

YIELD SPREAD*

*NOTE: SPREAD=30-YEAR BOND MINUS 3-MONTH BILL

SELECTED MARKET FACTORS

1 Nonfarm payroll employment was unexpectedly weak, rising by only 255,000 workers in September as goods-producing employment declined for a second consecutive month.

2 Fundamental support for the dollar eased, and foreign exchange dealers became pessimistic about the U.S. currency as it moved through a sixteen-week low against the yen with no central bank intervention.

3 The U.S. trade deficit widened by $2.6 billion to $10.6 billion, as a broad-based deterioration allowed imports to rise by 10.5% in August. Exports rose by a respectable 3.9% during the month.

4 Retail sales declined by 0.4% in September while industrial production remained unchanged for the month. Moreover, a 3.3% decline in finished energy prices kept the September PPI to a 0.4% gain.

5 On the final day of the October 19 statement period, which was smaller than expected, indicated an unanticipated tightening in reserve market conditions. The 1/8% uptick in the fed funds rate to 8 1/8% - 8 3/8% reflected a weakening dollar, and was initiated despite evidence of weak growth.

6 Both the central bank of Japan and the Bundesbank eased money market conditions in response to the dollar's weakness.

7 The Dow Jones Industrial Average fell 24.35 points as the recent LBO surge prompted a new wave of regulatory concern about the increased usage of debt financing. In fact, as a result of recent LBO activity, disorderly conditions have developed in the corporate debt new-issue market.

U.S. TREASURY YIELDS
(Bond Equivalent Yields)

	Fed Funds	3-Month Bill	6-Month Bill	1-Year Bill	2-Year Note	3-Year Note	5-Year Note	7-Year Note	10-Year Note	30-Year Bond	Spread*
October											
3	8.18	7.48	7.84	8.13	8.41	8.50	8.59	8.76	8.84	8.96	1.48
4	8.10	7.47	7.90	8.15	8.43	8.51	8.60	8.79	8.87	8.97	1.51
5	8.39	7.46	7.89	8.15	8.43	8.51	8.60	8.79	8.87	8.98	1.53
6	8.31	7.54	7.94	8.18	8.43	8.52	8.61	8.78	8.87	8.97	1.43
7	8.27	7.51	7.84	8.02	8.26	8.34	8.43	8.61	8.70	8.81	1.30
11	8.29	7.53	7.82	8.04	8.29	8.39	8.48	8.67	8.75	8.86	1.33
12	8.22	7.52	7.81	8.06	8.35	8.46	8.56	8.73	8.84	8.94	1.42
13	8.15	7.58	7.81	8.11	8.36	8.46	8.55	8.73	8.84	8.94	1.36
14	8.14	7.56	7.79	8.07	8.33	8.43	8.52	8.70	8.81	8.90	1.34
17	8.37	7.57	7.80	8.08	8.33	8.43	8.50	8.68	8.79	8.88	1.31
18	8.33	7.60	7.94	8.09	8.33	8.39	8.49	8.67	8.78	8.87	1.27
19	8.64	7.68	7.99	8.14	8.38	8.44	8.53	8.71	8.82	8.91	1.23
20	8.38	7.70	7.98	8.13	8.38	8.44	8.52	8.69	8.79	8.85	1.15
21	8.29	7.69	8.00	8.15	8.40	8.46	8.54	8.72	8.83	8.89	1.20
24	8.31	7.76	8.04	8.19	8.42	8.48	8.54	8.72	8.83	8.93	1.17
25	8.26	7.69	7.96	8.17	8.42	8.48	8.53	8.72	8.83	8.93	1.24
26	8.24	7.66	7.92	8.12	8.34	8.43	8.48	8.68	8.79	8.92	1.26
27	8.27	7.62	7.88	8.08	8.27	8.35	8.41	8.60	8.72	8.84	1.22
28	8.30	7.61	7.89	8.07	8.27	8.35	8.40	8.57	8.69	8.80	1.19
31	8.39	7.60	7.89	8.06	8.25	8.32	8.37	8.52	8.65	8.74	1.14

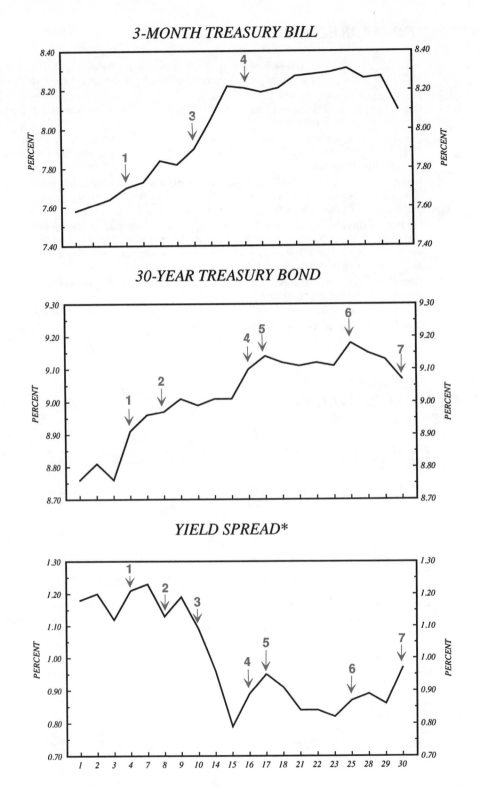

3-MONTH TREASURY BILL

30-YEAR TREASURY BOND

YIELD SPREAD*

*NOTE: SPREAD=30-YEAR BOND MINUS 3-MONTH BILL

SELECTED MARKET FACTORS

1   The bullish economic data released over the September-to-October period ended with the October payroll employment report. A combination of factors including a 323,000 October job gain, sizable upward revisions to the prior two months, and a 0.7% rise in earnings revealed a strong tone to economic growth.

2   The Treasury's large $30 billion refunding operation began, despite the absence of a bond offering.

3   According to *The Wall Street Journal*, Lee Hoskins, President of the Cleveland Federal Reserve Bank, expressed growing concern about emerging inflation pressures, especially after the release of October payroll report.

4   Speaking at the National Economic Commission, Federal Reserve Chairman Greenspan warned of the destabilizing effects of not addressing the budget deficit position.

5   The Treasury auctioned $9 billion in long bonds following President Reagan's approval of the Technical Tax Correction Bill.

6   OPEC reached a workable production accord at 18.5 million barrels output ceiling and $18 per barrel target. The output for Iran and Iraq was set at 2.4 million barrels per day.

7   According to the Fed's latest regional survey of the economy, the summer slowing in real growth remains firmly in place, and price pressures have eased as capacity constraints lessened in a number of key industries.

U.S. TREASURY YIELDS
(Bond Equivalent Yields)

	Fed Funds	3-Month Bill	6-Month Bill	1-Year Bill	2-Year Note	3-Year Note	5-Year Note	7-Year Note	10-Year Note	30-Year Bond	Spread*
November											
1	8.35	7.58	7.87	8.05	8.25	8.33	8.38	8.55	8.68	8.76	1.18
2	8.63	7.61	7.89	8.08	8.29	8.37	8.44	8.60	8.73	8.81	1.20
3	8.27	7.64	7.89	8.07	8.27	8.35	8.42	8.56	8.69	8.76	1.12
4	8.27	7.70	8.04	8.22	8.39	8.52	8.58	8.71	8.85	8.91	1.21
7	8.35	7.73	8.11	8.31	8.50	8.60	8.66	8.79	8.91	8.96	1.23
8	8.33	7.84	8.17	8.34	8.53	8.56	8.66	8.79	8.91	8.97	1.13
9	8.29	7.82	8.19	8.36	8.57	8.63	8.71	8.83	8.91	9.01	1.19
10	8.27	7.90	8.23	8.40	8.60	8.64	8.72	8.84	8.90	8.99	1.09
14	8.95	8.05	8.30	8.45	8.62	8.68	8.76	8.84	8.91	9.01	0.96
15	8.44	8.22	8.39	8.55	8.69	8.72	8.78	8.86	8.92	9.01	0.79
16	7.37	8.21	8.42	8.60	8.75	8.79	8.87	8.93	9.00	9.10	0.89
17	8.33	8.19	8.39	8.57	8.75	8.82	8.90	8.98	9.06	9.14	0.95
18	8.29	8.21	8.41	8.58	8.77	8.83	8.91	8.99	9.05	9.12	0.91
21	8.37	8.27	8.44	8.63	8.81	8.85	8.92	8.99	9.04	9.11	0.84
22	8.40	8.28	8.53	8.71	8.88	8.93	8.99	9.04	9.09	9.12	0.84
23	8.34	8.29	8.52	8.70	8.87	8.93	8.97	9.04	9.08	9.11	0.82
25	8.43	8.31	8.59	8.78	8.98	9.03	9.07	9.14	9.17	9.18	0.87
28	8.55	8.26	8.59	8.76	9.00	9.04	9.06	9.13	9.16	9.15	0.89
29	8.39	8.27	8.56	8.74	8.96	9.00	9.02	9.10	9.13	9.13	0.86
30	8.50	8.10	8.42	8.62	8.84	8.87	8.91	9.02	9.06	9.07	0.97

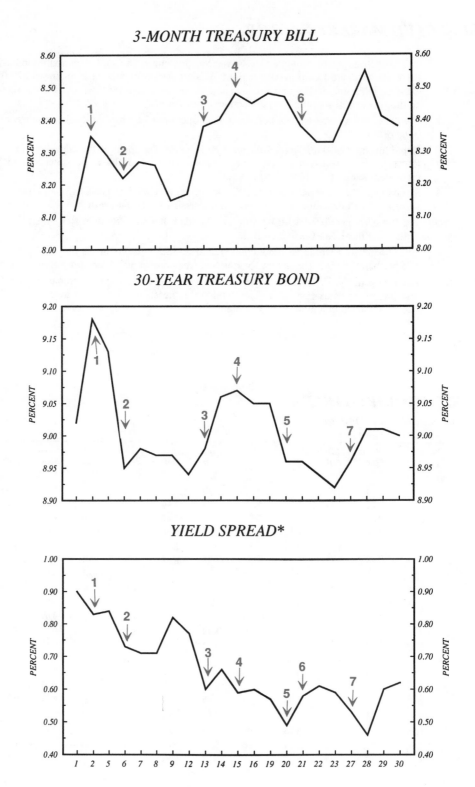

3-MONTH TREASURY BILL

30-YEAR TREASURY BOND

YIELD SPREAD*

*NOTE: SPREAD=30-YEAR BOND MINUS 3-MONTH BILL

SELECTED MARKET EVENTS

1   A 77,000 rise in manufacturing jobs contributed to November's 463,000 payroll employment figure. The 351,000 average gain in jobs over the last two months confirms a reacceleration in economic growth.

2   Well-informed sources leaked a story that the Soviet Union would unilaterally withdraw troops from Eastern Europe. These rumors prompted speculation about a possible move to cut the budget by slashing defense outlays.

3   Following a strong October sales performance, retail sales increased by +1.1% in November. The October sales rate was placed at +1.6%, up from an originally reported 0.9% increase.

4   The Bundesbank raised its Lombard rate from 5.0% to 5.5%, reflecting an increased policy drive to restrain inflation in Germany by holding M3 growth to 5.0% in 1989. In fact, the central bank of West Germany had exceeded its money supply targets for the last three years.

5   An unexpected 0.3% decline in apparel prices slowed the month-to-month increase in consumer prices to a respectable 0.3% in November, after rising by an average of 0.4% over the previous four months.

6   In the brief period between the corporate tax date and the end-of-the-quarter, technical pressures in the market for reserves eased temporarily.

7   As a result of purchases by last minute Christmas shoppers, what initially appeared to be a disappointing holiday sales period, registered a 5% to 6% gain over 1987.

U.S. TREASURY YIELDS
(Bond Equivalent Yields)

	Fed Funds	3-Month Bill	6-Month Bill	1-Year Bill	2-Year Note	3-Year Note	5-Year Note	7-Year Note	10-Year Note	30-Year Bond	Spread*
December											
1	8.54	8.12	8.45	8.66	8.86	8.88	8.88	8.99	9.01	9.02	0.90
2	8.63	8.35	8.72	8.96	9.12	9.13	9.11	9.17	9.18	9.18	0.83
5	8.65	8.29	8.71	8.94	9.09	9.09	9.07	9.12	9.13	9.13	0.84
6	8.59	8.22	8.61	8.80	8.88	8.91	8.88	8.94	8.95	8.95	0.73
7	8.49	8.27	8.65	8.84	8.93	8.97	8.93	8.99	9.00	8.98	0.71
8	8.50	8.26	8.67	8.90	9.00	9.03	9.01	9.04	9.02	8.97	0.71
9	8.52	8.15	8.67	8.95	9.03	9.05	9.05	9.10	9.07	8.97	0.82
12	8.58	8.17	8.69	8.96	9.05	9.07	9.07	9.11	9.08	8.94	0.77
13	8.39	8.38	8.80	9.08	9.16	9.16	9.15	9.18	9.15	8.98	0.60
14	8.51	8.40	8.81	9.13	9.20	9.21	9.19	9.22	9.19	9.06	0.66
15	8.81	8.48	8.72	9.18	9.20	9.22	9.21	9.22	9.19	9.07	0.59
16	8.90	8.45	8.71	9.13	9.18	9.20	9.18	9.20	9.17	9.05	0.60
19	8.96	8.48	8.71	9.11	9.18	9.18	9.16	9.18	9.15	9.05	0.57
20	8.85	8.47	8.74	9.04	9.11	9.10	9.09	9.11	9.08	8.96	0.49
21	8.79	8.38	8.61	8.98	9.09	9.09	9.08	9.10	9.07	8.96	0.58
22	8.85	8.33	8.65	8.95	9.04	9.11	9.09	9.11	9.07	8.94	0.61
23	8.74	8.33	8.64	8.94	9.04	9.11	9.08	9.11	9.05	8.92	0.59
27	8.84	8.44	8.79	9.06	9.15	9.20	9.17	9.20	9.13	8.96	0.52
28	9.39	8.55	8.85	9.12	9.23	9.23	9.22	9.27	9.21	9.01	0.46
29	9.64	8.41	8.72	9.08	9.18	9.20	9.19	9.22	9.18	9.01	0.60
30	9.04	8.38	8.67	9.02	9.14	9.18	9.14	9.18	9.14	9.00	0.62

1989

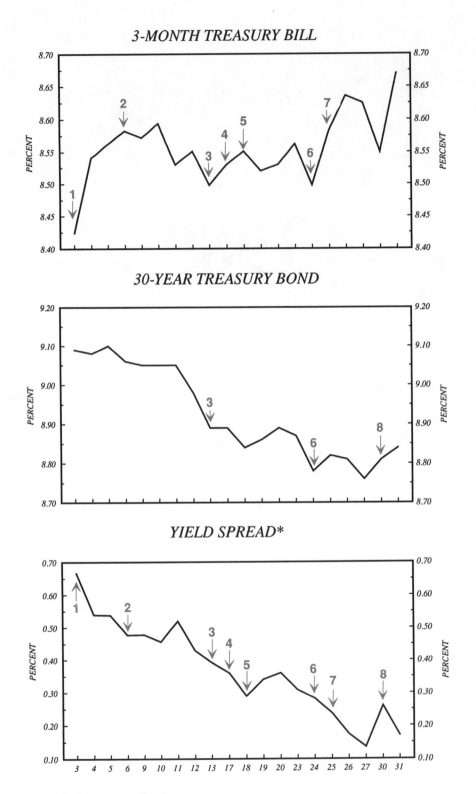

3-MONTH TREASURY BILL

30-YEAR TREASURY BOND

YIELD SPREAD*

*NOTE: SPREAD=30-YEAR BOND MINUS 3-MONTH BILL

SELECTED MARKET FACTORS

1 Large gains in production and new orders boosted the National Association of Purchasing Managers' Index from 56.6% in November to 58.1% in December.

2 A sharp 34,000 rise in manufacturing payroll employment during December lent support to a *Wall Street Journal* article which claimed that the Federal Reserve had tightened fed funds to 9%.

3 Despite strong retailer reports and a surge in late-December automobile sales, the monthly retail sales report revealed a disappointing 0.2% gain in consumer activity.

4 The Bundesbank provided a clear sign of tightening money market conditions by executing a 28-day repo with open rather than fixed-rate terms. This move preceded a 50 basis point rise in the Lombard rate to 6%, and a discount rate increase to 4% within two days.

5 With exports slipping by 2.3% and imports rising by 5.9%, the November trade deficit widened from $8.9 billion to $11.0 billion.

6 The Employment Cost Index rose by 1% in the fourth quarter after increasing by 1% in the three months that ended September. Despite this stable one-quarter gain, the year-over-year increase in wages and benefits accelerated to 5% year-over-year.

7 According to the latest "Tan Book" survey, the U.S. economy grew at a rapid pace late last year as consumer spending and production accelerated.

8 In sharp contrast to the weak December retail sales report, consumption spending during the month rose by a sharp 0.9% as farm subsidy payments pushed income up by a similar 0.9%.

U.S. TREASURY YIELDS
(Bond Equivalent Yields)

January	Fed Funds	3-Month Bill	6-Month Bill	1-Year Bill	2-Year Note	3-Year Note	5-Year Note	7-Year Note	10-Year Note	30-Year Bond	Spread*
3	9.40	8.42	8.77	9.11	9.21	9.26	9.25	9.28	9.23	9.09	0.67
4	9.35	8.54	8.87	9.14	9.25	9.26	9.24	9.28	9.22	9.08	0.54
5	9.00	8.56	8.97	9.22	9.32	9.34	9.32	9.34	9.27	9.10	0.54
6	9.04	8.58	8.98	9.20	9.32	9.35	9.30	9.32	9.25	9.06	0.48
9	9.19	8.57	9.00	9.18	9.29	9.34	9.30	9.32	9.23	9.05	0.48
10	9.15	8.59	8.93	9.15	9.25	9.32	9.29	9.31	9.24	9.05	0.46
11	9.10	8.53	8.91	9.17	9.29	9.31	9.28	9.30	9.24	9.05	0.52
12	9.15	8.55	8.88	9.06	9.20	9.23	9.20	9.20	9.14	8.98	0.43
13	9.10	8.50	8.80	8.99	9.14	9.15	9.10	9.10	9.06	8.89	0.39
17	9.26	8.53	8.85	9.03	9.16	9.17	9.11	9.10	9.06	8.89	0.36
18	9.07	8.55	8.78	8.95	9.13	9.12	9.07	9.04	8.99	8.84	0.29
19	8.98	8.52	8.75	8.91	9.09	9.11	9.06	9.05	9.00	8.86	0.34
20	8.97	8.53	8.76	8.93	9.13	9.15	9.11	9.07	9.03	8.89	0.36
23	9.10	8.56	8.77	8.95	9.13	9.13	9.06	9.05	9.00	8.87	0.31
24	9.10	8.50	8.74	8.91	9.07	9.04	8.98	8.97	8.93	8.78	0.28
25	9.32	8.58	8.82	9.00	9.10	9.11	9.05	9.03	8.99	8.82	0.24
26	9.25	8.64	8.85	9.03	9.14	9.17	9.07	9.04	8.99	8.81	0.17
27	9.17	8.63	8.84	8.98	9.07	9.09	9.03	9.00	8.95	8.76	0.13
30	9.18	8.57	8.86	9.00	9.10	9.13	9.07	9.05	9.00	8.83	0.26
31	9.14	8.69	8.91	9.04	9.12	9.13	9.08	9.03	9.01	8.84	0.15

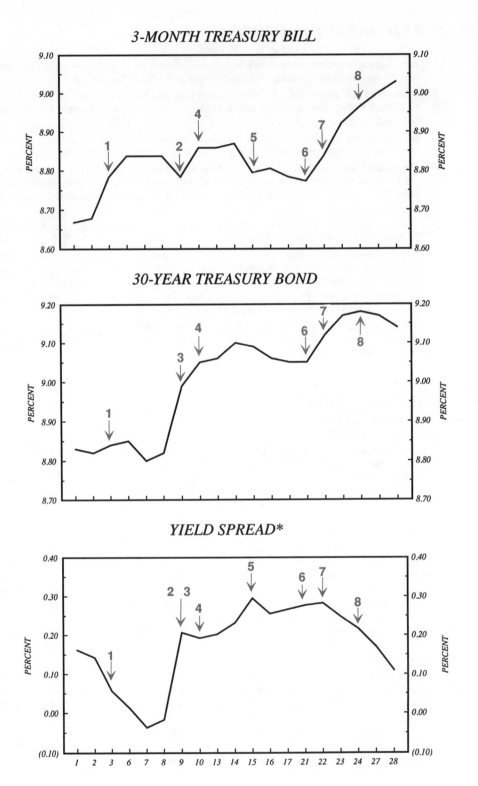

3-MONTH TREASURY BILL

30-YEAR TREASURY BOND

YIELD SPREAD*

*NOTE: SPREAD=30-YEAR BOND MINUS 3-MONTH BILL

SELECTED MARKET FACTORS

1 The nation's retailers recorded strong (6% to 10%) sales gains in January as overall payroll employment expanded by 408,000 jobs.

2 New money flooded the short end of the Treasury yield curve as Kohlberg Kravis & Co. completed its $25 billion purchase of RJR Nabisco.

3 Investors showed little response to a huge new issue of 30-year government bonds, pushing yields up sharply. In fact, bond prices experienced a 1 3/8 point decline, the largest one-day drop in about eight months.

4 Following a disastrous 1.0% pop in January wholesale prices, commercial banks raised the prime lending rate, which has been in place since late November 1988, from 10.5% to 11.0%.

5 Industrial production rose by 0.3% in January, following a revised December gain of 0.5%. The January gain, which was weaker than expected, was produced by a sharp deceleration in consumer durables.

6 Gold sales by the Soviet Union soared during the past few weeks, pushing the price of gold lower. Market sources claim the Soviets sold nearly 500,000 ounces, or almost 6% of their annual exports.

7 In his monetary policy report to Congress, Federal Reserve Chairman Greenspan served notice that he would push rates higher to head off inflation. The CPI rose by 0.6% in January after 0.3% in the previous month.

8 The Federal Reserve raised the discount rate from 6.5% to 7.0% in response to growing inflation pressures in the economy.

U.S. TREASURY YIELDS
(Bond Equivalent Yields)

	Fed Funds	3-Month Bill	6-Month Bill	1-Year Bill	2-Year Note	3-Year Note	5-Year Note	7-Year Note	10-Year Note	30-Year Bond	Spread*
February											
1	9.02	8.67	8.89	9.02	9.12	9.13	9.05	9.03	8.99	8.83	0.16
2	9.03	8.68	8.90	9.03	9.12	9.12	9.05	9.02	8.98	8.82	0.14
3	9.08	8.78	9.02	9.17	9.23	9.19	9.10	9.06	9.01	8.84	0.06
6	9.08	8.84	9.05	9.18	9.25	9.22	9.11	9.06	9.01	8.85	0.01
7	9.00	8.84	8.98	9.10	9.19	9.17	9.06	9.01	8.96	8.80	-0.04
8	9.38	8.84	8.97	9.12	9.21	9.19	9.06	9.01	8.95	8.82	-0.02
9	9.31	8.78	8.96	9.12	9.28	9.27	9.21	9.20	9.15	8.99	0.21
10	9.19	8.86	9.05	9.22	9.37	9.36	9.28	9.25	9.19	9.05	0.19
13	9.30	8.86	9.08	9.27	9.39	9.37	9.29	9.26	9.20	9.06	0.20
14	9.29	8.87	9.13	9.31	9.43	9.39	9.34	9.30	9.23	9.10	0.23
15	9.40	8.80	9.08	9.29	9.41	9.38	9.33	9.29	9.22	9.09	0.29
16	9.35	8.81	9.06	9.25	9.37	9.36	9.32	9.27	9.21	9.06	0.26
17	9.31	8.78	9.03	9.25	9.37	9.31	9.32	9.26	9.20	9.05	0.27
21	9.33	8.77	9.02	9.28	9.41	9.28	9.34	9.28	9.22	9.05	0.28
22	9.81	8.84	9.01	9.35	9.48	9.38	9.43	9.35	9.29	9.12	0.28
23	9.60	8.92	9.10	9.48	9.60	9.49	9.47	9.44	9.36	9.17	0.25
24	9.79	8.96	9.24	9.51	9.66	9.51	9.49	9.45	9.38	9.18	0.22
27	9.92	9.00	9.23	9.46	9.62	9.48	9.47	9.42	9.36	9.17	0.17
28	9.87	9.03	9.23	9.40	9.55	9.43	9.42	9.39	9.32	9.14	0.11

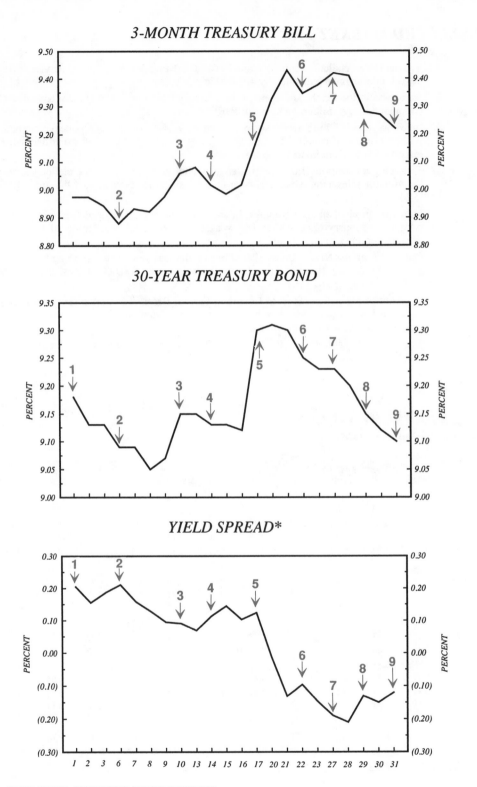

NOTE: SPREAD=30-YEAR BOND MINUS 3-MONTH BILL

SELECTED MARKET FACTORS

1. Federal Reserve Chairman Greenspan defended the recent move to push up rates (February 24 discount rate boost) and suggested the feasibility of even higher interest rates.

2. The National Association of Purchasing Managers' Index slipped for a second consecutive month from 53.2% in January to 53.0%, while the price index moved decidedly lower from 71.6% in February to 66.0% in March.

3. Payroll employment rose by a relatively moderate 289,000 workers in February; however, the civilian unemployment rate tumbled by 0.3% or 5.4% of the labor force.

4. A sharp 1.3% drop in durable goods orders for February offset a temperate 0.1% rise in non-durable sales and produced a 0.4% slide in overall retail activity.

5. For the second consecutive month, wholesale prices rose by a sharp 1.0% in February. A combination of accelerating food and energy prices added to the 0.6% rise in the underlying rate of finished goods prices.

6. Non-defense capital goods orders moved sharply lower in February (-8.9%), after combined gains of over 12% during the December-to-January period.

7. Brent crude prices soared through $19 per barrel in Tokyo trading after a tanker spill in the Port of Valdez closed the key Alaskan harbor to all shipping.

8. The February reading on the Index of Leading Indicators showed a 0.3% decline in the government's economic barometer following a 0.7% revised increase in the previous month.

9. The economy continued to slow in March according to the latest National Association of Purchasing Managers' survey as the Association's composite index slipped by 2.6% to 50.4%, the lowest level for the index in 32 months. Moreover, the N.A.P.M data revealed a decelerating upward move in prices paid by the Association's members.

U.S. TREASURY YIELDS
(Bond Equivalent Yields)

March	Fed Funds	3-Month Bill	6-Month Bill	1-Year Bill	2-Year Note	3-Year Note	5-Year Note	7-Year Note	10-Year Note	30-Year Bond	Spread*
1	9.82	8.98	9.18	9.40	9.55	9.42	9.43	9.41	9.36	9.18	0.21
2	9.83	8.98	9.18	9.38	9.52	9.42	9.38	9.37	9.31	9.13	0.16
3	9.70	8.94	9.19	9.36	9.50	9.40	9.38	9.35	9.31	9.13	0.19
6	9.77	8.88	9.18	9.32	9.46	9.36	9.34	9.31	9.26	9.09	0.21
7	9.59	8.93	9.18	9.34	9.48	9.38	9.35	9.30	9.26	9.09	0.16
8	10.50	8.92	9.17	9.35	9.48	9.37	9.34	9.28	9.23	9.05	0.13
9	9.89	8.98	9.17	9.35	9.48	9.42	9.35	9.29	9.24	9.07	0.10
10	9.82	9.06	9.33	9.58	9.66	9.60	9.48	9.40	9.34	9.15	0.09
13	9.82	9.08	9.32	9.56	9.64	9.58	9.48	9.40	9.35	9.15	0.07
14	9.78	9.02	9.28	9.54	9.64	9.58	9.45	9.38	9.32	9.13	0.11
15	9.84	8.99	9.24	9.52	9.62	9.57	9.45	9.38	9.31	9.13	0.15
16	9.79	9.02	9.26	9.48	9.61	9.55	9.43	9.37	9.30	9.12	0.10
17	9.81	9.18	9.47	9.72	9.84	9.76	9.64	9.57	9.49	9.30	0.12
20	9.85	9.32	9.60	9.84	9.90	9.84	9.71	9.61	9.53	9.31	-0.01
21	9.80	9.43	9.68	9.85	9.92	9.88	9.75	9.63	9.53	9.30	-0.13
22	10.18	9.35	9.54	9.71	9.81	9.78	9.65	9.55	9.45	9.25	-0.10
23	9.92	9.38	9.58	9.70	9.81	9.81	9.65	9.53	9.43	9.23	-0.15
27	9.90	9.44	9.64	9.75	9.85	9.79	9.67	9.54	9.44	9.23	-0.21
28	9.88	9.41	9.69	9.77	9.86	9.80	9.66	9.52	9.41	9.20	-0.21
29	9.84	9.29	9.61	9.69	9.80	9.74	9.60	9.47	9.36	9.15	-0.14
30	9.89	9.28	9.60	9.70	9.79	9.71	9.59	9.44	9.34	9.14	-0.14
31	9.79	9.23	9.54	9.64	9.73	9.66	9.53	9.40	9.30	9.11	-0.12

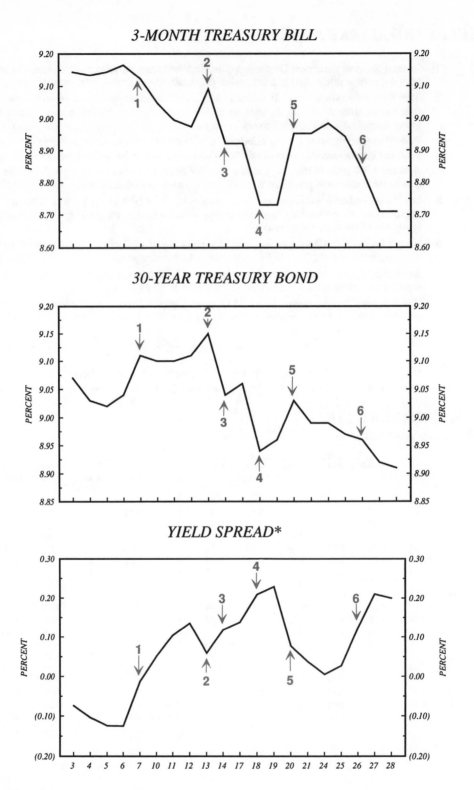

*NOTE: SPREAD=30-YEAR BOND MINUS 3-MONTH BILL

SELECTED MARKET FACTORS

1   A 0.2% drop in the civilian unemployment rate to 5.0% of the labor force was recorded in March despite the slowing in non-farm payroll employment to only a 180,000 job gain for the month.

2   The National Bank of Switzerland raised its discount rate by 50 basis points to 4 1/2% and lifted the Lombard rate to 7.0%, after seriously underestimating domestic growth and inflation pressures.

3   A sharp deceleration in the underlying rate of wholesale inflation (+0.3% vs. +0.6%) prompted a 0.4% March PPI increase, which was smaller than expected. Industrial production held steady in March for a second consecutive month, while a 5.3% surge in imports pushed the trade deficit up to $10.5 billion during the month.

4   In contrast to a softer March PPI, the CPI climbed to 0.5% as food and energy price gains accelerated.

5   Following an acceleration in West German producer prices in March (+3.4% year-over-year vs. 3.1% in February), the Bundesbank raised both the discount rate (4.5%) and the Lombard rate (6.5%) by 50 basis points.

6   Aggressive open market operations in the face of a soft fed funds market prompted speculation about a Federal Reserve easing. In addition to executing several rounds of system repo, the Federal Reserve purchased bills for its own account on Wednesday, April 26.

U.S. TREASURY YIELDS
(Bond Equivalent Yields)

April	Fed Funds	3-Month Bill	6-Month Bill	1-Year Bill	2-Year Note	3-Year Note	5-Year Note	7-Year Note	10-Year Note	30-Year Bond	Spread*
3	9.92	9.14	9.41	9.50	9.56	9.50	9.39	9.29	9.21	9.07	-0.07
4	9.52	9.13	9.27	9.42	9.47	9.44	9.31	9.24	9.17	9.03	-0.10
5	9.28	9.14	9.24	9.42	9.45	9.40	9.31	9.24	9.17	9.02	-0.12
6	9.85	9.17	9.29	9.49	9.54	9.47	9.35	9.30	9.20	9.04	-0.13
7	9.83	9.12	9.31	9.52	9.57	9.54	9.42	9.38	9.27	9.11	-0.01
10	9.85	9.05	9.29	9.49	9.57	9.53	9.43	9.38	9.27	9.10	0.05
11	9.79	9.00	9.31	9.50	9.57	9.53	9.42	9.38	9.27	9.10	0.10
12	9.78	8.98	9.30	9.51	9.59	9.56	9.44	9.39	9.29	9.11	0.13
13	9.84	9.09	9.37	9.59	9.66	9.62	9.50	9.41	9.34	9.15	0.06
14	9.83	8.92	9.12	9.33	9.43	9.40	9.29	9.25	9.18	9.04	0.12
17	9.89	8.92	9.16	9.37	9.48	9.44	9.33	9.27	9.20	9.06	0.14
18	9.71	8.73	8.90	9.14	9.28	9.24	9.14	9.10	9.06	8.94	0.21
19	10.71	8.73	8.88	9.17	9.30	9.27	9.17	9.13	9.08	8.96	0.23
20	9.89	8.95	8.99	9.37	9.46	9.41	9.32	9.26	9.20	9.03	0.08
21	9.87	8.95	9.11	9.33	9.44	9.37	9.27	9.21	9.15	8.99	0.04
24	9.88	8.99	9.17	9.36	9.46	9.37	9.26	9.21	9.15	8.99	0.01
25	9.85	8.94	9.19	9.28	9.41	9.32	9.21	9.16	9.12	8.97	0.03
26	9.82	8.84	9.12	9.22	9.34	9.29	9.18	9.15	9.11	8.96	0.12
27	9.85	8.71	9.00	9.13	9.23	9.18	9.10	9.07	9.05	8.92	0.21
28	9.82	8.71	9.00	9.12	9.22	9.15	9.06	9.04	9.02	8.91	0.20

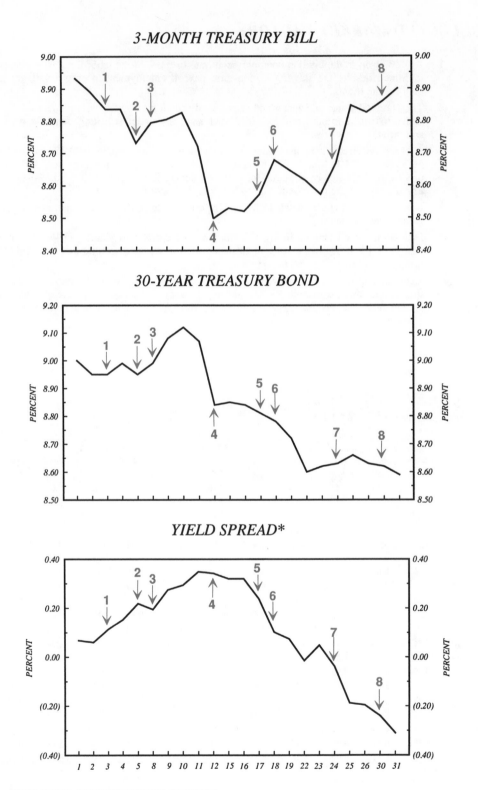

3-MONTH TREASURY BILL

30-YEAR TREASURY BOND

YIELD SPREAD*

*NOTE: SPREAD=30-YEAR BOND MINUS 3-MONTH BILL

SELECTED MARKET FACTORS

1   Petroleum prices fell by as much as $1 a barrel in response to concern that an oil glut might recur. The largest price drop occurred in West Texas Intermediate field postings, which fell to $19.25 dollars a barrel as the market focused on a $20.9 million barrel OPEC output.

2   A 9,000 drop in manufacturing employment and a sharp deceleration in service-producing jobs produced a slow 117,000 gain in April payroll employment. The small payroll gain more than offset a 0.7% rise in hourly earnings and a 0.3 of an hour lengthening in the factory work week to 41.3 hours.

3   Bethlehem Steel reached a tentative accord with the United Steel Workers Union on a 20% wage and benefits increase for their new three-year contract beginning June 1, 1989.

4   Wholesale prices rose by 0.4% in April after a 0.7% increase in March as energy prices rose by 7.2% and food prices slipped 0.6%. At the same time, a 2.8% drop in passenger car prices pushed the excluding food and energy component down by 0.1% for the month. On the same day, President Bush ordered U.S. troops into the Panama Canal zone and student protests in China began to threaten the government's stability.

5   A 7.4% rise in exports offset a 3.2% increase in imports to produce a surprisingly small March trade deficit of $8.8 billion. The improved trade outlook and the lack of coordinated currency intervention resulted in the dollar rising to a 29-month high against the yen.

6   Unlike the April PPI, consumer prices for the month increased by 0.7% as energy costs surged by 5.1%.

7   The Bank of England pushed up the commercial bank lending rate by 1% to 14% as a result of domestic inflation pressures. Later the same day, the Federal Reserve drained reserves through 7-day matched sales, highlighting the Federal Reserve's reluctance to ease in response to the sharp rise in the dollar.

8   In a long-awaited move, the Bank of Japan raised the discount rate by 75 basis points to 3.25%. This marked the first increase in the rate in many years. China's leaders appeared to be cracking down on worker support for student demonstrators in Beijing.

U.S. TREASURY YIELDS
(Bond Equivalent Yields)

	Fed Funds	3-Month Bill	6-Month Bill	1-Year Bill	2-Year Note	3-Year Note	5-Year Note	7-Year Note	10-Year Note	30-Year Bond	Spread*
May											
1	9.85	8.93	9.19	9.30	9.36	9.30	9.19	9.16	9.14	9.00	0.07
2	9.83	8.89	9.07	9.22	9.27	9.20	9.11	9.10	9.08	8.95	0.06
3	10.15	8.84	8.98	9.15	9.21	9.19	9.10	9.07	9.06	8.95	0.11
4	9.91	8.84	9.00	9.14	9.21	9.19	9.09	9.07	9.06	8.99	0.15
5	9.90	8.73	8.87	8.97	9.04	9.01	8.96	8.96	8.99	8.95	0.22
8	9.84	8.80	8.92	9.04	9.09	9.09	9.02	9.02	9.04	8.99	0.20
9	9.79	8.81	9.00	9.18	9.23	9.16	9.17	9.15	9.15	9.08	0.28
10	9.77	8.83	9.05	9.20	9.27	9.23	9.21	9.20	9.16	9.12	0.29
11	9.74	8.72	8.93	9.06	9.14	9.11	9.10	9.12	9.10	9.07	0.35
12	9.67	8.50	8.67	8.75	8.82	8.81	8.80	8.81	8.81	8.84	0.34
15	9.79	8.53	8.77	8.85	8.91	8.87	8.85	8.83	8.82	8.85	0.32
16	9.76	8.52	8.76	8.90	8.95	8.90	8.87	8.84	8.82	8.84	0.32
17	9.92	8.57	8.82	8.89	8.96	8.90	8.87	8.83	8.80	8.81	0.24
18	9.80	8.68	8.88	8.94	9.00	8.93	8.88	8.82	8.78	8.78	0.10
19	9.73	8.65	8.85	8.89	8.94	8.89	8.82	8.75	8.71	8.72	0.07
22	9.70	8.62	8.78	8.78	8.84	8.78	8.71	8.62	8.58	8.60	-0.02
23	9.73	8.57	8.80	8.79	8.83	8.77	8.72	8.64	8.60	8.62	0.05
24	9.75	8.67	8.88	8.85	8.82	8.79	8.74	8.67	8.63	8.63	-0.04
25	9.76	8.85	8.98	8.94	8.92	8.88	8.75	8.72	8.67	8.66	-0.19
26	9.71	8.83	8.93	8.92	8.89	8.86	8.72	8.71	8.66	8.63	-0.20
30	9.77	8.89	8.92	8.88	8.87	8.81	8.68	8.68	8.64	8.63	-0.26
31	10.48	8.92	8.87	8.86	8.82	8.78	8.65	8.64	8.60	8.60	-0.32

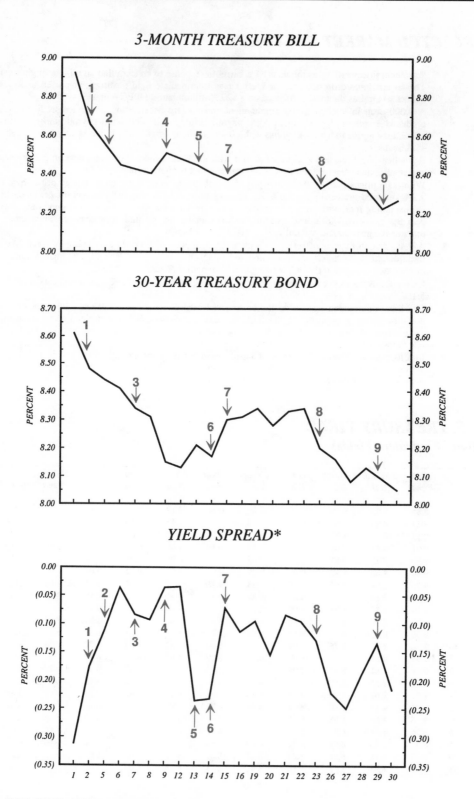

3-MONTH TREASURY BILL

30-YEAR TREASURY BOND

YIELD SPREAD*

*NOTE: SPREAD=30-YEAR BOND MINUS 3-MONTH BILL

SELECTED MARKET FACTORS

1. The Federal Reserve moved to ease rates by 25 basis points following a small 101,000 rise in May payroll employment. Although the April job gain was revised up by 96,000 workers to 206,000 jobs, the 33,000 drop in goods-producing employment and a 0.2% reduction in the factory work week confirmed the economic deceleration.

2. Citibank cut the prime lending rate from 11.5% to 11.0%. The Ayatollah Khomeini died at the age of 87, leaving his 49-year old son as spiritual leader. Government troops used violence to end the student demonstration in Tiananmen Square in Beijing, China.

3. By failing to execute matched sales with fed funds below 9 5/8%, the Federal Reserve confirmed speculation that it had recently eased monetary policy.

4. Wholesale prices rose by 0.9% in May as energy prices rose by 3.3%, while food prices gained by 0.8%. Excluding food and energy, wholesale prices rose by 0.5% versus a 0.1% decline in this component in April.

5. A 0.1% rise in overall retail sales emerged in May as non-auto sales slowed to only 0.1% following April's 0.7% increase.

6. Japan's Finance Ministry cautioned life insurance companies against speculating in dollars. Reports circulated that representatives of the Big Five insurance companies were called in to discuss their recent activity.

7. Both ends of the yield curve responded to different economic statistics reported that day. The short end rallied on an unchanged industrial production report, while bonds sold off in response to a $1.2 billion narrowing in the April trade deficit to $8.3 billion.

8. A 9.4% decline in transportation orders led a broad-based 4.2% drop in May durable goods orders. In addition to transportation, orders declined sharply for both electrical and non-electrical machinery, while primary metals on orders slipped by a smaller 1.5% during the month.

9. European central banks followed the Bundesbank in raising rates. In an unexpected move to halt the tide of rising global inflation pressures, the Bundesbank raised both the discount and Lombard rates by 50 basis points (5% and 7%, respectively).

U.S. TREASURY YIELDS
(Bond Equivalent Yields)

June	Fed Funds	3-Month Bill	6-Month Bill	1-Year Bill	2-Year Note	3-Year Note	5-Year Note	7-Year Note	10-Year Note	30-Year Bond	Spread*
1	9.84	8.92	8.87	8.87	8.82	8.78	8.65	8.65	8.61	8.61	-0.31
2	9.73	8.66	8.60	8.57	8.52	8.47	8.42	8.45	8.43	8.48	-0.18
5	9.64	8.55	8.49	8.46	8.44	8.39	8.33	8.38	8.36	8.44	-0.11
6	9.58	8.45	8.36	8.48	8.45	8.40	8.35	8.38	8.36	8.41	-0.04
7	9.48	8.42	8.25	8.39	8.38	8.35	8.28	8.31	8.27	8.34	-0.08
8	9.47	8.40	8.21	8.35	8.33	8.30	8.26	8.29	8.27	8.31	-0.09
9	9.36	8.51	8.33	8.32	8.28	8.23	8.16	8.17	8.15	8.15	-0.36
12	9.35	8.48	8.32	8.33	8.29	8.26	8.18	8.19	8.16	8.13	-0.35
13	9.30	8.45	8.27	8.45	8.41	8.38	8.30	8.31	8.25	8.21	-0.24
14	9.22	8.40	8.21	8.41	8.36	8.32	8.24	8.25	8.20	8.17	-0.23
15	9.46	8.37	8.32	8.49	8.48	8.46	8.36	8.37	8.33	8.30	-0.07
16	9.50	8.42	8.42	8.57	8.53	8.48	8.40	8.38	8.35	8.31	-0.11
19	9.44	8.44	8.42	8.57	8.55	8.49	8.41	8.42	8.37	8.34	-0.10
20	9.41	8.44	8.54	8.52	8.50	8.45	8.35	8.36	8.31	8.28	-0.16
21	9.55	8.41	8.57	8.57	8.53	8.49	8.40	8.40	8.37	8.33	-0.08
22	9.66	8.44	8.59	8.58	8.55	8.50	8.41	8.42	8.38	8.34	-0.10
23	9.57	8.33	8.41	8.39	8.39	8.34	8.27	8.29	8.25	8.20	-0.13
26	9.51	8.38	8.39	8.37	8.35	8.29	8.22	8.22	8.18	8.16	-0.22
27	9.55	8.33	8.21	8.35	8.27	8.25	8.14	8.16	8.11	8.08	-0.25
28	9.64	8.32	8.21	8.35	8.27	8.27	8.18	8.20	8.17	8.13	-0.19
29	9.69	8.22	8.16	8.19	8.16	8.14	8.09	8.13	8.12	8.09	-0.13
30	9.63	8.27	8.14	8.12	8.08	8.05	8.03	8.10	8.10	8.05	-0.22

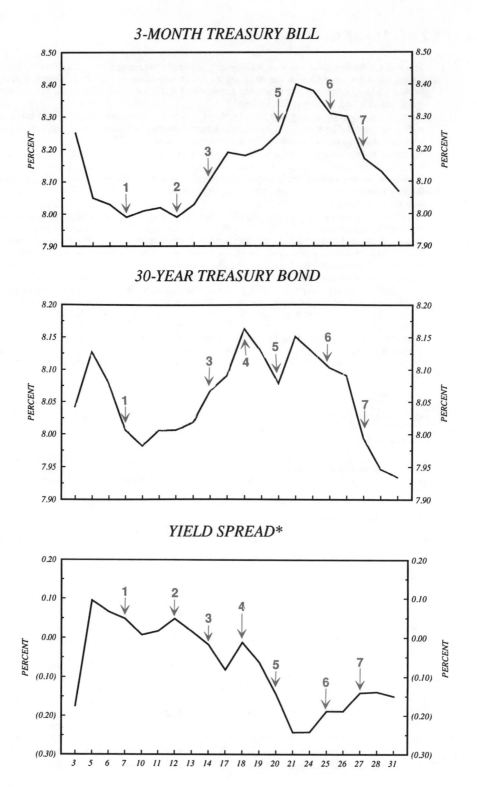

*NOTE: SPREAD=30-YEAR BOND MINUS 3-MONTH BILL

SELECTED MARKET FACTORS

1   Following a 180,000 rise in non-farm payroll employment for June, which was lower than expected, the fed funds rate dropped 25 basis points to 9 1/4% as the Federal Reserve moved to ease reserve market conditions.

2   The Federal Reserve executed a large $4.7 billion bill sale as currency market intervention disrupted the normal add/drain dynamics. Traditionally, currency growth creates a large add need during the summer months. This year, a surge in the Federal Reserve's currency holding, however, had produced a technical drain need. The bill sale also eased speculation about an acceleration in the Fed's drive to push short rates down.

3   Despite a 0.1% decline in June, wholesale prices and a 0.2% downturn in industrial production for the month, the Federal Reserve kept reserve market conditions tight prior to the mid-year policy report scheduled for July 20.

4   A 4.3% surge in imports and a disappointing 0.9% drop in exports produced a $1.9 billion widening in the trade deficit for May. In addition to the widening in the overall deficit, the trade shortfall with Japan increased to $4.3 billion as the deficit in non-auto capital goods deteriorated.

5   In his semi-annual report on monetary policy, Federal Reserve Chairman Greenspan clearly indicated that the members of the FOMC would tolerate a 4 1/2% to 5.0% inflation rate, if necessary, to avoid a recession. In fact, the focus of his report was on the increased risk of a downturn in the business cycle over that of an inflation acceleration.

6   The Federal Reserve failed to execute overnight matched sales with fed funds trading below 9 1/8%. This lack of a rate protest marked the first clear signal that the Federal Reserve was in the process of easing rates for a third time in two months. The latest easing moved the fed funds rate down to 9%.

7   Real GNP rose by a sluggish 1.7% in the second quarter as government spending and producer durable goods equipment purchases provided the bulk of the upward momentum to the economy. A smaller improvement in net exports restrained second-quarter growth.

U.S. TREASURY YIELDS
(Bond Equivalent Yields)

July	Fed Funds	3-Month Bill	6-Month Bill	1-Year Bill	2-Year Note	3-Year Note	5-Year Note	7-Year Note	10-Year Note	30-Year Bond	Spread*
3	9.49	8.25	8.12	8.04	8.02	8.00	7.99	8.09	8.09	8.07	-0.17
5	9.48	8.05	7.96	8.00	7.99	7.97	7.97	8.11	8.11	8.14	0.10
6	9.46	8.03	7.96	7.96	7.94	7.92	7.91	8.07	8.08	8.10	0.07
7	9.23	7.99	7.91	7.89	7.83	7.85	7.86	8.00	8.02	8.04	0.05
10	9.22	8.01	7.89	7.89	7.81	7.83	7.84	7.97	7.99	8.02	0.01
11	9.25	8.02	7.90	7.87	7.81	7.80	7.80	7.96	8.00	8.04	0.02
12	9.54	7.99	7.85	7.81	7.74	7.77	7.79	7.88	8.00	8.04	0.05
13	9.31	8.03	7.94	7.81	7.74	7.78	7.80	7.89	8.00	8.05	0.02
14	9.22	8.11	8.05	7.86	7.83	7.81	7.84	7.92	8.04	8.09	-0.02
17	9.28	8.19	8.11	7.92	7.85	7.86	7.85	7.95	8.05	8.11	-0.08
18	9.24	8.18	8.17	8.03	7.95	7.97	7.97	8.04	8.13	8.17	-0.01
19	9.21	8.20	8.13	7.96	7.90	7.92	7.90	8.01	8.09	8.14	-0.06
20	9.19	8.25	8.09	7.88	7.81	7.81	7.80	7.91	8.01	8.10	-0.14
21	9.20	8.40	8.24	8.02	7.91	7.91	7.89	7.97	8.07	8.16	-0.24
24	9.17	8.38	8.24	8.01	7.93	7.90	7.87	7.96	8.05	8.14	-0.24
25	9.14	8.31	8.01	7.92	7.84	7.82	7.79	7.91	8.01	8.12	-0.19
26	8.86	8.30	8.05	7.91	7.75	7.83	7.81	7.89	8.02	8.11	-0.19
27	9.00	8.17	7.97	7.77	7.65	7.70	7.69	7.80	7.92	8.03	-0.14
28	8.94	8.13	7.90	7.69	7.56	7.62	7.60	7.72	7.87	7.99	-0.14
31	8.94	8.07	7.85	7.65	7.53	7.58	7.56	7.68	7.82	7.92	-0.15

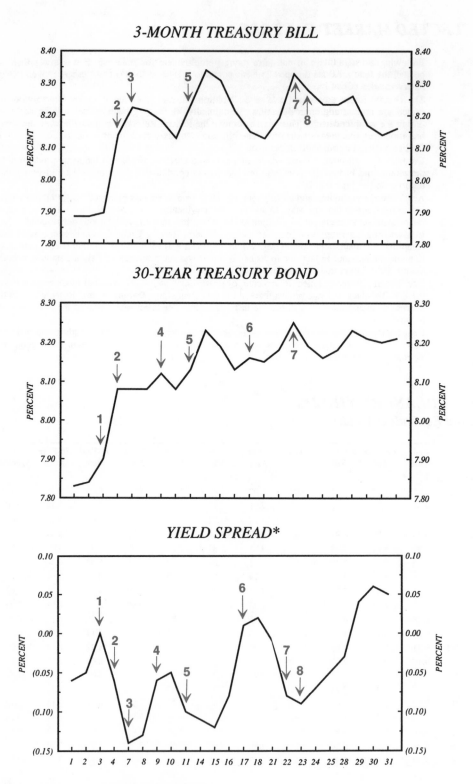

3-MONTH TREASURY BILL

30-YEAR TREASURY BOND

YIELD SPREAD*

*NOTE: SPREAD=30-YEAR BOND MINUS 3-MONTH BILL

SELECTED MARKET FACTORS

1   Late-July auto sales totaled 7.5 million units, assuring a 7.6 million unit average for the month, up 8.1% from June's 7.0 million level. This uptick in sales was credited to aggressive dealer incentives and early talk of large price increases in the 1990 models.

2   A 169,000 rise in payroll employment, combined with a rebound in manufacturing workers (+3,000), a lengthening in the factory workweek (41.0 hours), and a 0.8% surge in hourly earnings revealed a solid fundamental base to the economy. These payroll data were in sharp contrast to the recession view that prevailed in May and June.

3   Congress passed a compromise thrift bill lumping $20 billion in REFCO borrowing on-budget and $30 billion as off-budget financing. The on-budget portion of the bailout bill forced the Treasury to quickly announce a $5 billion addition to a previously announced $10 billion cash management bill.

4   Aggressive foreign interest in the Treasury's 10-year offering failed to materialize at the time of auction, producing the smallest cover in the past twelve issues.

5   Despite the surprisingly large 0.4% decline in wholesale prices reported for July, the Street opted to focus on a 0.9% rise in retail sales during the month, and a 0.3% upward revision to the June release. The market had been anticipating a 0.1% slide in retail sales for the month.

6   A 1.5% rise in merchandise exports, combined with a 3.6% drop in imports, produced a relatively narrow $8.2 billion trade deficit in June. Among the major trade components which improved in June, the $1.2 billion swing in the flow of non-auto capital goods was considered the most important factor.

7   A second consecutive +5.0% rise in non-defense capital goods orders in July more than offset a 1.9% slide in total orders for the month, which was larger than expected.

8   The execution of a customer repo late in the period, after several rounds of matched sales, surprised many Street analysts who retreated quickly from recession forecasts made in the spring and early summer months.

U.S. TREASURY YIELDS
(Bond Equivalent Yields)

	Fed Funds	3-Month Bill	6-Month Bill	1-Year Bill	2-Year Note	3-Year Note	5-Year Note	7-Year Note	10-Year Note	30-Year Bond	Spread*
August											
1	8.95	7.89	7.73	7.61	7.46	7.51	7.49	7.60	7.74	7.83	-0.06
2	8.95	7.89	7.74	7.63	7.53	7.59	7.57	7.65	7.76	7.84	-0.05
3	8.94	7.90	7.80	7.69	7.60	7.66	7.64	7.71	7.80	7.90	0.00
4	8.93	8.14	8.10	8.05	7.92	7.94	7.94	7.95	8.00	8.08	-0.06
7	8.95	8.22	8.19	8.16	8.01	8.05	7.98	7.98	8.03	8.08	-0.14
8	8.95	8.21	8.08	8.08	7.96	7.94	7.95	7.96	8.00	8.08	-0.13
9	9.24	8.18	8.01	8.10	7.99	7.98	7.96	7.98	8.05	8.12	-0.06
10	9.02	8.13	8.00	8.08	7.99	7.97	7.96	7.98	8.02	8.08	-0.05
11	9.00	8.23	8.09	8.18	8.12	8.10	8.10	8.08	8.09	8.13	-0.10
14	9.04	8.34	8.17	8.33	8.31	8.28	8.27	8.28	8.24	8.23	-0.11
15	9.19	8.31	8.31	8.33	8.29	8.26	8.24	8.23	8.21	8.19	-0.12
16	9.03	8.21	8.23	8.22	8.17	8.15	8.11	8.13	8.12	8.13	-0.08
17	8.95	8.15	8.26	8.35	8.26	8.22	8.20	8.20	8.18	8.16	0.01
18	8.93	8.13	8.30	8.29	8.26	8.24	8.20	8.17	8.15	8.15	0.02
21	8.94	8.19	8.35	8.35	8.32	8.27	8.27	8.24	8.20	8.18	-0.01
22	8.92	8.33	8.45	8.45	8.43	8.39	8.35	8.33	8.29	8.25	-0.08
23	9.44	8.28	8.35	8.38	8.37	8.36	8.23	8.29	8.25	8.19	-0.09
24	9.05	8.23	8.31	8.32	8.32	8.30	8.23	8.24	8.20	8.16	-0.07
25	8.98	8.23	8.33	8.32	8.34	8.32	8.23	8.24	8.21	8.18	-0.05
28	8.95	8.26	8.35	8.36	8.41	8.37	8.29	8.30	8.27	8.23	-0.03
29	8.92	8.17	8.28	8.37	8.44	8.41	8.30	8.31	8.27	8.21	0.04
30	8.89	8.14	8.24	8.34	8.41	8.37	8.28	8.29	8.25	8.20	0.06
31	8.92	8.16	8.21	8.28	8.42	8.37	8.27	8.30	8.26	8.21	0.05

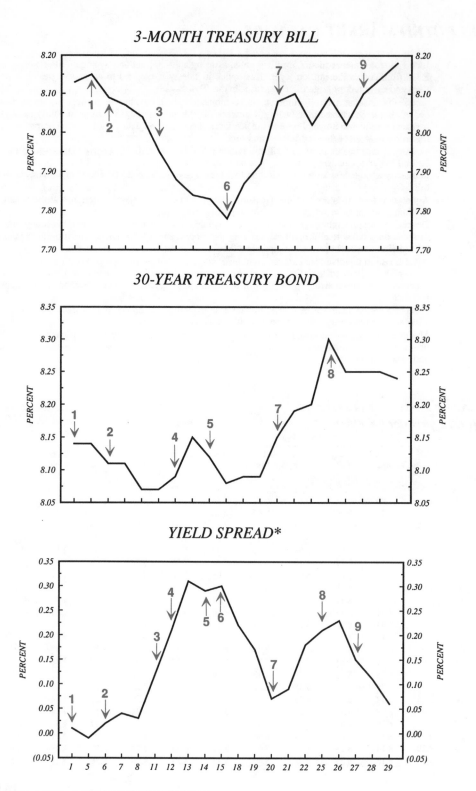

3-MONTH TREASURY BILL

30-YEAR TREASURY BOND

YIELD SPREAD*

*NOTE: SPREAD=30-YEAR BOND MINUS 3-MONTH BILL

SELECTED MARKET FACTORS

1   Strike-adjusted payroll employment rose by a strong 228,000 workers in August as manufacturing added 11,000 workers to their payrolls. The telephone workers' strike held the reported uptick in jobs to 110,000 workers.

2   The dollar climbed to its highest level in two and a half months, despite concerted attempts to halt its rise by at least a dozen central banks. In late-afternoon New York trading, the dollar was quoted at 1.9883 Deutsche marks, up from 1.910 Deutsche marks in Europe. The U.S. currency unit also rose to 146.84 yen versus 146.13 yen in Tokyo trading.

3   Rumors circulated in the market that Federal Reserve Chairman Greenspan had called an emergency FOMC meeting in response to the strength of the dollar. This report was later denied by a Federal Reserve spokesperson.

4   Market News Service carried a story citing Richmond Federal Reserve President Black and Kansas Federal Reserve President Guffey as indicating that the dollar would not dictate domestic monetary policy. They were reported to emphasize the Federal Reserve's focus on price pressures.

5   Junk bond prices plunged in reaction to Campeau Corp.'s growing cash crunch. As news that the big real estate and retail concern would be unable to meet its upcoming interest payment, the firm's bonds fell as much as 10 points during the day. Campeau Corp.'s problems dragged down overall junk bond debt prices.

6   For a third consecutive month, wholesale prices fell by 0.4%, reflecting a drop in energy prices and a slide in finished food prices. The market seemed to ignore a broad-based 0.5% rise in the excluding food and energy measure as the dollar traded on a further improvement in the U.S. trade shortfall (-$7.6B vs. -$8.0B) and a 0.3% rise in August industrial production.

7   The latest regional survey conducted by the St. Louis Federal Reserve Bank depicted an economy growing at a "moderate or slow" rate. This was perceived as the Fed's way of showing a slight pickup in the pace of business activities from that which existed in July.

8   Finance ministers and central bankers from the world's seven leading industrial nations stated that the rise in the exchange value of the dollar is "inconsistent with longer run economic fundamentals." Despite the strong wording in the G-7 communique, it failed to detail action which might be taken on interest rates. For the first time, the G-7 did aggressively intervene, however, in overseas markets in a coordinated strike on the dollar, a move that initially shocked the currency markets.

9   The Federal Reserve failed to execute a rate protest with funds above 9 1/8%. This absence of an overnight add allowed quarter-end pressures in the reserve market to be misinterpreted temporarily as a possible Federal Reserve tightening.

U.S. TREASURY YIELDS
(Bond Equivalent Yields)

	Fed Funds	3-Month Bill	6-Month Bill	1-Year Bill	2-Year Note	3-Year Note	5-Year Note	7-Year Note	10-Year Note	30-Year Bond	Spread*
September											
1	8.93	8.13	8.20	8.23	8.37	8.32	8.18	8.23	8.19	8.14	0.01
5	8.93	8.15	8.26	8.31	8.37	8.34	8.21	8.23	8.19	8.14	-0.01
6	9.14	8.09	8.26	8.29	8.35	8.31	8.19	8.21	8.17	8.11	0.02
7	9.00	8.07	8.24	8.26	8.35	8.28	8.19	8.22	8.17	8.11	0.04
8	8.98	8.04	8.21	8.20	8.27	8.23	8.14	8.19	8.14	8.07	0.03
11	8.95	7.95	8.08	8.10	8.20	8.17	8.10	8.16	8.13	8.07	0.12
12	8.93	7.88	8.02	8.10	8.18	8.13	8.07	8.16	8.13	8.09	0.21
13	8.89	7.84	8.01	8.11	8.20	8.16	8.11	8.18	8.18	8.15	0.31
14	8.90	7.83	7.98	8.03	8.09	8.08	8.05	8.12	8.13	8.12	0.29
15	9.02	7.78	7.94	7.99	8.06	8.03	8.01	8.09	8.09	8.08	0.30
18	8.96	7.87	8.04	8.08	8.13	8.08	8.04	8.11	8.10	8.09	0.22
19	8.94	7.92	8.04	8.07	8.17	8.13	8.05	8.11	8.09	8.09	0.17
20	9.48	8.08	8.16	8.22	8.27	8.23	8.14	8.18	8.15	8.15	0.07
21	8.97	8.10	8.17	8.26	8.32	8.26	8.19	8.24	8.20	8.19	0.09
22	8.99	8.02	8.17	8.25	8.34	8.27	8.20	8.26	8.22	8.20	0.18
25	9.09	8.09	8.25	8.33	8.43	8.41	8.32	8.38	8.32	8.30	0.21
26	9.05	8.02	8.26	8.34	8.36	8.39	8.29	8.34	8.30	8.25	0.23
27	9.03	8.10	8.26	8.36	8.39	8.40	8.31	8.36	8.30	8.25	0.15
28	9.20	8.14	8.28	8.41	8.41	8.42	8.34	8.37	8.30	8.25	0.11
29	9.24	8.18	8.34	8.48	8.46	8.46	8.36	8.40	8.31	8.24	0.06

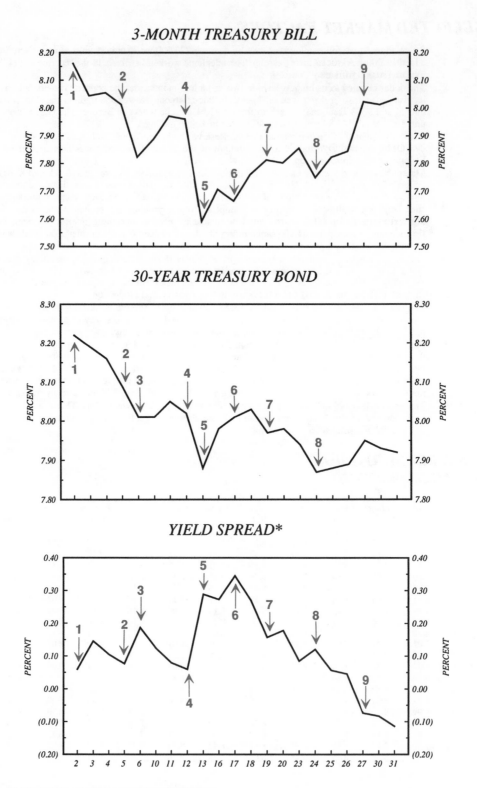

3-MONTH TREASURY BILL

30-YEAR TREASURY BOND

YIELD SPREAD*

NOTE: SPREAD=30-YEAR BOND MINUS 3-MONTH BILL

SELECTED MARKET FACTORS

1   The National Association of Purchasing Managers' Index rose from 45.2% to 46.0%. This was the fifth consecutive month that the index was below 50%, which translates into a contracting economy.

2   The Bundesbank raised the West German discount rate from 5% to 6%, and the Lombard rate from 7% to 8%. Inflationary pressures and excessive money supply growth were cited as reasons for the rate increases.

3   Total payroll employment for September was 209,000, while manufacturing payroll employment was down a large 108,000.

4   The junk bond market received more bad news yesterday when Ramada, Inc. withdrew its offering of high-yield bonds because of poor investor reception.

5   The Dow Jones Industrial Average fell 190.58 points following the announcement that a takeover group for UAL could not get financing for the leveraged buyout. Many risk arbitrageurs viewed this as a sign from commercial banks that they would no longer participate in risky buyouts. Quality spreads widened following the "flight to quality."

6   The August trade deficit was $10.8 billion, much worse than the $9.0 billion that had been anticipated.

7   The consumer price index for September rose by 0.2%, following a 0.2% increase in August.

8   Non-defense capital goods orders slipped by 5.6% in September after falling 10.3% in the previous month.

9   The Federal Reserve executed a second consecutive round of four-day matched sales with funds trading above the 8 3/4% perceived equilibrium level. This helped to eliminate market speculation about an imminent easing in monetary policy.

U.S. TREASURY YIELDS
(Bond Equivalent Yields)

October	Fed Funds	3-Month Bill	6-Month Bill	1-Year Bill	2-Year Note	3-Year Note	5-Year Note	7-Year Note	10-Year Note	30-Year Bond	Spread*
2	9.16	8.16	8.37	8.49	8.48	8.46	8.33	8.36	8.28	8.22	0.06
3	9.08	8.04	8.32	8.41	8.39	8.38	8.27	8.31	8.23	8.19	0.15
4	9.13	8.04	8.32	8.41	8.37	8.37	8.25	8.29	8.22	8.16	0.12
5	9.02	8.02	8.27	8.36	8.31	8.31	8.18	8.22	8.15	8.09	0.07
6	8.92	7.83	8.03	8.06	8.10	8.08	8.01	8.08	8.03	8.01	0.18
10	8.91	7.89	8.04	8.04	8.06	8.06	8.00	8.08	8.03	8.01	0.12
11	8.88	7.96	8.09	8.08	8.08	8.10	8.03	8.10	8.07	8.05	0.09
12	8.82	7.96	8.03	7.99	8.10	8.03	7.98	8.05	8.04	8.02	0.06
13	8.81	7.87	8.00	7.90	7.69	7.79	7.79	7.85	7.87	7.88	0.01
16	8.63	7.69	7.90	7.85	7.85	7.94	7.91	7.97	7.98	7.98	0.29
17	8.70	7.68	7.89	7.82	7.83	7.93	7.92	7.98	8.00	8.01	0.33
18	8.75	7.75	7.91	7.81	7.83	7.93	7.92	8.01	8.01	8.03	0.28
19	8.71	7.82	7.97	7.90	7.87	7.94	7.91	7.96	7.96	7.97	0.15
20	8.71	7.80	8.00	7.88	7.92	7.96	7.93	7.98	7.98	7.98	0.18
23	8.73	7.82	7.97	7.85	7.88	7.91	7.87	7.92	7.92	7.94	0.12
24	8.72	7.75	7.82	7.76	7.78	7.82	7.80	7.86	7.87	7.87	0.12
25	8.73	7.81	7.83	7.77	7.76	7.82	7.79	7.86	7.86	7.88	0.07
26	8.75	7.85	7.87	7.80	7.78	7.85	7.81	7.89	7.88	7.89	0.04
27	8.74	8.02	8.00	7.88	7.87	7.92	7.87	7.95	7.94	7.95	-0.07
30	8.75	8.01	7.99	7.87	7.85	7.91	7.86	7.92	7.92	7.93	-0.08
31	8.89	8.03	7.99	7.88	7.85	7.91	7.86	7.92	7.92	7.92	-0.11

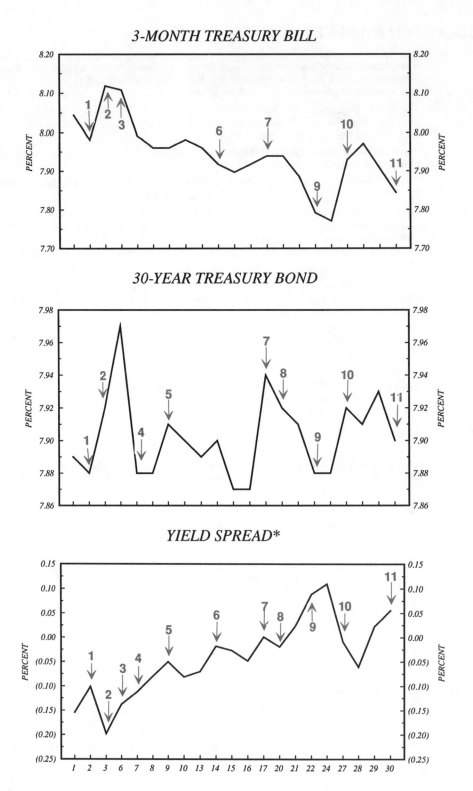

3-MONTH TREASURY BILL

30-YEAR TREASURY BOND

YIELD SPREAD*

*NOTE: SPREAD=30-YEAR BOND MINUS 3-MONTH BILL

SELECTED MARKET FACTORS

1 The Federal Reserve's latest regional survey of economic activity showed that the pace of economic activity was "slow to moderate" with some of the weakest sectors showing early signs of bottoming out.

2 Non-farm payroll employment expanded by 233,000 jobs in October as service-producing jobs, particularly teaching positions, were filled. The goods-producing sector slipped by 13,000 workers as the machinists' strike at Boeing cut the factory work week by 0.3 hours to 41.1 hours during the month.

3 A second consecutive round of overnight customer repo with fed funds trading at 8 5/8% signaled a renewed easing in monetary policy. The latest policy move established a 8 3/8% to 8 5/8% trading range on fed funds, some 25 basis points below the previous tolerance band implemented in October.

4 The Treasury postponed the November refunding as a result of debt limit restrictions.

5 Wholesale prices accelerated in October as food prices climbed by 1.4% during the month. This uptick in the PPI (+0.4%) was not anticipated by most market analysts.

6 The Boeing strike and the earthquake on the West Coast were cited as factors contributing to the 0.7% drop reported in industrial production for October. Despite the weak production report, the Treasury bond market experienced a moderate degree of dislocation following the auction of $10 billion in bonds.

7 October housing starts rebounded by 12.0% in October after a 4.6% slide in September. According to the latest FOMC minutes, the Federal Reserve refrained from easing rates at the October meeting because the makers of policy did not want the move to be perceived as having been undertaken in response to the dollar or the G-7 meeting.

8 Developments in Eastern Europe prompted the Bush administration to plan defense cuts as the likelihood of a full scale U.S.-Soviet conflict diminished.

9 The Treasury market misinterpreted the Fed's execution of a technical 5-day system repo, considering the move to have policy significance. As a result, speculation about an additional 25 basis point easing touched off rallies at both ends of the yield curve.

10 In order to reinforce the point that the November 22 system repo was merely technical, the Fed executed an unexpected overnight matched sales operation one hour earlier than the usual intervention time.

11 A 0.2% decline in October consumption spending was reported on the same day that initial unemployment claims were pushed upward by 46,000 applications to the 363,000 level.

U.S. TREASURY YIELDS
(Bond Equivalent Yields)

November	Fed Funds	3-Month Bill	6-Month Bill	1-Year Bill	2-Year Note	3-Year Note	5-Year Note	7-Year Note	10-Year Note	30-Year Bond	Spread*
1	8.98	8.04	7.94	7.86	7.87	7.91	7.86	7.92	7.91	7.89	-0.15
2	8.77	7.99	7.92	7.81	7.81	7.86	7.81	7.86	7.87	7.88	-0.11
3	8.74	8.11	8.10	8.01	8.01	8.02	7.93	7.95	7.96	7.92	-0.19
6	8.74	8.14	8.14	8.05	8.04	8.07	7.99	8.01	8.00	7.97	-0.17
7	8.64	8.01	7.99	7.88	7.87	7.92	7.85	7.87	7.90	7.88	-0.13
8	8.48	7.95	7.91	7.79	7.78	7.83	7.81	7.84	7.87	7.88	-0.07
9	8.42	7.96	7.99	7.82	7.80	7.79	7.84	7.86	7.90	7.91	-0.05
10	8.40	7.97	7.99	7.83	7.83	7.82	7.85	7.88	7.92	7.90	-0.07
13	8.44	7.96	7.97	7.80	7.82	7.82	7.85	7.88	7.89	7.89	-0.07
14	8.44	7.92	7.82	7.70	7.75	7.75	7.80	7.86	7.87	7.90	-0.02
15	8.73	7.90	7.78	7.66	7.69	7.69	7.74	7.80	7.82	7.87	-0.03
16	8.52	7.92	7.82	7.70	7.71	7.70	7.74	7.79	7.82	7.87	-0.05
17	8.45	7.94	7.86	7.69	7.77	7.75	7.82	7.87	7.88	7.94	0.00
20	8.47	7.94	7.86	7.69	7.77	7.74	7.80	7.86	7.86	7.92	-0.02
21	8.50	7.89	7.82	7.69	7.77	7.74	7.79	7.84	7.85	7.91	0.02
22	8.38	7.84	7.75	7.60	7.66	7.65	7.72	7.77	7.81	7.88	0.04
24	8.30	7.76	7.69	7.59	7.64	7.63	7.70	7.76	7.80	7.88	0.12
27	8.56	7.92	7.86	7.74	7.79	7.76	7.80	7.83	7.85	7.92	0.00
28	8.73	7.97	7.90	7.76	7.78	7.79	7.81	7.84	7.86	7.91	-0.06
29	8.99	7.92	7.85	7.77	7.80	7.80	7.78	7.87	7.88	7.93	0.01
30	8.60	7.84	7.78	7.72	7.75	7.75	7.74	7.83	7.84	7.90	0.06

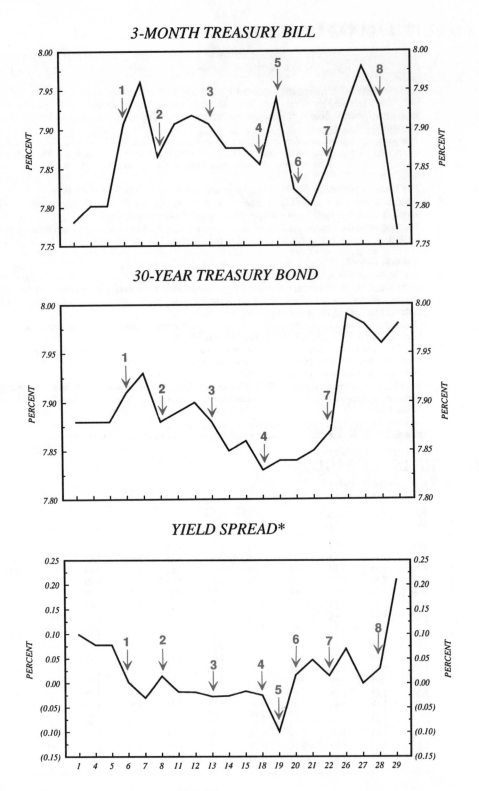

3-MONTH TREASURY BILL

30-YEAR TREASURY BOND

YIELD SPREAD*

*NOTE: SPREAD=30-YEAR BOND MINUS 3-MONTH BILL

SELECTED MARKET FACTORS

1 The late November survey of regional business conditions compiled by the Federal Reserve Bank of New York described the economy as "stable to moderately expanding." This summary statement implied a modest improvement in growth from the previous survey conducted six weeks earlier.

2 Non-farm payroll employment rose by 210,000 in November after a small 93,000 gain in October. The October employment total had previously been placed at 233,000 jobs. The bulk of this downward revision was concentrated in service jobs since the number of teachers hired in the month was cut sharply.

3 Early December automobile sales came in at a rate of only 5.5 million units. This represents a recessionary level for auto sales and prompted cuts in domestic Japanese production.

4 Heller Financial, Inc. told its clients to stop shipping merchandise to Campeau Corp.'s retail operations. This move reflected a recent analysis of the real estate firm's third-quarter financial statements.

5 A surge in food prices produced a 0.4% rise in consumer prices in November. Energy, which had been a major factor restraining consumer prices, edged only 0.1% lower, allowing a 0.4% rise in the trend rate of consumer prices to be reflected in the overall index.

6 The Federal Reserve eased reserve market conditions by executing an overnight system repo during a fundamental drain week. This move cut the fed funds rate target from the 8 1/2% level to 8 1/4% established in early November.

7 Durable goods orders surged 5.1% in November as transportation orders surged 10.5% and non-defense capital goods climbed by 8.3% for the month.

8 Aggressive adding of reserves by the Federal Reserve at the end of the year helped to offset technical reserve market distortions.

U.S. STREASURY YIELDS
(Bond Equivalent Yields)

December	Fed Funds	3-Month Bill	6-Month Bill	1-Year Bill	2-Year Note	3-Year Note	5-Year Note	7-Year Note	10-Year Note	30-Year Bond	Spread*
1	8.51	7.78	7.75	7.67	7.70	7.70	7.70	7.79	7.81	7.88	0.10
4	8.53	7.80	7.76	7.68	7.72	7.73	7.70	7.79	7.82	7.88	0.08
5	8.51	7.81	7.67	7.68	7.72	7.71	7.70	7.79	7.82	7.88	0.07
6	8.47	7.90	7.74	7.76	7.80	7.79	7.76	7.84	7.85	7.91	0.01
7	8.48	7.95	7.79	7.82	7.85	7.84	7.80	7.88	7.88	7.93	-0.02
8	8.46	7.87	7.71	7.73	7.78	7.77	7.73	7.83	7.82	7.88	0.01
11	8.44	7.90	7.73	7.74	7.78	7.76	7.74	7.83	7.83	7.89	-0.01
12	8.44	7.92	7.83	7.76	7.80	7.76	7.74	7.84	7.84	7.90	-0.02
13	8.58	7.95	7.83	7.77	7.82	7.76	7.73	7.84	7.82	7.88	-0.07
14	8.51	7.88	7.78	7.71	7.75	7.70	7.68	7.80	7.79	7.85	-0.03
15	8.56	7.88	7.78	7.65	7.75	7.70	7.70	7.82	7.80	7.86	-0.02
18	8.56	7.85	7.78	7.62	7.75	7.69	7.67	7.79	7.77	7.83	-0.02
19	8.50	7.93	7.88	7.72	7.72	7.73	7.69	7.81	7.78	7.85	-0.08
20	8.42	7.82	7.78	7.63	7.64	7.70	7.67	7.78	7.77	7.84	0.02
21	8.27	7.81	7.78	7.64	7.68	7.71	7.67	7.80	7.77	7.86	0.05
22	8.19	7.84	7.83	7.70	7.74	7.77	7.75	7.86	7.82	7.88	0.04
26	8.49	7.92	7.83	7.83	7.88	7.91	7.89	8.01	7.94	7.99	0.07
27	8.45	7.98	7.99	7.82	7.89	7.91	7.89	7.99	7.93	7.98	0.00
28	8.45	7.93	8.00	7.76	7.86	7.86	7.85	7.95	7.91	7.96	0.03
29	7.97	7.77	7.85	7.81	7.83	7.86	7.83	7.98	7.93	7.98	0.21